THE INDIAN KITCHEN

MONISHA BHARADWAJ

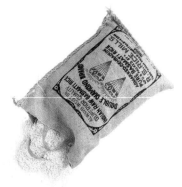

Monisha Bharadwaj was born in Bombay and has earned recognition as a stylish hostess, cook and food journalist. She has worked as a food consultant in India and Britain. She has also written for The Times of India group of newspapers. Her books include *The Prestige Festival Cookbook*, *Exotic Curries of the Orient* and *Great Diamonds of India*. Her most recent book for Kyle Cathie is *Inside India: Quintessential Indian Style*. Monisha lives between Bombay and London with her husband and their two children.

THE INDIAN KITCHEN

MONISHA BHARADWAJ

TED SMART

This book is for my parents, Aai and Baba, who have always encouraged me to pursue excellence, for my husband Nitish who has supported my endeavours, and for baby Arrush, with all my love.

First published in hardback as The Indian Pantry in Great Britain, 1996 by Kyle Cathie Limited

This edition produced for The Book People Ltd, Hall Wood Avenue, Haydock, St Helens WA11 9UL

ISBN 1 85626 224 3

Text © 1996 Monisha Bharadwaj
Recipe photography © 1996 Julie Dixon
Home economy by Kathy Man
Cut-out photography of ingredients © 1996 by Jacqui Hurst
Selected views of India © 1995 Jean Cazals; © 1994 Marcus Grover
Book design © 1996 Geoff Hayes

Monisha Bharadwaj is hereby identified as the author of this work in accordance with Section 77 of the Copyright, Designs and Patents Act 1988.

A CIP catalogue record for this title is available from the British Library.

Printed and bound in Singapore by Kyodo Printing Co. Pte. Ltd.

Acknowledgements

The Indian Council of Agricultural Research, Ministry of Food and Agriculture, New Delhi, Spices Export Promotion Council, Kerala and National Sugar Institute, Kanpur, were all helpful in providing information. I am grateful to my relatives, especially my grandmother, Mrs Sumati Patil, who enlightened me on rural produce, my father, Prabhakar Patil who helped in more ways than I can mention and my mother, Vimla Patil who gave me support, encouragement and suggestions. In spite of very busy schedules of their own, all of them willingly and patiently answered all my questions. Also a big thank you to my agent Teresa Chris for her perseverance and dedication. Finally, grateful thanks to Kyle Cathie for her belief in me and her very relevant questions about all things Indian, and to Kate Oldfield who put endless, endless hours of work into the editing

The publishers would like to thank Thomas Goode & Co. (London) Ltd, and Graham and Green, London, NW1 for the loan of some of china and glassware for this book

CONTENTS

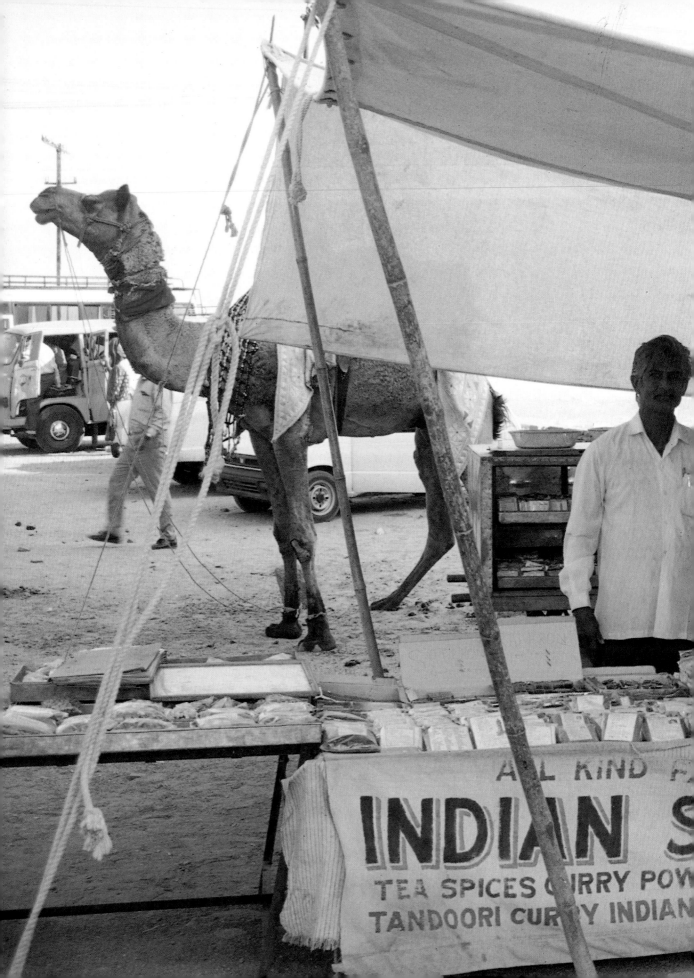

INTRODUCTION

India's history of a flourishing spice trade, which lead to conquest and colonisation, is reflected in the country's cuisine, renowned for its clever blend of exotic spices, delicate herbs, meats, vegetables and cereals. The best Indian dishes are a swirl of textures and flavours, mysteriously fiery yet beautifully subtle, and today Indian food is celebrated as one of the world's fastest growing and most varied cuisines; Indian restaurants dot the streets of every major city in the world and devoted gourmets haunt the better ones with unmatched passion.

Indian food is now finding its way into the kitchens and homes of people everywhere, from Europe and the United States to Africa and Australia. Previously exotic ingredients like tamarind and jaggery are now widely available in supermarkets and stores, so the creation of exciting and authentic Indian fare outside India is a very real possibility. With judicious shopping and well-planned storage, genuine Indian meals are simple and quick to prepare. The results are always tasty and nutritious. In this book, I have brought together over 100 readily available, yet often less familiar, Indian ingredients, and for each I offer tips on how to recognise and select the best quality products and suggest recipes that reveal their versatility.

In India, more so than in any other country, food cannot be separated easily from its social context. I have, therefore, examined each pantry 'ingredient' in terms of its distinctive properties and features, which often extend beyond the culinary realm to the medicinal and even the mythological. I have tried to encourage the reader to look into the world beyond the pantry itself, seeing how the ingredient is grown, harvested and sold in the colourful markets that are so essential to Indian life to provide, what I hope is, a vivid insight into a great and vital culinary tradition.

There is no doubt that all Indians love food. In a country where there are as many cuisines as there are states, people spend an amazing amount of time and energy buying, making, eating or even just discussing food. For this reason, the kitchen can be the most fascinating room in an Indian home. Here, iridescent spices sparkle alongside huge boxes of Himalayan snow-washed rice, earthy lentils accentuate plump, dry fruits and rich, musky nuts sit next to jars of pearly sago and subja seeds. Bread is rolled out each day on creamy marble boards and homemade yoghurt, stiff enough to slice, is set in earthy terracotta pots.

Fresh foods are highly valued and seasonal ones are preserved for later use. In the heat of the summer, when heaps of amber and gold-dusted mangoes fill every fruit stall, a clever Indian cook selects the choicest fruit to make jam, pulp, cakes and *panha* (a saffron and mango-flavoured drink that can be stored for months). Indians are diligent about the storage of food and their store cupboards contain ingredients that are colourful, nutritious and wonderfully fragrant.

The secret of good Indian cooking lies in a well-stocked pantry. It is from this source of spices, herbs, nuts, flours and essences that the Indian cook can create culinary masterpieces like Spicy Lemonade, mouthwatering sweets like crunchy *Karanjis*, delightful salads like *Aam ka Sasam* and countless other delicacies, many of which are featured in this book. The store cupboard in any Indian home, contains many durable ingredients that can be mixed, matched and interchanged in a vast range of delicious recipes.

The kitchen and pantry are the Indian

housewife's pride. Cleanliness and order are of utmost importance and the kitchen is scrubbed until it sparkles after the preparation of each meal. In most Indian households, the kitchen is considered almost sacred. In orthodox homes, the lady of the house will wake up early, bathe and put on a pure silk sari before entering the kitchen. After this purification, she will not allow anyone who has not bathed to touch her, not even her own children, until she has finished preparing the meal.

A typical village kitchen, Vishala, near Amdebad

For centuries, the kitchen has been the stronghold of the Indian woman. It is here that she shares her deepest secrets, fears and joys with her friends, or keeps a watchful eye on her children as she cooks. Here she passes on advice to her daughters and manages the finances of the house. A large majority of Indian women control their household's expenses and at times the kitchen becomes more like a personnel office. This room witnesses much bartering over the price of fruit and vegetables, and in some parts of India people selling fresh produce, household appliances and even saris will come to meet the lady of the house at the kitchen door to ply their trade. This constant activity and the endless stream of people who come to the kitchen at some point during the day means that the Indian kitchen is rarely quiet. Work starts at dawn with the preparation of breakfast which is a significant meal. Fruits, fried titbits, pancakes or eggs and sweet dishes are served, and usually the women will eat after the men and children have been fed. Of course, in urban India, professional men and women find increasingly that their jobs make demands on their time which prevent them continuing these traditional practices, and as in all other metropolises of the world many people skip breakfast altogether.

All meals in India are equally important. Lunch is served with as much care as supper and teatime sees another spread of sweet and savoury dishes on the table. The evening meal, however, is the most interesting meal of the day. This is the time for the family to get together, exchange news and gossip and a sense of sharing and togetherness prevails. As this is perhaps the only time in the day that the family gets to relax together, this meal is the most elaborate. Traditionally, Indians do not have separate courses but serve all the main dishes together. Even soups are served at the same time. *Thalis*, or platters which offer bowls of different food, are quite popular throughout India and on special occasions the contents of the thali become richer and more varied. However, it is equally easy to find people who eat a simple meal of *dal-roti* – lentils and bread – with a big spoonful of mango pickle. In the cities, as Westernisation becomes more and more evident, international cuisines, especially Chinese, Italian and Anglo-American, are finding their way into a growing number of homes.

Indians love eating out and every city, town and village abounds in excellent places to eat.

Slimming diets are frowned upon and society collectively discourages any kind of food self-denial. People are complimented when they look 'healthy', which usually means pleasantly plump, and with the constant availability of delicious food in India it is very easy to put on extra weight.

A NOTE ON INGREDIENTS

The mystery and magic of Indian cooking is rapidly unfolding on the shelves of supermarkets worldwide, where a huge range of ingredients is now available. However, using these ingredients correctly to get authentic results still remains a question of trial and error to many cooks. Although most people in India use fresh produce, it is quite acceptable and timesaving to use frozen vegetables and meats like peas, sweetcorn and chicken, paying careful attention to thawing and cooking instructions. Tinned tomatoes and tomato purée make a good alternative to fresh tomatoes in most dishes. Many busy cooks use ready-made ginger or garlic paste, tinned chickpeas or red kidney beans and tinned coconut milk. Tamarind, which is also available as a ready-made paste, still needs to be diluted in a little water. It may not dissolve completely but this will not affect the dish as it invariably blends with the other ingredients during cooking. The only way of making fresh coconut milk is by blending warm water and fresh, grated coconut in a blender and squeezing out the thick milk by hand.

Many of the methods in this book involve frying masala pastes and spices. Always remember to cook blended spice mixtures and powders on a very low heat or they will burn. To determine that a blended spice paste is cooked, just wait for the mixture to separate from the oil in which it is fried. Adding a few drops of water (watch out for the sizzle that erupts!) hastens this process and reduces the chances of scorching. Adding spices at different times during cooking gives a variety of flavours, from subtle to deep and heavy. Always add salt during cooking so that its flavour suffuses through the heart of the dish.

ESSENTIAL EQUIPMENT IN A MODERN INDIAN KITCHEN

A rural Indian kitchen and an urban one are quite different in the way that they function, but some essential and functional tools and utensils are found in every Indian kitchen, throughout the world. A spice-box is a must. This handy box has small compartments and tiny individual spoons for the main spices used in everyday cookery, including turmeric, chilli powder, cumin, coriander, black mustard seeds and asafoetida.

Most Indian cooks prefer to use a selection of stainless steel, aluminium, brass and iron utensils and, due to the intense cooking processes involved, the bases of these pots and pans are reinforced with a thick layer of the same metal or one of copper. A *kadai*, or Indian wok, is found in every kitchen. Ideal in shape and thickness, it can be used for stir-frying or deep-frying and ensures even, non-stick cooking. Kadais are available in many sizes and qualities. Look for a thick, heavy aluminium one with handles that make it easier to work with. Highly decorative, kitchen-to-table enamel kadais look pretty but they are not very heavy and can heat up too quickly. Other popular utensils are rimmed, straight-sided, upright vessels called *degchis*.

No Indian kitchen can function without a grinder of some sort. The vast panorama of spice pastes and powders, chutneys and masalas demand a heavy-duty method of reducing whole spices, fruits, herbs and nuts to a smooth blend. Stone slabs with a heavy, rounded grinding stone or huge stone bowls with an oval grinding stone are still used but are being rapidly replaced by powerful electric blenders. These have various attachments for

In India people still buy whole wheat and take it to the nearest *chakki*, or mill, to be ground

dry and wet grinding and can pulverise the hardest spices to a fine, soft powder. In the absence of such a strong ally, you can use a coffee-grinder to grind small quantities of spices very effectively. However, remember to wash it well after use or you might end up with coriander-flavoured coffee the next time you use your machine! Very small amounts of spice seeds, made brittle by dry-roasting, can also be ground in a mortar. Food processors that can grate, chop and knead are also becoming more and more popular in Indian kitchens, though many cooks genuinely believe that traditional methods produce tastier food.

In India, where coconut inspires the cuisine of many states, a coconut-scraper is found in the majority of homes. This is a flat, wooden base to which a sickle-shaped blade is attached. This has a serrated fan at the end, which is used to scrape out the white flesh from the coconut shell. The blade is also used to chop meat and vegetables. This whole device is placed on the floor and one has to sit on the plinth to use it. Coconut can also be effectively grated in a food processor after breaking open the shell and prising away the flesh. Small stainless steel or brass graters are used for grating ginger and garlic. You can also use a garlic press.

One of the most versatile tools available to an Indian cook is a pressure cooker. Although they seem to have gone out of fashion in the West, they are seen in almost every kitchen in India and are used to make everything from curries to puddings. As they drastically reduce cooking times and give a perfectly finished product, they are invaluable to anyone who wants to rustle up a meal in minutes.

Another must is a refrigerator. As Indian food retains its flavour even after freezing, it can be prepared well in advance and stored for later use. In very hot weather, along with the usual meat, milk and vegetables, flour goes into the fridge too.

'A Guest is Equal to God'

'Atithi Devo Bhava' is an ancient Sanskrit saying that has been handed down through the ages and one that holds true even today. It means that a guest is equal to God and should be treated as such. Despite the hustle and bustle of modern life, this is still the basic concept that underlies all Indian hospitality. Even the poorest home in India will offer a guest a meal and it is considered an insult to the host if his congenial offer is not accepted. In fact the principles of perfect Indian entertaining dictate that as an ideal host you must provide your guest with good food, good music and good conversation.

That one should provide a guest with food is a reflection of the important role food plays in India. Throughout Indian history food has always had very strong social, religious and medicinal associations, playing a central role during festivals and sacraments, and in the treatment of the weak and the sick. And food becomes the focal point of many social occasions, such as the festival of *Makara Sankranti* which falls in January each year. This day celebrates the beginning of the sun's journey from the tropic of Cancer to the tropic of Capricorn and the start of the harvesting season in much of agricultural India. The air is cold and misty and special sweets made from jaggery and sesame seeds, both considered warming, are distributed and eaten. Kite-flying competitions are organised to bring people together and a feast is prepared from the newly harvested food grains. Families exchange plates full of warming, gingery sweets and wish each other luck, prosperity and good health in the forthcoming years.

Indian gods too have their favourite foods. Lord Krishna, the dark, handsome god with the peacock feather in his crown, is said to love milk, butter and yoghurt. Countless mythological tales relate his passion for these foods, describing how, as a child he would steal into his mother's kitchen to eat them. Because of these associations these foods are considered both healthy and sacred, and every Hindu feast features them.

All religious food in India must only include those ingredients which are considered acceptable. An awareness of what is and what is not acceptable is inculcated in each generation through word of mouth. Milk, ghee, coconut, fruits, certain vegetables, rice and yoghurt are considered suitable for Hindu feasts (the food at all religious feasts is offered to the gods first and then is eaten as a blessing). Meat, fish, eggs, alcohol, onions and garlic are not allowed. But different communities and religious sects have different beliefs about food, and many people from north India will happily include a garlic-based curry at a religious feast, whereas south Indians will make sure that there is not a single clove of garlic to be found in the kitchen where such a meal is being prepared!

Alcohol is generally considered taboo and is banned from a majority of religious celebrations. Indeed there is no Indian tradition of drinking alcohol with a meal and Ayurvedic belief states that alcohol should not be consumed with food. Almost always Indians drink water, and plenty of it. Of course Indians do drink alcohol, mainly beer and whisky, but

Young girls celebrating the birth of Lord Krishna, Coimbatore, near Madras

only at social events and even then it is usually the men who partake, leaving most women to sip a soft drink. Heavy drinking is considered wrong and society gossips will be quick to criticise any one who is overindulgent.

Much of India is vegetarian, mainly because of the Hindu way of life. Hinduism as a religion promotes respect towards life and living creatures and therefore animals are considered sacred. It is probably for this reason that Indian cuisine has a limitless choice of vegetarian fare. Hindus do not eat beef and the Muslim population avoids pork, so Indian non-vegetarian fare centres around chicken, fish lamb and goat.

Every Indian knows the nutritional values and health aspects of different foods and these play an important part in simple household medicine and in the Hindu science of Ayurveda, which promotes a balanced diet and the use of herbal remedies to maintain health and happiness. In India, Ayurveda is regarded

as a viable, efficient way of life that has been tried and tested for 3000 years. Ayurvedic wisdom is passed from mother to child, advising which foods to eat and which to avoid – for example fish and yoghurt should not be eaten together as the combination is said to cause skin problems. (Although the two are eaten together quite happily in western Bengal because here they believe that it is milk and fish that is the wrong combination.) There is a broad awareness of the qualities of food and the effects on the body. Excessive warmth in the body is thought to be the root cause of many maladies and therefore 'heating' and 'cooling' foods are balanced in an Indian meal. Foods like yoghurt, rice and ghee are cooling to the body, whereas meat, mangoes, pineapple and cashew nuts – amongst many others – are considered heat-inducing and are consumed in moderation. So embedded have these beliefs become in society that many people accept them as natural customs.

I could write a whole new book on the role food plays in the fabric of Indian society and there is not enough space here to do the subject justice. I have realised as I have been researching and writing this book that it is impossible to reflect the immense diversity of Indian cuisine. Each state in India has its own language, cuisine, dress and climate. It is even possible that within single villages people will have differing concepts of how life should be lived. I have endeavoured to present as wide a picture as possible, but often when I have put pen to paper to write about a particular aspect of culinary culture the kaleidoscope has turned and the picture in front of me changes. Anyone familiar with India will know what I mean. There is a common thread which holds all of this together: the love of traditions. The enduring traditions are energetic and exciting.

I have tried to include ingredients and recipes from those parts of India which are rarely represented in the West. The reader will find many recipes from the south which should extend the culinary repertoire of those who know only the more generally accepted north Indian tandoori dishes. Some of the recipes here may never have left India before.

Lastly, I would like to emphasise two points. This book is the fruition of years of research, and yet it represents only the tiniest tip of the iceberg. I am aware that some people will feel that their approach to cooking is different from that found in my methods. There is seldom one way of doing things in India. Furthermore I would encourage my readers, as lovers of Indian food, to consider this book only a starting point on an exciting and ongoing culinary journey.

Author's notes on the recipes
It would have taken up too much valuable space to cross-reference all the ingredients used in this book. Therefore I suggest that the cook use the index whenever an unfamiliar ingredient is listed.
In India there is no set way of cooking dishes, and so my methods often don't give a cooking time. I ask all cooks to use their eyes and their own judgment which, after all, is real cooking.

FROM THE
SPICE BOX

Anethum sowa/Anethum graveolens

DILL

(SOWA)

Dill has been in cultivation for more than 2000 years. The ancient Greeks and Romans were aware of its special properties and are believed to have covered their heads with dill leaves to induce sleep. In the Middle Ages, Europeans considered dill to be a herb with magic qualities and used it in brews to counteract witchcraft. There are two main species of dill – European dill (*Anethum graveolens*) and Indian dill (*Anethum sowa*).

Market stalls, Kashipur

Indian dill resembles European dill but its seeds are longer and narrower

HOW IT GROWS

Indian dill is found practically all over India. It is an annual or biennial herbaceous plant with silky, wispy leaves, clusters of small yellow flowers and oval, flattened fruits. The single stalks grow to a height of about 1m (3ft). To harvest the fragrant seeds, the fruits are left to ripen on the plant until they become yellow-brown. The seeds are then extracted, threshed and dried.

APPEARANCE AND TASTE

Indian dill resembles the European plant but the ripe, dried seeds are longer and narrower, and they taste slightly different due to the differing amounts of essential oil they contain. Dill seeds are light brown and are flat and oval in shape. They are especially easy to recognise because of their weightlessness – 10,000 seeds weigh about 25g (1oz). Dill has an aroma that is slightly reminiscent of caraway – warm, aromatic and tingly.

BUYING AND STORING

The most commonly available forms of dill are leaves and seeds. The seeds are sometimes sold ground. You can release the essential oil in the seeds by crushing them, but do this just before using them in the recipe. The best way to store dill seeds is whole and in a cool, dry place.

MEDICINAL AND OTHER USES

Dill is well known for its medicinal qualities, and is especially useful for preventing stomach disorders like flatulence and colic. It is equally effective for colds and bronchitis, when a hot infusion of the seeds mixed with honey will bring instant relief. Dill is also believed to stimulate and regulate menstrual flow, stimulate breast milk in nursing mothers and delay ovulation to help natural birth control. Dill water, which is a mild infusion of seeds, is a miracle-drink, relieving hiccups, colic and flatulence in babies and inducing restful sleep. Dill oil is used in the manufacture of insecticides. The dried residue left after the distillation of the essential oil from the seeds is used as a cattle feed.

CULINARY USES

Dill seeds are used in breads, soups, processed meats, sauces and even in cakes and pastries. The seeds are also used as a substitute for caraway. The green herb with its unique, fresh taste is a versatile kitchen plant and goes beautifully with fish, meats, salads and lentils.

This recipe that follows is a speciality of the Sindhi community and is a tasty, nutritious *mélange*. It is best eaten with hot rotis or served over plain boiled rice. A fresh green salad is all that is needed to complete the meal.

SAIBHAJI
(DILLED SPINACH AND LENTILS)

Serves 4
Preparation time 30 minutes
Cooking time 20 minutes

4 tablespoons sunflower oil
1 teaspoon cumin seeds
1 teaspoon dill seeds
1 teaspoon ginger paste
1 teaspoon garlic paste
4 tablespoons split gram lentils (channa dal), *washed and drained*
600g (1¼lb) spinach, *washed and chopped*
4 tablespoons coriander leaves, *chopped*
4 tablespoons dill leaves, *chopped*
2 medium tomatoes, *chopped*
1 small potato, *peeled and chopped*
2 small aubergines (*available from Indian grocers*), *chopped*
2 carrots, *peeled and chopped*
150ml (5fl oz) water
1 teaspoon chilli powder
1 teaspoon turmeric powder
Salt

1 Heat the oil in a pan. Add the cumin and dill seeds. When they begin to change colour, add the ginger and garlic pastes.

2 Give it a good stir then drop in the lentils, herbs and vegetables. Pour in the water and cook until completely softened.

3 Sprinkle in the chilli and turmeric powders and season with salt. Stir-fry until well blended.

4 Remove from the heat and churn with an egg-beater to blend until smooth. (You should aim to achieve a thick, dropping consistency.) Serve very hot.

This recipe is for a dish that can be enjoyed with beer for lunch on a warm Sunday or served with salad and a steaming hot, fragrant pulao for dinner.

SUVAWALE CHOPS
(DILLED LAMB CHOPS)

Serves 4
Preparation time 30 minutes
Cooking time 1 hour

300g (10oz) potatoes, boiled and peeled
1 teaspoon turmeric powder
1 teaspoon chilli powder
2 teaspoons coriander powder
2 teaspoons cumin powder
4 tablespoons coriander leaves, *chopped*
2 teaspoons dill seeds
Salt
8 thinly cut lamb chops, trimmed
1 teaspoon ginger paste
1 teaspoon garlic paste
220g (8oz) gram flour
½ teaspoon bicarbonate of soda
Sunflower oil for frying

1 Mash the potatoes with the turmeric, chilli, coriander and cumin powder, coriander leaves, dill seeds and salt.

2 Simmer the chops with the ginger and garlic pastes, salt and enough water to cover for 1 hour, until cooked, then drain completely.

3 Cover each chop with the potato paste and reserve for 10 minutes to make firm.

4 Meanwhile, make a fairly thick batter with the gram flour, bicarbonate of soda, water as needed and some salt.

5 Heat the oil until it smokes. Dip each chop in the batter and deep fry until golden.

6 Drain on absorbent paper, serve hot with tomato ketchup and mint chutney (page 103).

Suvawale Chops

Celery seeds enhance the flavour of tomatoes

Apium graveolens dulce

CELERY SEED

(AJMUD)

Though celery seed is an important minor spice in India, it is not very prolifically used. The celery that is grown now is an evolved descendant of a wild herb called smallage which grew all over Europe. Indian celery is quite different to European. Slender stalks bear small leaves and the flavour is slightly more subtle.

 HOW IT GROWS

Celery grows to a height of 60–80cm (2–3ft) and has conspicuously jointed stems. Celery seed is the dried ripe fruit of this herb. Celery grows in Scandinavia, Africa, Asia and the USA. In India it grows wild and is cultivated in the north-west.

 APPEARANCE AND TASTE

Celery seeds are tiny and extremely light. They are tobacco-brown in colour with 5 longitudinal ridges. The seeds have a powerful smell. They taste somewhat bitter, with a faint flavour of cumin.

BUYING AND STORING

Celery is available fresh as bright-yellow to green stalks with leaves, or as dried seeds which can be ground to a powder. It is a good idea to buy whole celery seeds – they are rarely used ground anyway. Also the powder is sometimes adulterated with linseed meal or worthless vegetable seeds. Store in a dry jar and use within 6 months.

MEDICINAL AND OTHER USES

Celery seeds are believed to be a tonic for asthma. An infusion of the seeds in water in the ratio 1:20 is said to relieve rheumatism and calm the nerves. Celery seeds are often added to commercial birdseed. The essential oil is used in perfumery, to make celery salt, and to impart warmth and aroma to tonics.

 CULINARY USES

The seeds seem to complement the tangy flavour of tomato and are used in several tomato-based Indian curries. They are also sprinkled over breads before baking to give bite and fragrance.

Commercial birdseed often contains celery seeds

The following recipes come from 2 different parts of India. The first is from the north and is one of the countless rotis made there.

DANA ROTI
(CELERY SEED BREAD)

Serves 4
Preparation time 15 minutes
Cooking time 30 minutes

450g (1lb) wholewheat flour
2 teaspoons ghee
2 tablespoons coriander leaves,
  chopped finely
Salt
2 teaspoons celery seeds
Sunflower oil for brushing

1 Make a soft dough with the flour, ghee, coriander, salt, celery seeds and water as needed.

2 Divide the dough into equal-sized balls about 3cm (1in) in diameter. Roll out each ball into a flat disc, dusting the board with flour as necessary.

3 Heat a griddle and place the roti on it. Reduce the heat and cook until little bubbles appear on the surface. Turn over and do the other side, brushing the roti with oil.

4 Continue with all the rotis in this manner. Serve hot with a curry, yoghurt and savoury pickle.

This recipe is from the south and can be served as a soup before the main meal.

TOMATOCHE SAAR
(THIN TOMATO CURRY)

Serves 4
Preparation time 15 minutes
Cooking time 20 minutes

10 medium tomatoes
1 tablespoon sunflower oil
1 teaspoon black mustard seeds
1 teaspoon cumin seeds
16 curry leaves
1 teaspoon celery seeds
1 teaspoon sugar
Salt
2 tablespoons coriander leaves,
  chopped finely

1 Blanch the tomatoes in boiling water, remove skins and liquidise to a thick purée.

2 Heat the oil in a pan and add the mustard seeds. When they pop, add the cumin seeds and the curry leaves. Stir once and add the celery seeds.

3 After one more stir, pour the tomato purée into this spice mixture.

4 Add the sugar and salt, dilute with 300ml (½pt) of water and bring to the boil. Simmer until blended, about 5 minutes, and remove from the heat.

5 Serve hot, sprinkled with fresh coriander leaves.

Dana Roti

Brassica nigra/Brassica juncea/
Sinapsis alba/Brassica hirta

MUSTARD

(RAI)

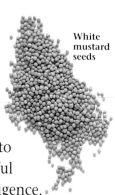

White mustard seeds

Mustard is widely used in the preparation of auspicious fare in Indian homes and temples. It is believed to possess the ability to calm the mind, create a peaceful personality and sharpen intelligence.

Dressing hair with oils in classical Indian statuary

HOW IT GROWS

There are 3 main varieties of mustard: white, brown and black. All 3 varieties grow in India as well as in Argentina, Austria, Chile, Denmark, Great Britain, Japan and the USA. They are all annuals which bear clusters of bright yellow flowers. In fact, from a distance, mustard fields in bloom look like huge, velvety golden carpets.

APPEARANCE AND TASTE

The seeds of the plant are the spice. White mustard seeds are a pale tan in colour and have a smooth matte finish. Black mustard seeds are larger than the other 2. The seeds of

Black mustard seeds

all 3 varieties are tiny and notoriously energetic. If you ever drop a packet of mustard seeds on the floor, you will find the odd seed even after weeks of cleaning. Raw mustard seeds have almost no smell, but on cooking, they acquire a distinctive, acrid, baked-earth aroma that dominates any dish. The seeds are sharp, nutty, slightly bitter and aromatic in taste. Their heat is often misjudged, so be careful when adding them to recipes. Mustard paste has a unique flavour that hits you in the nose and then sings in your veins!

BUYING AND STORING

Mustard is available as whole seeds, split seeds or mustard *dal*, powder and paste. Indian cooking does not use commercially blended mustards but they can make a reasonable substitute for homemade mustard paste. Mustard oil is a popular cooking medium in regional Indian cookery. Buy small amounts of the seeds and store in a clean, dry jar. Mustard seeds form clumps when wet which makes them difficult to use when cooking. Stored properly, they last up to a year.

MEDICINAL AND OTHER USES

Warm mustard oil is an excellent liniment and is used to relieve arthritic pain. In north India mustard oil massaged into the scalp is thought to promote lustrous and bountiful hair growth. Mustard is also believed to ward off evil and Indian women ritually cancel any negative forces that surround their children by wishing over them with a handful of mustard seeds.

CULINARY USES

In the south of India and along the coast, mustard is used primarily in the tempering or *baghar* of spices. This simple procedure of heating oil until very hot, dropping in the mustard seeds and cooking them until they pop and crackle, gives many dishes a distinctive flavour. In Bengal, mustard seeds are crushed to a paste for use in fiery marinades and curries that can shock the senses. Mustard is an excellent preservative and split seeds, which look like tiny lentils, are widely used for pickling.

All three main varieties of mustard grow in India

Mustard oil

To anyone belonging to the Bengali community of India, a meal of fish and rice is one of life's pleasures. The following recipe for fish curry is an all-time Bengali favourite.

MACHHER JHOL
(FISH IN MUSTARD SAUCE)

Serves 4
Preparation time 20 minutes
Cooking time 15 minutes

Mustard oil for frying
4 pieces cod or any white fish,
*   cut into 3cm (1¼in) chunks*
2 teaspoons ginger, shredded
2 teaspoons green chilli,
*   chopped*
1 teaspoon turmeric powder
2 tablespoons black mustard
*   seeds*
2 teaspoons panch phoron
Salt
150ml (¼pt) water

1 Heat the oil in a kadai or wok and fry the fish for 2-3 minutes. Set aside in its juices.

2 Make a fine paste of the ginger, chilli, turmeric and mustard seeds with a little water in a food processor.

3 Heat 3 tablespoons of oil in a pan. Add the panch phoron. When the seeds crackle, add the mustard paste and salt. Cook for 5 minutes stirring all the while.

4 Add the fish, its juices and the rest of the water and simmer for 3 more minutes. Serve hot with boiled rice.

This recipe is for a salad that is served with any spicy meal to tone down the burn.

KHIRA TAMATER KA RAITA
(CUCUMBER AND TOMATO IN YOGHURT)

Serves 4
Preparation time 15 minutes
Cooking time 0

150g (5oz) cucumber, chopped
*   finely*
150g (5oz) tomatoes, chopped
*   finely*
300ml (10fl oz) yoghurt, beaten
Salt
1 teaspoon sugar
2 teaspoons sunflower oil
1 teaspoon black mustard seeds
1 teaspoon cumin seeds
2 teaspoons coriander leaves,
*   chopped*

1 Mix together the cucumber, tomatoes, yoghurt, salt and sugar.

2 Heat the oil in a small pan. Add the mustard and cumin seeds. As soon as they finish crackling, pour the seeds and the oil over the yoghurt.

3 Serve cold with a sprinkling of coriander.

Machher Jhol

Capsicum annuum/Capsicum frutescens

CHILLIES

(LAL MIRCH/HARI MIRCH)

Green chillies

Indian food without chillies is like summer without sunshine. That is not to say that all Indian food scorches the taste buds, rather that it is an amicable blend of heat, fragrance and flavour. Given the importance of this spice today, it is surprising that until about 400 years ago, chillies were unknown in India. They were first introduced by the Portuguese at the end of the 15th century. Chillies were first domesticated in Mexico in about 7000 BC and it is generally believed that Columbus introduced the fruit to the Europeans. By 1650 they had spread all over the world and were adopted into the cuisines of most of the tropical countries. Beautiful to look at and endowed with the power of fire, this fruit belongs to the *Solanaceae* family, which includes such tranquil relatives as the tomato and the aubergine.

Anaheim chilli

Scotch Bonnets

taste ranges from mild to dynamite. The level of heat is dependent on the amount of capsaicin present in the seeds, veins and skin of the chillies and is not diminished by cooking, storing, or freezing. Chillies actually cool down the system in hot weather. The capsaicin dilates blood vessels to increase circulation and encourage perspiration. However, if you do suffer, don't reach for a jug of water – capsaicin is insoluble in water (like oil). Dairy products have the power to neutralise capsaicin so try yoghurt, or milk to douse the fire.

Birdseye chillies

HOW IT GROWS

Chillies are cultivated mainly in tropical and sub-tropical countries with India undoubtedly the largest producer and major exporter. Commercially, chillies, which are fruits of the capsicum species, may be classified on the basis of their colour, shape and pungency, but on the whole, two major varieties – *Capsicum annuum* and *Capsicum frutescens* – are grown and eaten all over the world. The *c.annuum* bush is an annual which grows up to a height of 1m (3ft) and bears

fruit that are large, mild and pendant, like sweet peppers. The *c. frutescens* plant is a perennial which grows up to 2m (6ft) and has smaller, pungent pods, which grow pointing away from the stem. Examples are birdseye and tabasco chillies. When the fruits mature, they are picked and dried in great mounds in the sun, or in huge mechanical driers. They are then sorted according to their size, pungency and colour.

Red chillies

APPEARANCE AND TASTE

Fresh unripe chillies come in various shades of green from lime to olive. The ripe fruits are red and these are dried until they look like dark crumpled rubies. Mexican chillies like the serrano, jalapeno, cascabel and ancho are short and thick. Habanero chillies from the West Indies are lantern shaped and various Indian chillies are long and fat, round like cherries, or small and slender. Chillies have a strong, smarting aroma and their

Heaps of drying chillies

Chilli powder is one of the most important spices in Indian cuisine

dry, dark place. Exposure to light can spoil the colour. You can buy several forms of chilli powder like paprika which is mild but does not store well and cayenne which is extremely hot. However, Indian chilli powder is widely available and needs no alternative.

MEDICINAL USES

Chillies are very high in vitamins A and C and have more vitamin C per gram than many oranges. Capsicum preparations are used as counterirritants for lumbago and rheumatic disorders. They are also added to medicines which relieve sore throats. However, an inordinate intake of chillies can burn the lining of the stomach, so beware of overindulgence.

BUYING AND STORING

Chillies are available fresh, dried, powdered, flaked, in oil, in sauce, bottled and pickled. When buying fresh chillies, look for crisp, unwrinkled ones that are waxy and green. Make sure they are bright and unbroken. The pungency can vary from the mild Kashmir chilli to the dried south Indian varieties which have incredible firepower. As with all ground spices, chilli powder loses its strength and sparkle after a few months. Whole dried chillies will keep for up to a year if stored in a

CULINARY USES

Chillies or chilli powder are used in virtually every savoury dish in India. All chillies need to be treated with respect. The capsaicin in chillies is highly irritant to skin, so be careful when preparing them. Try to avoid contact with the inside of the fruit and wash hands with soap and water immediately after use or wear rubber gloves when chopping. Keep hands away from the face. To reduce the pungency of chillies, discard the seeds and soak them in cold salted water. For maximum fire, slice the chillies and leave the seeds in. To prepare dried chillies, also wash in cold water, dry, remove stems and shake out the seeds. They can be torn, soaked in warm water and ground to a paste.

Chillies are cultivated mainly in tropical and sub-tropical countries with India undoubtedly the largest producer and exporter

It is very difficult to find recipes that will best represent the use of chillies in Indian cookery, but the following ones are known for their tasty firepower. The chillies add to the taste of the main ingredient and enhance the overall flavour. The chicken comes from the Mughal repertoire and the potatoes are a speciality of the west coast of India.

MURGH ROGHNI
(CHICKEN IN ALMOND AND CASHEW SAUCE)

Serves 4
Preparation time 30 minutes
Cooking time 1 hour

12 chicken drumsticks, skinned
150ml (5fl oz) yoghurt
Salt
1 teaspoon sugar
150ml (5fl oz) sunflower oil
60g (2oz) unsalted cashew nuts, soaked in hot water for 10 minutes
60g (2oz) almonds, soaked in hot water for 10 minutes
1 teaspoon cumin seeds
1 teaspoon ginger paste
1 teaspoon garlic paste
2 large onions, chopped finely
10 tablespoons tomato purée
2 teaspoons chilli powder
1 teaspoon turmeric powder
2 teaspoons garam masala powder
4 eggs, hard-boiled, shelled, halved
2 tablespoons double cream

1 Marinate the chicken in the yoghurt and salt for 30 minutes.

2 Heat the sugar in a heavy pan until it browns. Add half the oil and blend into the caramel.

3 Place the chicken in the pan and fry until well browned. Meanwhile grind the nuts to a paste.

4 In a separate pan, heat the remaining oil and sprinkle in the cumin seeds. When they turn brown add the ginger and garlic pastes. Stir a couple of times and add the onion. Fry until golden.

5 Add the tomato purée and nut paste and simmer until the oil separates then add the powdered spices.

6 Add the fried chicken and cook until tender, adding a little water to prevent burning.

7 Check the seasoning and serve hot, garnished with the eggs and a swirl of cream.

BATATA TALASANI
(SPICY POTATO STRAWS)

Serves 4
Preparation time 15 minutes
Cooking time 15 minutes

4 tablespoons sunflower oil
2 teaspoons garlic, crushed
6 large potatoes, peeled and cut into thin chips
Salt
1 teaspoon chilli powder

1 Heat the oil in a kadai or wok. Add the garlic and stir for half a minute.

2 Add the potato chips and stir-fry until translucent. Add the salt and chilli powder and mix well.

3 Then add a little water and cook on a low heat until the potatoes are done to your satisfaction. Serve hot with rotis or as a spicy alternative to chips.

Batata Talasani

Opposite: chillies drying in a Rajasthani village street

Carum carvi

CARAWAY

(SIYA JEERA)

Outside India, caraway is often confused with the more popular cumin, but it is nevertheless quite distinctive. Though used infrequently over most of India, it is an essential ingredient in north Indian cookery. Its special qualities were known to the ancient Egyptians, Greeks and Romans who used it to make love potions, believing that it prevented lovers from straying. Caraway was especially popular in the Medieval Europe when it was added to breads, cakes and roasted apples.

In India caraway grows wild in the northern Himalayas and is cultivated in the hills of Kumaon, Garhwal and Chamba

HOW IT GROWS

The caraway plant is a biennial herb with a fleshy root and slender, branched stems that grow up to 0.6m (2ft). It has wispy leaves and small white and apple-green flowers. The seeds ripen in summer into narrow, curved, elongated and ridged kernels. Caraway is native to Asia but also grows well in Holland (which is the world's largest producer), Canada, Great Britain, Poland, Germany, Morocco and the USA. In India it grows wild in the northern Himalayas and is cultivated in the hills of Kumaon, Garhwal and Chamba. It also seems to thrive in the alpine astringency of the Kashmiri summers.

APPEARANCE AND TASTE

Caraway seeds are brown, hard and sharply pointed at the ends. They are about 4–7mm (¼–⅓in) long and have five longitudinal, tan-coloured ridges. The seed has a pleasant, warm odour and an aromatic, pungent and slightly bitter flavour. The sharp taste seems to leave a warm feeling in the mouth.

BUYING AND STORING

Caraway is available whole or ground. It is very easy to grind the seeds at home as a light roasting makes them brittle. Store in a cool, dry place or it will form clumps and become fusty.

Old Delhi spice market

MEDICINAL AND OTHER USES

Caraway is considered a 'spring cleaner' for the body, relieving flatulence and colic, activating the kidneys, freshening the breath and nullifying the nauseating effect of some medicines. A tiny bit can be chewed to relieve a griping stomach, but beware of the sharp seeds and stinging flavour. The essential oil is used to scent soaps and mouthwashes. The husks and stalks of the seeds are used as cattle fodder.

CULINARY USES

Caraway is used to flavour bread, cakes and cheese. Caraway-flavoured Indian cheese is popular but is available only in certain parts of India. The famous liqueur kümmel is laced with the extract of caraway. In Indian cookery it is used to complement meat or rice dishes.

Caraway seeds

Ground caraway

The following recipes can be served together. The first makes a tasty change from ordinary boiled rice. The second dish is a legendary delicacy. It is a Mughal speciality that has been absorbed into the Indian repertoire and is now served in many north Indian restaurants.

TAMATER PULAO
(TOMATO-FLAVOURED RICE)

Serves 4
Preparation time 30 minutes
Cooking time 35 minutes

4 tablespoons sunflower oil
1 teaspoon caraway seeds
1 teaspoon black peppercorns
10 curry leaves
300g (10oz) basmati rice,
  washed
150g (5oz) tomatoes, chopped
4 tablespoons tomato purée
Salt
600ml (1pt) hot water
4 tablespoons coriander leaves,
  chopped

1 Heat the oil in a heavy pan. Add the caraway seeds and peppercorns. Stir a few times. Then add the curry leaves and the rice. Reduce the heat and stir-fry until the rice grains turn shiny.

2 Drop in the tomatoes, tomato purée and salt. Increase the heat, mix well and pour in the hot water. Give it a good stir, cover and cook on a low heat until the rice is fluffy and dry.

3 Serve hot with a sprinkling of coriander.

MURGH MASSALAM
(CHICKEN IN RICH ALMOND SAUCE)

Serves 4
Preparation time 2 hours
Cooking time 1 hour

1 large chicken, whole, skinned
  and cleaned

For the marinade:
2 teaspoons garlic paste
2 teaspoons ginger paste
2 teaspoons green chilli, minced
150ml (5fl oz) natural yoghurt
1 teaspoon salt

For the stuffing:
6 tablespoons basmati rice
2 large eggs, hard boiled,
  chopped
6 tablespoons onion, chopped
  finely
2 tablespoons almonds, chopped
4 tablespoons coriander leaves,
  chopped
Salt

For the sauce:
5 tablespoons sunflower oil
2 large onions, sliced, boiled until
  translucent, drained and
  ground to a paste
2 teaspoons ginger paste
2 teaspoons garlic paste
4 cardamom
8 cloves
16 black peppercorns
2 teaspoons caraway seeds
2 bay leaves
Salt
1 teaspoon chilli powder
1 teaspoon turmeric powder
2 teaspoons coriander powder
2 tablespoons flaked almonds
2 tablespoons raisins
450ml (15fl oz) yoghurt

For the garnish:
4 tablespoons coriander leaves,
  chopped
1 teaspoon saffron strands
2 tablespoons single cream

1 Mix together the marinade ingredients and pour over the chicken. Reserve for an hour.

Murgh Massalam

2 To make the stuffing, cook the rice until soft. Drain and mix with all the other ingredients.

3 Remove the chicken from the marinade and stuff with the prepared mixture. Reserve the marinade.

4 To make the sauce, heat the oil in a pan. Add the onions, ginger and garlic pastes and fry until golden. Add the whole spices and bay leaves then stir. Fry until the oil separates from the sauce. Then add the salt and the powdered spices. Stir well.

5 Add the rest of the sauce ingredients and the reserved marinade. Cook until the oil separates again.

6 Now put the chicken in a heavy-bottomed pan and pour the sauce over. Cover and cook until done (roughly 40 minutes, depending on the size of your chicken), basting from time to time.

7 Soak the saffron in the cream for 10 minutes.

8 Pour the saffron cream over the chicken just before serving and serve hot, garnished with coriander leaves.

Cassia bark is much harder and coarser than cinnamon

Cinnamomum cassia

CASSIA

(JUNGLI DALCHINI)

The Indian name dalchini comes from the Arabian term *dar-al-chini* meaning 'wood of China', as one of the most ancient and largest producers of the spice was China. However, cassia is native to north-east India and Burma. Often confused with cinnamon because of its appearance and name (cinnamon in Hindi is *dalchini*), the two are interchangeable in certain dishes. Cassia is used widely around the Indian subcontinent. There are several varieties of cassia, all fairly similar, but the Chinese is considered the best.

Cassia buds

HOW IT GROWS

Cassia comes from a tropical tree of the laurel family that grows to a height of 3m (10ft). It bears pointed, glossy leaves and tiny, yellow flowers. The flowers give way to a small fruit called buds. The bark of the tree, which comprises the spice, is layered, dark and rough on the outside and smooth and lighter on the inside. The harvesting is done in the monsoon when the bark is easy to prise off. The outer roughness is scraped off and discarded and the bark is dried into large curls called quills. It is cultivated in China, Burma, Indonesia, Central America and India.

APPEARANCE AND TASTE

Cassia bark is brown and rough on the outside and light and smooth on the inside. It is much harder and coarser than cinnamon. The buds are small and round and are sold dried with the stalk attached. The smell is similar to cinnamon but is less pronounced. The taste is woody, and bitter sweet.

BUYING AND STORING

Cassia is available as small pieces or as a powder. If you need cassia powder buy it, as you will ruin the blade of your grinder if you try to grind the bark at home. Buy cassia buds that are unbroken and tan-coloured with a dark stalk. Look for good, fragrant cassia and store in an airtight jar to preserve its flavour. In

Selling chillies in Bombay

China, some people tie the bark and buds in muslin cloth for prolonged storage.

MEDICINAL AND OTHER USES

Cassia is used to treat colic and diarrhoea and is said to relieve flatulence. Added to spicy pot-pourri blends, the oil, available in aromatherapy shops, is used in perfumes and cosmetics. The wood of the tree is sometimes polished and used to make furniture.

CULINARY USES

In India, cassia is used exactly like cinnamon, in curries, rice and vegetables. It is not added to sweets because of its astringency. The Chinese use it in their blend of five-spice powder. Cassia buds are used in cooking as well as in *paan* – a betel leaf filled with nuts, seeds and spices and eaten after a rich meal to freshen the breath. A single bud often fastens the leaf envelope to hold in the contents.

Kolhapur is a town not far from Bombay, known for its fiery, dried red chillies and chilli powder.

KOLHAPURI RASSA
(LAMB IN HOT COCONUT SAUCE)

Serves 4
Preparation time 40 minutes
Cooking time 40 minutes

For the marinade:
150ml (5fl oz) yoghurt
1 teaspoon turmeric powder
1 teaspoon chilli powder
1 teaspoon garam masala
* powder*
2 teaspoons ginger paste
2 teaspoons garlic paste
Salt

For the curry:
600g (1¼lb) lean lamb,
* trimmed and cubed*
150ml (5fl oz) sunflower oil
4cm (1½in) cassia stick
10 black peppercorns, crushed
6 cloves
1 teaspoon aniseed
2 onions, chopped finely
300g (10oz) coconut, grated if
* fresh, or desiccated*
150g (5oz) tomatoes, chopped

1 Mix the marinade ingredients and add the lamb. Stir well and reserve for 30 minutes.

2 Heat 2 tablespoons of the oil in a heavy pan and add the whole spices. Fry for a minute and add the onion. Fry until pale and golden and add the coconut. Fry well until brown. Add the tomatoes, stir and take off the heat.

3 Cool this mixture and grind to a coarse paste in a food processor.

4 Heat the remaining oil in another heavy pan. Take the lamb out of the marinade and fry until brown. Add the marinade and a little water, cover and cook until nearly done.

5 Add the ground paste and simmer for 5 minutes. Check the salt and remove from the heat.

6 Serve very hot with plain boiled rice or rotis.

This recipe comes from the north which grows cassia as well as a special variety of carrot that is almost wine-coloured and full of flavour. If you do manage to get deep-coloured carrots for this recipe, so much the better.

GAJAR KA PULAO
(CARROT-FLAVOURED RICE)

Serves 4
Preparation time 10 minutes
Cooking time 20 minutes

5 tablespoons sunflower oil
6cm (2½in) cassia stick
6 cloves
10 black peppercorns
300g (10oz) Indian rice
150g (5oz) carrots, grated
4 tablespoons cashew nuts
Salt
600ml (1pt) hot water

1 Heat the oil in a heavy pan. When it is hot, add the whole spices and fry for a minute.

2 Add the rice and fry until translucent. Drop in the carrots and the cashew nuts.

3 Fry for a couple of minutes. Add the salt and hot water. Bring to the boil, lower the heat, cover and cook until the rice is fluffy but each grain is still separate.

4 Serve hot with a curry, salad and a poppadom.

Kolhapuri Rassa

Cinnamomum verum/Cinnamomum zeylanicum

CINNAMON

(DALCHINI)

Ground cinnamon

Although cinnamon is native to Sri Lanka and is mentioned in the records of that country dating back to the 13th century, the oldest description available is in the Jewish religious text, the Torah. The Portuguese colonised Sri Lanka for its cinnamon but were defeated by the Dutch who controlled world prices by limiting its supply. In India, its medicinal properties have been well known since before the 8th century.

HOW IT GROWS

Cinnamon is an evergreen tree of the laurel family. Sri Lanka is the largest producer and cinnamon from Sri Lanka and the Seychelles is considered the best in the world. The tree grows to 10m (35ft). The leaves of the cinnamon tree are large, leathery and shiny, the tiny flowers are lemon-white and the oblong fruits are dark purple and have one seed.

APPEARANCE AND TASTE

The dried inner bark of the cinnamon tree is the spice used in cooking. The longest, unblemished pieces of bark are rolled by hand to form compact curls and then dried. The long thin scrolls called quills are camel-coloured and very brittle. Sometimes during processing some quills fragment and these are sold as quillings. The sweet, woody scent of the spice is quite special, very easy to recognise and is the main flavouring in many desserts. The taste is warm, sharply sweet and aromatic.

BUYING AND STORING

Cinnamon is commonly available as quills, quillings or ground into fine powder. Sometimes cinnamon buds are also used as a spice. When buying bags of cinnamon, check that there are no chippings and that the quills are fairly long and whole. Cinnamon is easy to grind at home but if you buy ground cinnamon remember that it loses its verve fairly quickly, after which it looks, tastes and smells like sawdust, so buy small amounts and consume within a month.

MEDICINAL AND OTHER USES

Cinnamon was known to ancient physicians before 2700 BC. Cinnamon infused in warm water is effective in curing the common cold, preventing nervous tension, checking nausea and stimulating digestion. Cinnamon oil cures gastric debility and is commonly used as an inhalation for colds and sinusitis. Local application is said to relieve certain rheumatic pains. Cinnamon is used in making incense, toothpaste and perfumes. Cinnamon bark oil is used in some pharmaceuticals, germicides and soaps. Cinnamon leaf oil is also used in perfumery. Cinnamon oil is used extensively in food processing and in flavouring soft drinks.

CULINARY USES

Cinnamon is used to flavour rice, curries, desserts and meats. It is also an essential part of the standard blend of garam masala which includes cardamom, cloves and peppercorns. Garam masala is the magic spice mixture which gives many Indian dishes that rich, heady fragrance. *Masala chai* is tea with milk and sugar, which is liberally laced with cinnamon.

The cinnamon tree grows up to 10 metres (35 feet) high

Cinnamon sticks

This dish evokes the splendour of old Delhi where it is eaten in the shade of ancient, copper-burnished forts and turrets.

GOSHT SHAHJANI
(RICH, BROWN LAMB)

Serves 4
Preparation time 45 minutes
Cooking time 1 hour

600g (1 ¼lb) boneless lamb, trimmed and cubed
150ml (5fl oz) yoghurt
2 teaspoons ginger paste
2 teaspoons garlic paste
10 tablespoons coriander leaves, chopped
10 tablespoons tomato purée
1 teaspoon chilli powder
1 teaspoon turmeric powder
1 teaspoon cinnamon powder
Salt
8 tablespoons sunflower oil
4 potatoes boiled, peeled and quartered
3 large onions, peeled and quartered
8 cloves

1 Marinate the meat in a mixture of yoghurt, ginger, garlic, coriander leaves, tomato purée, powdered spices and salt for 30 minutes.

2 Heat 3 tablespoons of oil in a heavy pan and stir-fry the potatoes until golden. Drain and reserve.

3 In the same pan stir-fry the onions until golden. Drain and reserve.

4 Heat the remaining oil. Add the cloves. When they pop, add the meat mixture and stir.

5 Add a little water and cook on a low flame until the meat is tender and the oil separates from the gravy.

6 Add the fried potatoes and onions and cook for 5 more minutes. Serve hot with naan or roti.

This is a rice dish that comes from the grand kitchens of the Maharajas of India where a normal day meant cooking for 50 people, not including the retinue of servants. It is scaled down here to manageable proportions.

RATAN PULAO
(JEWELLED VEGETABLE RICE)

Serves 4
Preparation time 30 minutes
Cooking time 30 minutes

6 tablespoons sunflower oil
1 teaspoon cumin seeds
4cm (1 ½in) stick cinnamon
8 cloves
16 black peppercorns
8 cardamom
4 fresh green chillies, chopped finely
150g (5oz) carrot, diced finely
150g (5oz) green peas
90g (3oz) French beans, chopped
90g (3oz) sweetcorn
90g (3oz) mushrooms, sliced
Salt
300g (10oz) basmati rice, washed and drained
2 tablespoons raisins
1 sheet edible silver foil (optional)

1 Heat the oil in a heavy pan and add the cumin seeds. When they pop add the whole spices.

2 Stir a couple of times and add the green chillies, all the vegetables and salt. Stir-fry for 2-3 minutes.

3 Add the rice and fry until translucent. Add 600ml (1pt) of hot water, mix gently and bring to the boil then lower heat, cover and cook until all the vegetables are soft but still crisp.

4 Serve hot garnished with raisins and edible silver foil.

Coriandrum sativum

CORIANDER

(DHANIA)

Most Indian cooks will not allow a savoury dish to leave their kitchen without a good sprinkling of fresh, fragrant coriander leaves. This pretty herb is the most commonly used garnish in India, and adds a dewy-green touch to red or brown curries. Seeds of the coriander plant are the spice. Coriander is perhaps one of the first spices known to man and has been around for over 3000 years. It finds mention in ancient Sanskrit texts and in the Bible where the colour of manna is likened to that of coriander seeds.

Coriander seeds

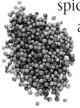

HOW IT GROWS

Coriander is both an annual and perennial herb which grows up to 20cm (8in) and has many branches. The plant bears whitish-pink lacy flowers which mature into seeds. These seeds are picked when ripe, dried, threshed and sieved, taking care to keep them whole.

Ground coriander seeds

APPEARANCE AND TASTE

Coriander leaves are compound and fragile. The stem, which is pale green and tender, is also used in cookery. The seeds which constitute the spice are round, 1cm (½in) in diameter and have fine, longitudinal ridges. The herb and the spice are completely different from one another with regard to aroma and flavour. The leaves taste and smell fresh and fruity with a hint of ginger.

The seeds, on the other hand, have a sweet, heady aroma with a subtle whiff of pine and pepper.

BUYING AND STORING

Little bunches of fresh coriander tied with string are commonly available at greengrocers. It looks quite like parsley but the test lies in the aroma – parsley has a gentle scent, coriander's is vibrant. Coriander seeds as well as ground coriander are also available. Make your own coriander seed powder in a mortar or food processor after dry-roasting – it is fresh, unadulterated and considerably more fragrant than ready-made. Coriander oil is sometimes sold.

MEDICINAL AND OTHER USES

Coriander seeds are said to be diuretic, antibilious, and carminative. An infusion of the seeds is cooling and helps reduce fever. It also helps lower blood cholesterol and makes an excellent eyewash. Coriander juice is rich in vitamins A, B and C and in iron. Caution: asthma sufferers should use coriander sparingly. Coriander oil is valuable in perfumery as its spicy note blends beautifully with rich oriental scents. It is also used to flavour medicines as it retains its pleasant aroma longer than any other oil of its kind.

An infusion of coriander is a traditional Indian beauty aid

CULINARY USES

Suited to almost every savoury Indian dish, coriander the spice and the herb is used daily in curries, chutneys, soups and drinks. Roasted coriander powder is an indispensable item in the spice box and cool yoghurt-based salads and drinks like raita and lassi are dusted with it for a delicious zing. An apple-green chutney made by grinding coriander leaves, coconut, ginger, garlic and spices is a popular sandwich spread or meal accompaniment. The volatile oil is used to flavour liqueurs and chocolate.

The coriander plant bears lacy flowers which mature into seeds

Fresh coriander

This recipe comes from Maharashtra. It is a favourite farm meal, along with rotis, and often uses fresh aubergines straight off the plant, cooked in front of visitors.

BHARWA BAINGAN
(STUFFED AUBERGINES)

Serves 4
Preparation time 30 minutes
Cooking time 40 minutes

8 tablespoons sunflower oil
8 cloves
8 black peppercorns
2 tablespoons coriander seeds
2 large onions, sliced
150g (5oz) coconut, grated if
    fresh (or desiccated)
8 small aubergines (available
    from all Indian grocers)
4 tablespoons coriander leaves
1 teaspoon chilli powder
1 teaspoon turmeric powder
1 teaspoon tamarind paste
4 tablespoons unsalted
    cashew nuts
½ teaspoon sugar
Salt
12 small shallots, peeled
8 new baby potatoes, peeled

1 Heat 2 tablespoons of the oil in a pan, add the cloves, peppercorns, and coriander seeds. Fry for a minute then add the sliced onion and cook until brown.

2 Add the coconut. Stir until well browned, then remove, cool and grind to a paste in a blender, adding a little water if required.

3 Slit each aubergine lengthwise into four, keeping the stem end intact.

4 Mix the coconut paste with the coriander leaves, powder spices, tamarind, cashewnuts, sugar and salt. Stuff this mixture into the aubergines, reserving some.

5 Roll the whole potatoes and onions in the remainder of the mixture.

6 Heat the oil in a pan until it smokes, lower the heat and add the vegetables. Cover and cook on a low heat without burning, adding a little water as necessary, until you can easily slide a skewer through the vegetables.

7 Serve hot with rotis.

This recipe comes from Kerala in south India and the addition of the coconut milk transforms an otherwise common dish into something special.

ANDE KI BHURJI
(EGG MASALA)

Serves 4
Preparation time 30 minutes
Cooking time 15 minutes

8 eggs
150g (5oz) fresh coconut,
    grated(or a tin of coconut
    milk)
Salt
4 teaspoons sunflower oil
1 small onion, chopped finely
60g (2oz) mushrooms,
    chopped
2 green chillies, minced
6 tablespoons tomato, chopped
½ teaspoon turmeric powder
1 teaspoon coriander powder

1 Beat the eggs. Then make coconut milk by adding hot water to the coconut and liquidising it in a blender. Squeeze out the milk through a sieve or in a piece of muslin and discard the residue. (Alternatively, use tinned coconut milk.) Blend this along with the salt into the beaten egg.

2 Heat the oil in a non-stick pan and stir-fry the onions until golden.

3 Add the mushrooms, chillies and lastly, the tomato. Stir-fry until cooked, then add the turmeric and coriander powder.

4 Pour the egg mixture over, cover and cook on a very low heat until set.

5 Garnish with coriander leaves and cut into fingers to serve with naan.

Bharwa Baingan

Crocus sativus
SAFFRON
(KESAR)

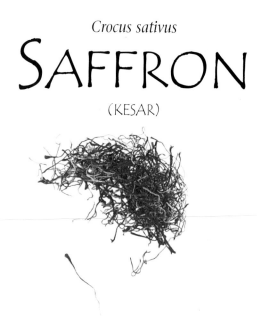

Saffron is the dried stigmas of *Crocus sativus*

Kesar, zaffran, crocus, saffron . . . by whatever name, this golden spice has evoked an aura of romance, richness and rarity through the ages. In India, saffron is worth its weight in gold, its vibrant colour and heady bouquet making it pure ambrosia. In earlier times, its scent was so valued that the Romans are believed to have perfumed the streets of Rome with saffron oil before Nero entered it. Alexander the Great is said to have wept tears of joy when he first saw the beautiful saffron fields in India. The Mughal emperors of Delhi were known to relax to their favourite music in the saffron-scented splendour of their marble palaces. Even today, saffron reigns in the spice kingdom, beautiful, fragile and infinitely precious.

HOW IT GROWS

At one time, saffron is known to have grown wild in Persia and Asia Minor. India and Spain are today the only major producers of the spice. In India it only grows in Pampore in the valley of Kashmir and Kishtwar in Jammu. Saffron is the dried stigmas of the *Crocus sativus*, a perennial bulb which flowers for just two weeks in late October. In India the lavender-blue blossoms are plucked at dawn before the hot sun wilts them. Then comes the delicate task of prising out the delicate stigmas from within each flower, a job done by skilful women by hand. The stigmas are dried artificially or in the sun; in Spain the stigmas are toasted over charcoal.

APPEARANCE AND TASTE

Saffron is made up of fine, orange-gold threads that are so light that 750,000 hand-picked flowers yield only about 450g (1lb). When fresh, saffron is bright and glossy, but exposure to light and air makes it dull and brittle. Pure saffron is believed to be able to colour and flavour 70,000 times its weight in liquid. Its intense, musky aroma suffuses any room in which a box of saffron is opened and the taste is slightly bitter but richly perfumed.

BUYING AND STORING

Saffron is sold loosely matted like a lace of dark amber strands. It is also available ground into a deep orange powder. The best saffron is rich in colour and highly fragrant. You will need very small quantities. It loses its zest with keeping; indeed, prolonged periods of hoarding can degenerate it into a

Saffron dye

cake of characterless threads. Store saffron away from light which can bleach it to a faded yellow, and in an airtight jar to keep in its fragrance. It is the most expensive spice in the world due to its scarcity, fragility and flavour. That is why the temptation to adulterate it is considerable – look out for copies. The usual adulterant is safflower, aptly called bastard saffron. Cheaper and with thicker strands than saffron, it will turn food golden but will not flavour it.

MEDICINAL AND OTHER USES

Saffron is prescribed for flatulent colic, urinary disorders, skin and menstrual problems. It has featured in the pharmacopoeia of several cultures as a cure for fevers and melancholia. Adding to its romanticism is the fact that it is believed to be a powerful aphrodisiac and is used in the preparation of several sweets and drinks that are thought to stimulate and strengthen libido. In India saffron has a special place in ceremonial worship. Traditionally used as a paste to paint a religious mark on the forehead, it is reserved for rituals of birth or marriage. Famous temple deities are anointed daily with generous amounts of its paste to scent and decorate them. The spice also gets special sanctity from its use as a dye for the robes of Hindu and Buddhist priests.

CULINARY USES

Saffron enhances savoury food as well as sweet. A few strands soaked in a little warm water or milk and added along with the liquid to the dish adds a fragrant richness. It especially complements milk desserts, rice and chicken. A superb summer drink, mango panha, is made by boiling raw mangoes and sugar together, straining the concentrate and flavouring it with saffron.

Hindu deities Krishna and Radha are traditionally annointed with saffron

The crocuses are picked before the sun wilts them then the stigmas are pulled out by hand and dried

Even the most simple dish can be transformed into something magical by the addition of saffron. The recipes on the following page are for dishes that are rich in themselves but depend on saffron for unmatched flavour. The first dish is a sumptuous rice that evokes the old-world Muslim ambience of the city of Lucknow, where beautiful women would sit behind filigreed windows while the men played chess on ancient mother-of-pearl chessboards.

LUCKNOW MURGI BIRYANI
(CHICKEN BIRYANI LUCKNOW STYLE)

Serves 4
Preparation time 40 minutes
Cooking time 1½ hours

For the rice:
6 tablespoons sunflower oil
4 cloves
8 black peppercorns
4cm (1½in) stick cinnamon
2 cloves garlic, peeled
4cm (1½in) piece ginger, peeled
300g (10oz) basmati rice, washed
Salt

For the curry:
300g (10oz) boneless chicken, cubed
300ml (½pt) yoghurt
70ml (2½fl oz) single cream
Salt
1 teaspoon ginger paste
1 teaspoon garlic paste
1 teaspoon cumin powder
1 teaspoon chilli powder
1 teaspoon turmeric powder
6 tablespoons sunflower oil

1 teaspoon black cumin seeds (sahjeera)
2 large onions, chopped
4 tablespoons tomato, chopped
2 teaspoons garam masala powder

For the garnish:
2 tablespoons sunflower oil
1 large onion, sliced thinly
1 teaspoon saffron strands soaked in 2 teaspoons of milk
4 tablespoons coriander leaves, chopped
1 teaspoon rose-water
4 tablespoons mint leaves, chopped

To make the rice:
1 Heat the oil in a pan and fry the cloves, peppercorns and cinnamon. Keep stirring until the spices begin to change colour. Then add the garlic and ginger and stir.

2 Drain the rice and add to the mixture with 600ml (1pt) hot water. Season with salt and mix well.

3 Cook until soft and fluffy then drain. Remove and discard the ginger and garlic. Keep warm.

To make the curry:
1 Mix the chicken with the yoghurt, cream, salt, ginger, garlic, cumin, chilli and turmeric powders.

2 Heat the oil and fry the black cumin until it pops.

3 Add the onion and cook until brown, then add the tomato and garam masala. Cook until blended and add the chicken mixture.

4 Stir-fry until the oil separates, then add 300ml (½pt) hot water. Reduce the heat and cook until the chicken is tender.

To serve:
1 In a deep dish, arrange layers of rice and chicken curry, ending with a rice layer.

2 Heat the oil in a small pan and fry the onion until brown and crisp. Sprinkle on top of the biryani along with the saffron, coriander, rose-water and mint leaves and cover.

3 Place in a hot oven for 10 minutes until heated through. Serve with plain yoghurt and fried whole potatoes.

This recipe is for a dessert whose very name means 'ambrosia of the gods'. Its silvery smoothness and creamy richness make it one of India's best-loved sweets.

SHRIKHAND
(CREAMY YOGHURT DESSERT)

Serves 4
Preparation time 40 minutes
Chilling time 4 hours

1200ml (2pt) set yoghurt
1 teaspoon saffron strands
2 tablespoons milk
220g (8oz) caster sugar
½ teaspoon nutmeg powder
½ teaspoon cardamom powder
2 tablespoons pistachio nuts, chopped
2 tablespoons raisins
2 teaspoons chirongi nuts

1 Hang up the yoghurt in a clean muslin or cotton cloth overnight. Discard the whey.

2 Soak the saffron in the milk.

3 Place the drained yoghurt in a bowl. Add the sugar and beat until blended.

4 Add the saffron to the yoghurt and blend. Put into 4 serving bowls. Sprinkle with the nutmeg, cardamom, pistachios, raisins and chirongi. Serve chilled.

Shrikhand

Curcuma longa

TURMERIC

(HALDI)

One of the most traditional and versatile of spices used in Indian cooking, turmeric is the very heart and soul of any curry. This key ingredient is used daily in every part of India as its unique colour and flavour enriches every regional cuisine. Turmeric is used prolifically in a host of Indian dishes ranging from starters, lentils, meats and vegetables. It has also been used for centuries as a curative and cleansing agent. Since early times, it has been associated with purification so that even today, an Indian bride and groom are ritually anointed with turmeric as part of a cleansing ceremony, after which they do not leave the house until the wedding. Turmeric is stored in every Indian house – its use as a quick antiseptic, as a beauty aid and, of course, as a versatile cooking spice makes this condiment a truly exceptional part of the traditional Indian spice box.

Turmeric powder

the underground root or rhizome of the plant. Though turmeric is grown over vast areas for commercial use, it is also often grown at home in rustic terracotta pots, mainly for its fragrant leaves which are used to flavour some Indian sweets. As for the root, only cured turmeric has the aroma and colour (chiefly due to the presence of the pigment curcumin) necessary for cooking. Curing is only carried out commercially so the fresh, home-grown rhizome is used solely for medicine or as a beauty aid. The rhizomes are boiled in water for about 45 minutes, drained and then dried in the sun for 10 to 15 days until they become hard and dry. They are then cleaned, polished and ground into a powder.

Fresh turmeric

HOW IT GROWS

A member of the ginger family, turmeric grows best in a tropical climate. India is the world's largest producer and exporter. About 180,000 tonnes of cured turmeric are produced in India annually, of which 92% is consumed within the country and 8% is exported to about 64 countries worldwide. The main turmeric growing states are Andhra Pradesh, Maharashtra, Orissa, Tamil Nadu, Karnataka and Kerala. Other countries which grow turmeric are China, Haiti, Jamaica, Japan, Malaysia, Peru, Sri Lanka and Vietnam. The plant, which is a herbaceous perennial and grows to a height of over 1m (3ft), bears large, pretty leaves and spikes of clustered flowers. Turmeric the spice is

Hill turmeric plant in flower

Traditional spice box including turmeric

Rajasthani spice market

APPEARANCE AND TASTE

Fresh turmeric looks deceptively dull. Within its rough, brown skin, which can be easily·peeled, lies the most beautiful golden-yellow root. This root is exported in its dried form which resembles tough, bright yellow wood. The most widely available form of turmeric is the flamboyant golden powder that frequently shimmers next to the bright red chilli powder on shop shelves. In fact, Marco Polo noted on one of his travels that its colour resembled that of saffron. Turmeric has an earthy, sensual fragrance reminiscent of the aridness of vast fields parched in a hot Indian summer. On its own, it has a musky, dry taste, but it is used wholeheartedly in Indian cooking for its wonderful quality of enhancing and balancing the flavours of all the other ingredients. However, be careful not to use turmeric when cooking green vegetables as they will turn grey and taste bitter.

BUYING AND STORING

Turmeric is available as a powder or as a dried root that, with some difficulty, can be powdered at home. It is easiest to buy the ready-ground powder and save time and bother. Store the spice in a dry jar and use within four months or it may lose its vibrancy. Be careful while storing and using turmeric; it will stain hands and clothes quite quickly.

MEDICINAL AND OTHER USES

Turmeric paste is used as a quick household antiseptic for minor burns and wounds. Consumption of it is said to help purify blood and to soothe inflamed sinuses. Turmeric boiled with milk and drunk last thing before going to bed is considered to be the best medicine for an irritating dry cough. Mixed with water, it is also used as a depilatory and its skin-cleansing and polishing properties make it an ideal face mask when mixed with milk for an oily skin or with cream for a dry skin. Turmeric is also considered sacred by Hindus. On festive days, Hindu women apply an auspicious dot of red powder (*sindoor*) and one of turmeric on each other's foreheads as a mark of respect, friendship and goodwill. Turmeric has been used as a dye for centuries and is still used to colour silk, cotton, medicines, confectionery, paints and varnishes. Laboratories use turmeric paper to test alkalinity.

The turmeric root is cured commercially to produce turmeric powder

CULINARY USES

Turmeric is used in virtually every Indian meat, lentil and vegetable (except greens) dish. It is an excellent preservative and therefore it is used extensively in pickles. It can be added to foods for its colour, taste or as a thickening agent. If it is added to the oil before the vegetable, meat or lentil, it imparts a deep colour and pungent taste to the dish. Added after the main ingredient, it lends a subtler flavour and a paler, lemony hue. The leaves of the turmeric plant can be dried and used to flavour ghee. The leaves can also be used to wrap foods like fish or sweets before steaming. Unlike the powder which has a musky dry smell, the leaves smell rich and sweet.

Turmeric dye

The first dish that follows comes from Bengal, where it is served as part of a traditional wedding feast along with a sumptuous array of fish and rice creations. It also makes a good starter.

BHAJA BAINGAN
(CRISP FRIED AUBERGINES)

Serves 4
Preparation time 10 minutes
Cooking time 15 minutes

1 teaspoon turmeric
1 teaspoon red chilli powder
1 teaspoon coriander powder
1 teaspoon cumin powder
Salt
4 tablespoons semolina
2 large aubergines
Sunflower oil for frying

1 Mix together the spices, salt and semolina. Then cut the aubergine into discs, 0.5cm (¼in) thick.

2 Heat a little oil in a frying pan. Coat each disc with the spiced semolina and fry in hot oil, turning over until both sides are crisp and golden.

3 Remove with a slotted spoon and drain on absorbent paper.

4 Serve immediately. Discs tend to become soggy when cold so do not fry in advance.

This recipe is a delicacy from Maharashtra and its heady fragrance conjures up visions of sun-soaked afternoons in the rich green fields of the countryside. It is an ideal accompaniment to boiled rice and a vegetable dish.

AAMTI
(MAHARASHTRIAN LENTILS)

Serves 4
Preparation time 10 minutes
Cooking time 15 minutes

280g (8oz) split mung beans (moong dal)
600 ml (1pt) water
3 tablespoons sunflower oil
1 teaspoon black mustard seeds
Large pinch asafoetida
1 teaspoon turmeric
1 teaspoon cumin seeds
10 curry leaves
4 green chillies, sliced just enough to reveal seeds
150g (5oz) tomatoes, chopped
6 tablespoons coriander leaves, chopped
Salt

1 Bring the lentils to a boil in the water and simmer until soft and mushy. Have the rest of the ingredients ready.

2 Heat the oil in a small pan. Add the mustard seeds. When they pop, quickly add the asafoetida, turmeric, cumin, curry leaves and chillies. Fry for a minute and add the cooked lentils.

3 Bring to the boil. Add the tomatoes and coriander and salt and turn off the heat. Keep covered.

4 Serve hot with plain boiled rice.

Aamti

Cuminum cyminum

CUMIN

(JEERA)

Enter a spice market in India and you will be overwhelmed by the rich ambers, blacks and sages and the warm, acrid aromas which fill the air. Among the heaps of spices, you will find one that is used in the regional cookery of every part of India. This gentle spice can be tasted in the rich meat curries of northern Kashmir and in the hot coconut curries of the south, in the exquisite vegetarian fare of Gujarat as well as in the river fish preparations of Bengal. This spice is cumin, known to man since Biblical times. Sometimes confused with caraway or nigella, cumin is an important spice in its own right and one that makes a happy addition to almost every Indian savoury.

Driving to market, Jaipur

HOW IT GROWS

Cumin is the seed of a small, slender annual herb of the coriander family, native to the Nile valley. The plant grows to a height of 30–45cm (12–18ins). It is grown extensively in India, Iran, Morocco, China, Russia, Indonesia, Japan and Turkey.

APPEARANCE AND TASTE

Cumin seeds are really the fruits of the herb. These are elongated, oval and 5–6mm (¼in) long. They range from sage-green to tobacco-brown in colour and have longitudinal ridges. During the drying process, some fine stalks invariably get left on, so cumin appears slightly bristly. Another variety of cumin is black cumin or *kala jeera*. The seeds are dark brown to black and are smaller and finer than cumin. The smell of cumin is distinctive. It has been described as peculiar, strong and bitter and is usually loved or hated. Cumin has a warm, somewhat bitter taste. Black cumin is not as bitter in flavour.

Cumin seeds are really the dried fruits of the herb

BUYING AND STORING

Available whole as seeds, cumin is also found crushed to a powder which is often blended with coriander seed powder to form a widely used mixture called *dhana-jeera*. This combination is one of the essential spice blends used in Indian cookery. Every packet of cumin has fine dried stalks, but avoid those that have the reed like, thicker stems as well. These are slightly yellowish and quite easy to recognise. It is not at all difficult to make cumin powder at home. Roast the seeds on a griddle until they change colour and crush them into a fine toasty powder. Roasting the cumin releases and enriches its earthy flavour. Store cumin in a dry place away from light. The powder must be used within 3 months.

MEDICINAL AND OTHER USES

Known for its miraculous curative properties, it is prescribed for indigestion, biliousness and flatulent colic. Hot cumin water is excellent for colds and fevers and is made by boiling a teaspoon of roasted seeds in 3 cups of water. Honey can be added to soothe a sore throat. It is believed that cumin seeds scattered between the folds of linen or wool keep insects away. The essential oil of cumin is used in perfumery to complement flowery tones like hyacinth and violet. It is also used in the manufacture of soaps.

CULINARY USES

Suited to almost any cuisine in the world, cumin is used in North African dishes like couscous, Middle Eastern ones like kebabs, in Spanish stews and in American pies. In India most curries start off with a loud crackle as cumin seeds hit the hot oil, before the meat or vegetables are added. Roasted cumin powder is sprinkled on top of salads or yoghurt as a dark, contrasting, aromatic garnish. It is also the very essence of *jaljeera* – a tasty digestive drink. It is also used in spice blends like panch phoron and tandoori masala.

A warm, dusky evening is the best time to have this fresh, sweet-sour drink which has the flavour of fun.

JALJEERA
(CUMIN SEED COOLER)

Serves 4
Preparation time 45 minutes
Cooking time 0

4 tablespoons whole tamarind (soaked in 300ml (½pt) of water)
600ml (1pt) water
6 tablespoons jaggery, grated
Salt
1 teaspoon chilli powder
1 teaspoon rock salt
2 teaspoons cumin powder (dry-roasted)
4 tablespoons mint leaves
4 tablespoons coriander leaves, chopped

1 Squeeze the thick juice from the soaked tamarind and discard the pith and fibres.

2 Add the water to dilute then stir in the jaggery, salt, chilli powder, rock salt and

Jaljeera

cumin powder and blend completely.

3 Chill thoroughly.

4 Before serving, add the mint and coriander leaves and serve ice-cold.

This recipe is for a dish that serves as an accompaniment, starter or main course and is delicious eaten hot with rotis and lentils.

BHARWAN MIRCH
(STUFFED LONG CHILLIES)

Serves 4
Preparation time 30 minutes
Cooking time 20 minutes

8 long Kenyan chillies
4 tablespoons chickpea flour
Large pinch of asafoetida
2 teaspoons cumin powder
2 teaspoons lemon juice
½ teaspoon turmeric powder
½ teaspoon chilli powder
Salt
2 tablespoons sunflower oil
1 teaspoon cumin seeds

1 Slit the chillies lengthways and carefully remove and discard all the seeds.

2 Mix the chickpea flour, asafoetida, cumin powder, lemon juice, turmeric and chilli powder with salt, and add a little water to make a thick paste.

3 Smear this paste on the inside of each chilli.

4 Heat the oil in a pan until it is hot and add the cumin seeds. When they pop, add the chillies one by one and stir-fry. Lower the heat and cook until they are soft. Serve hot with rotis.

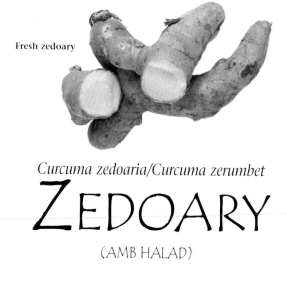

Fresh zedoary

Curcuma zedoaria/Curcuma zerumbet

ZEDOARY

(AMB HALAD)

Zedoary is found extensively in India and Indonesia and is hardly known outside these countries. Great heaps of it are sold in October and November and it is seen pickled on many Indian tables in winter. Zedoary is an ancient spice and is believed to have been used as a perfume and medicine several centuries ago.

Dried zedoary

HOW IT GROWS

Zedoary, a close relative of turmeric, is a rhizome or underground stem of a plant with long fragrant leaves. There are 2 types of zedoary seen in Indian markets – *Curcuma zedoaria* which is small and fat like ginger and *Curcuma zerumbet*, which is long and slender like tumeric. In India, zedoary grows all over Maharashtra, Gujarat and in areas which have a moist climate. It is often grown in kitchen gardens for home use.

APPEARANCE AND TASTE

The rhizome has a thin brown skin and a bright orange, hard interior. Zedoary has a smell reminiscent of turmeric, ginger and mango. In fact, it is because of this strong aroma of mango that it is called *amb halad* in many Indian languages (*amb* means mango). The taste is crisp and gingery with a bitter after-taste.

BUYING AND STORING

Zedoary is sold as a fresh root or dried slices. The fresh root is more popularly used in India. Buy plump rhizomes that show no signs of shrivelling or wilting. They can be stored in the refrigerator for up to 2 weeks. Pickled zedoary lasts for up to a month.

MEDICINAL AND OTHER USES

Zedoary is highly valued for its ability to purify the blood. Zedoary, like turmeric, is an antiseptic and a paste applied locally to cuts and wounds helps healing. It is used in Indian perfumes called *ittars* as well as in some drinks. A paste of a little zedoary and cream makes a good face mask and keeps the skin clear and shining.

CULINARY USES

Zedoary enhances some soups and chutneys. However, its main use is in a pickle which must be eaten quickly. It adds flavour as well as colour to a dish and, cut into little squares, it can make a pretty garnish for salads. Use sparingly as the taste is powerful, and be careful while handling it as its bright colour can stain clothes and fingers, just like turmeric.

The following recipes are for dishes that remind me of Bombay's clement winters. The pickle and the soup are both eaten from November to January and are believed to add a glow to dull, winter skin. They are both very easy to make and their fresh, mango fragrance holds a promise of the summer months to come.

AMB HALAD KA ACHAR
(HOT AND SOUR PRESERVE)

Serves 4
Preparation time 30 minutes
Cooking time 0

4 teaspoons zedoary, peeled and chopped finely
2 teaspoons ginger, chopped finely
1 teaspoon garlic, chopped finely
½ teaspoon green chilli, minced
6 tablespoons lemon juice
Salt

1 Mix all the ingredients. Put in an airtight jar and shake well to blend.

2 Serve in tiny quantities with rice and curry.

Street market in Jaipur

AMB HALAD KA SHORBA
(ZEDOARY SOUP)

Serves 4
Preparation time 45 minutes
Cooking time 30 minutes

6 tablespoons french beans, chopped finely
6 tablespoons carrots, chopped finely

6 tablespoons peas
6 tablespoons sweetcorn
4 tablespoons sunflower oil
2 onions, chopped finely
6 tablespoons tomatoes, blanched, skinned and chopped
Salt
1 teaspoon sugar
4 tablespoons distilled vinegar
4 tablespoons coriander leaves
1 teaspoon zedoary, chopped finely

1 Simmer the vegetables in 600ml (1pt) water until cooked but firm. Reserve along with the cooking fluid.

2 Heat the oil in a separate pan and add the onion. Fry until golden.

3 Add the tomatoes, salt and sugar. Stir until the tomatoes become mushy.

4 Add the vegetables with the broth, vinegar, chopped coriander leaves and zedoary.

5 Bring to the boil and take off the heat. Serve very hot.

Amb Halad ka Achar

Elettaria cardamomum

CARDAMOM

(ELAICHI)

One of the most popular spices in the world, cardamom is called the 'queen of spices', second only to black pepper, the king. Known to man since ancient times, it is mentioned in Greek literature of the 4th century BC. The Mughal emperors of India carried tiny silver boxes of cardamom pods which were chewed as a mouth freshener, a tradition that exists even today amongst the rich and famous of the country. The spice reached Europe through the caravan routes and through the Portuguese, French, Dutch and British merchants who fought endless battles to gain a monopoly of the lucrative trade.

The best cardamom is grown in Kerala

HOW IT GROWS

There are many varieties of cardamom, the true one being the green cardamom. India, Sri Lanka, Guatemala and Thailand are the major producers of cardamom. The fat, green pods grown in Kerala, south India, are considered the best in the world. Cardamoms are the dried fruits of a herbaceous perennial of the ginger family, growing up to 5m (15ft) tall. The fruits are picked just before they ripen, and then dried in drying houses or in the sun.

APPEARANCE AND TASTE

Cardamom pods differ according to the variety. They are all oval capsules containing between 10 to 40 hard,
dark brown seeds that are sticky and cling together. The best variety is the bright lime-green cardamom – smooth, unblemished and unopened. White cardamom pods are green cardamom pods bleached with sulphur fumes and brown cardamom pods are bigger and hairy. In fact they look like tiny, fibrous coconuts. Cardamom is prized for its seeds, while the skins of the pod are thrown away. Whole cardamom seeds have a sweet flavour and a mild, pleasant aroma. As soon as they are crushed, they release a strong, camphorous fragrance and if chewed, the taste is bitter-sweet, aromatic and lingering. Brown cardamom is rather medicinal in flavour. It is also available as seeds or ground to a powder.

BUYING AND STORING

Buy the whole pods with the freshness sealed in. The seeds are easy to use and the powder needs to be used up so quickly that buying it ready-made is a waste of time. Grind the seeds in a mortar or in a small food processor. Buy pods that are plump, fresh and evenly coloured. Cardamom stores well if whole – a clean, dry jar kept in a dark place is all that is needed.

Bleached green cardomom pods

Brown cardamom pods

MEDICINAL AND OTHER USES

Cardamom is used to relieve stomach disorders and heartburn. Gargling with cardamom water soothes a sore throat. Cardamom tea is a useful remedy for headache. The spice, boiled in milk and sweetened with honey, is thought to correct impotency. Cardamom can be seen in *supari* blends – a mouth-freshener made of spices and betel nuts, often chewed after heavy, onion- and garlic-based meals. Many Indians serve cardamoms coated with edible silver foil after a heavy meal, as a scented digestive. It is also used for pharmaceutical purposes, in perfumery and to make liqueurs and bitters.

CULINARY USES

Indian savouries and sweets are both flavoured with cardamom. This fragrant spice is used in rich, red curries and milky desserts. In India tea and coffee are sometimes spiked with cardamom. Around the world, it is used in spiced cakes and breads. Brown cardamom is used only in savouries, especially in rice dishes like biryani. Along with green cardamom, it is an essential ingredient in garam masala.

Cardamom is of special value in the following dishes which are served on festive days. Rice kheer is considered one of the most auspicious of all Indian foods and finds a place of distinction at every feast.

CHAAVAL KI KHEER
(INDIAN RICE PUDDING)

Serves 4
Preparation time 20 minutes
Cooking time 1½ hours

150g (5oz) basmati rice, washed and drained
600ml (1pt) milk
4 tablespoons almond powder or ground almonds
300ml (½pt) evaporated milk
Sugar to taste
2 tablespoons raisins
2 tablespoons pistachio nuts, chopped
1 teaspoon cardamom powder
Red rose petals to garnish

1 Bring the rice to the boil with the milk in a heavy pan then allow to simmer for an hour or until mushy. Mash the rice roughly with a whisk while still on the heat.

2 Blend the almonds into the evaporated milk and add to the rice. Stir until thick and creamy.

3 Add the sugar, raisins and pistachios. Sprinkle the cardamom powder over and stir well.

4 Serve chilled, garnished with rose petals.

Koftas are a north Indian speciality and make a rich, tasty accompaniment to rotis.

MALAI KOFTA
(MEATBALLS IN CREAM SAUCE)

Serves 4
Preparation time 30 minutes
Cooking time 1 hour

For the meatballs:
600g (1¼lb) lamb mince
4 slices bread, soaked in water and squeezed dry
1 teaspoon chilli powder
1 teaspoon turmeric powder
1 teaspoon garam masala powder
1 teaspoon ginger paste
1 teaspoon garlic paste
2 tablespoons white poppy seeds
Salt
Pinch of bicarbonate of soda
1 teaspoon raisins
Sunflower oil for frying

For the sauce:
6 tablespoons sunflower oil
4 large onions, sliced
2 tablespoons ginger, chopped
2 tablespoons garlic, chopped
1 teaspoon cumin seeds
8 green cardamom
1 teaspoon chilli powder
1 teaspoon turmeric powder
1 teaspoon garam masala powder
6 tablespoons tomato purée
1 teaspoon sugar
Salt
300ml (½pt) single cream

For the garnish:
2 tablespoons coriander leaves, chopped

1 To make the meatballs, knead the mince with all the other ingredients except the oil. Make equal sized balls, pressing them hard to bind the ingredients.

2 Steam for 10 minutes or until cooked.

3 Heat the oil in a kadai or wok and fry the meatballs until brown. Take care while lowering them into the hot oil as they will splatter.

4 Then, to make the sauce, heat 2 tablespoons of the oil and fry the onions, ginger and garlic. Blend to a paste in a food processor.

5 Heat the remaining oil in a heavy pan and add the cumin and cardamom. Stir once. Then add the onion paste and fry until golden. Add all the powder spices and tomato purée.

6 Sprinkle in the sugar and salt and keep stirring until well blended. The oil should separate from the sauce. Add a little water if necessary, to achieve a creamy consistency. Take off the heat, stir in the cream and gently slide in the meatballs.

7 Reheat before serving, adding a little water if required. Serve sprinkled with coriander.

Chaaval ki Kheer

Eugenia caryophyllus/Syzygium aromaticum

CLOVES

(LAUNG)

Cloves are one of the most ancient and valuable spices of the Orient. Early references to them can be found in Chinese literature dating back to 266 BC. They found their way to Europe along the caravan routes in 1265, but their source and place of origin were a mysterious secret. In the 16th century the Portuguese discovered the Moluccas or Spice Islands, now part of Indonesia, and thus started a new chapter in clove lore. In 1770, the French took a clove tree into Mauritius from where the spice reached Zanzibar and Madagascar. Cloves were established in Sri Lanka in 1796 and in India in 1800 by the East India Company. The word 'clove' is derived from the French 'clou' and the English 'clout', both broadly meaning nail, from the likeness of the spice to a large-headed nail.

Clove powder

Cloves are one of the most ancient spices of the Orient

HOW THEY GROW

Lovers of a tropical environment, clove trees are 12–15m (36–45ft) tall, evergreen and straight-trunked. The clove of commerce is the air-dried, unopened flower-bud of the tree and grows in small clusters. The fully grown but unopened buds are picked green and dried in the sun until they turn dark brown and woody.

APPEARANCE AND TASTE

Good cloves are dark brown in colour. The buds have a long cylindrical base, crowned by a plump, beige ball which is encircled by a four-toothed calyx. Richly aromatic, cloves tend to leave a spectrum of sensations on the palate if chewed on their own. Beginning with a sharp tingling, they go on to taste woody and bitter and finally leave the mouth numb and warm. The flavour is so powerful that if too many cloves are used, the other flavours in the dish are completely lost, so they must be used carefully.

BUYING AND STORING

Cloves are almost always used whole but they form an

Cloves are the dried buds of the tree

important ingredient of blended spice mixtures when ground to a powder. Most people do not actually eat the whole cloves encountered in the finished dish. When buying cloves, look for examples that are rich in colour and have their round crowns intact. Good cloves should leave a trace of oil if pinched hard. Whole spices, including cloves, store well for up to a year in a clean, cool place.

MEDICINAL AND OTHER USES

Clove oil was grandmother's remedy for a toothache and is still widely used to cure aches and pains. Clove water checks the symptoms of cholera and asthma. The anaesthetic action of cloves helps numb the digestive system and reduces gastric irritability. Cloves are used in Indonesian cigarettes which are a heady combination of spices and tobacco. Clove oil is used in the manufacture of perfumes, soaps, bath salts and as a flavouring agent in medicine and dentistry.

CULINARY USES

Used in cooking the world over, they can be tasted studded in baked hams, in breads and cakes and in mulled wine. In India they are added to rice, meats and sweets. *Paan* or betel leaf is filled with aromatic spices and sweeteners and held together by a single, whole clove. This betel quid is a common mouth freshener and tiny *paan* shops dot every street corner in any city in India.

The following recipes are strongly flavoured with cloves. The first dish is a dry, spicy delicacy from the west coast of India and the second is a north Indian delight.

SUKHI KOLMI
(MAHARASHTRIAN PRAWNS)

Serves 4
Preparation time 15 minutes
Cooking time 20 minutes

600g (1¼lb) raw prawns,
  shelled and cleaned
1 teaspoon chilli powder
1 teaspoon turmeric powder
2 teaspoons coriander powder
Salt
4 tablespoons sunflower oil
4 cloves
4 cardamom
12 black peppercorns
2 large onions, chopped finely
150g (5oz) fresh fenugreek
  leaves (discard stems),
  chopped

1 Drain the prawns and mix with the powder spices and salt.

2 Heat the oil in a kadai or wok. Add the whole spices and stir a few times, add the onion and stir-fry until golden. Then add the prawns and cook until they turn pink.

3 Drop in the fenugreek and stir well. Cook on a low heat until the prawns are done. The dish should be dry but should have a creamy flavour because of the fried onions.

Mewa Pulao

MEWA PULAO
(RICE STUDDED WITH DRY FRUIT)

Serves 4
Preparation time 10 minutes
Cooking time 30 minutes

2 teaspoons sugar
4 tablespoons sunflower oil
10 cardamom
6 cloves
2 bay leaves
4cm (1½in) stick cinnamon
10 black peppercorns
450g (1lb) basmati rice, washed
  and drained
2 tablespoons raisins
2 tablespoons flaked almonds
2 tablespoons pistachio nuts,
  roughly chopped
4 tablespoons unsalted
  cashew nuts
900ml (1½pt) hot water
1 teaspoon saffron strands
Salt
4 tablespoons fresh coriander
  leaves, chopped
2 teaspoons glacé cherries,
  chopped

1 Heat a heavy-bottomed pan. Drop in the sugar and allow it to caramelise to a rich brown.

2 Spoon in the oil and blend. When the oil is hot, add the whole spices and stir until they change colour.

3 Then add the rice and fry well. Stir in the raisins and nuts and continue frying until they turn golden. Pour in the water and sprinkle in the saffron and salt. Give it a last stir, cover and cook on a low heat until the rice is fluffy and dry.

4 Mix gently with a slotted spoon to avoid breaking the rice grains.

5 Serve garnished with coriander leaves and glacé cherries. This rice goes well with a meat or chicken curry and a fresh salad.

Ferula asafoetida/Ferula narthex

ASAFOETIDA

(HING)

Although not native to India, asafoetida has for ages been an essential part of Indian cookery and medicine. It was also believed to enhance the musicality of the voice. It is said that in the days of the Mughal aristocracy, the court singers of Agra and Delhi would wake before dawn, eat a spoonful of asafoetida with butter and practice on the banks of the river Yamuna. Asafoetida gets its name from the Persian *aza* or resin and the Latin *foetidus* or stinking. Due to its offensive smell it is also sometimes referred to as 'devil's dung'.

Asafoetida powder

Most commonly available boxed as powder or as granules, asafoetida is also sold as a hard lump that needs to be crushed. It is best to buy a branded box of powder – it is airtight and keeps the sulphurous odour of the spice locked in. Having a strong flavour, asafoetida keeps well for up to a year.

MEDICINAL AND OTHER USES

Asafoetida is said to help flatulence and it is also prescribed for respiratory problems like whooping cough and asthma. Some European cultures believe that a small piece of asafoetida tied around a child's neck will protect it from disease, the fetid smell of the gum acting as a deterrent to germs. Despite its overpowering smell, asafoetida is used in some perfumes.

HOW IT GROWS

Asafoetida is the dried latex from the rhizomes of several species of *ferula* or giant fennel. It is grown chiefly in Iran and Afghanistan from where it is exported to the rest of the world. In India it is cultivated in Kashmir. Asafoetida is the product of a tall, smelly, perennial herb, with strong, carrot-shaped roots. The 2–4m (6–12ft) tall plant bears fine leaves and yellow flowers. In March or April, just before flowering, the stalks are cut close to the root. A milky liquid oozes out, which dries to form asafoetida. This is collected and a fresh cut is made. This procedure lasts for about 3 months from the first incision, by which time the plant has yielded up to 1kg (2lb) of resin and the root has dried up.

APPEARANCE AND TASTE

Fresh asafoetida is whitish and solid and gradually turns pink to reddish-brown on exposure to oxygen. It is ochre when sold commercially and the most widely used form is the fine yellow powder or granules. Asafoetida has a pungent, unpleasant smell quite like that of pickled eggs, due to the presence of sulphur compounds. On its own it tastes awful but it is added to most Indian savouries as it can complete the flavour of a dish.

CULINARY USES

Its powerful aroma complements lentils, vegetables and pickles. Asafoetida is used widely in south India – a surprising fact considering that it does not grow there at all. It is always used in small quantities – a tiny pinch added to hot oil before the addition of the other ingredients is enough to flavour a dish for 4. In India, asafoetida is always fried to calm its overpowering smell.

Asafoetida is supposed to help the voice and is traditionally eaten by singers who practise on the riverbanks

This recipe is a typical north Indian delicacy and is served with hot poories or fried, puffed bread, especially at Punjabi weddings which are occasions of great merry-making.

PUNJABI CHHOLE
(SPICY CHICK PEAS)

Serves 4
Preparation time 30 minutes + overnight soaking
Cooking time 30 minutes.

300g (10oz) white chickpeas, soaked in plenty of water with a pinch of bicarbonate of soda
6 tablespoons sunflower oil
1 teaspoon cumin seeds
½ teaspoon asafoetida
3 onions, chopped finely
1 teaspoon ginger paste
1 teaspoon garlic paste
1 teaspoon green chillies, shredded finely
150g (5oz) tomatoes, chopped finely
1 teaspoon chilli powder
1 teaspoon turmeric powder
1 teaspoon mango powder
1 teaspoon garam masala powder
1 teaspoon pomegranate seeds (arnardana), *crushed*
Salt
4 tablespoons coriander leaves, chopped
4 lemon wedges

1 Cook the chickpeas, in enough water to cover them, with the bicarbonate of soda until they are soft. (The peas should retain their shape.)

2 In a separate pan, heat the oil and add the cumin seeds and asafoetida. When the seeds pop, add the onion, ginger and garlic pastes and green chillies. Fry until golden.

3 Add the tomatoes and fry. Mash as you stir, making a paste. Then add the chilli, turmeric, mango and garam masala powders and pomegranate seeds. Cook this paste until blended and brown.

4 Add the chickpeas with the cooking water and blend, mashing a few to thicken the gravy. Simmer and season with salt.

5 Serve garnished with coriander leaves and a lemon wedge for each portion.

Punjabi Chhole

This recipe is a lentil dish eaten in Maharashtra, both in tiny, peasant homes and opulent city apartments.

VARAN
(MILD LENTIL CURRY)

Serves 4
Preparation time 30 minutes
Cooking time 45 minutes

220g (8oz) yellow lentils (toor dal), soaked in water for 30 minutes and drained
1 teaspoon turmeric powder
1 teaspoon cumin seeds, bruised
1 teaspoon asafoetida
Salt
2 tablespoons ghee

1 Cook the lentils in 750ml (1¼pt) hot water until they are very soft.

2 Add the turmeric powder, cumin seeds, asafoetida and salt. Simmer for 5 minutes.

3 Serve over boiled plain rice with a spoonful of ghee.

Foeniculum vulgare

FENNEL

(SAUNF)

Fennel is a common and much-loved spice in India. Served roasted after a meal as a digestive or used in countless home remedies for babies, it is also sold fresh, still on its fine, bright green stalks, outside schools where children buy it to chew on its fragrant, juicy sweetness. Known to Indian herbalists for centuries, it still forms a part of every Indian housewife's household medicine chest.

HOW IT GROWS

Fennel is the dried, ripe fruit of a biennial or perennial herb. The plant has wispy leaves and clusters of tiny yellow flowers on fine stalks. Fennel is native to the Mediterranean but also grows in Argentina, Bulgaria, Denmark, Egypt, France, Germany, Great Britain, India, Italy, Japan, Rumania and the United States.

APPEARANCE AND TASTE

Fresh fennel seeds are vibrant green. They are small and cylindrical, 6–7mm (½in) long, straight or slightly curved and have fine, longitudinal ridges. They are dried for storage and turn to a dull, greenish-yellow. The entire fennel plant is aromatic and is used in various ways in the kitchen. The seeds have a warm, sweet and intense flavour which turns slightly mellow and bitter on roasting.

BUYING AND STORING

Fennel is available fresh on the stalk and as dried or ground seeds. Look for fennel seeds which are evenly greenish-yellow and not brown, and avoid bags that are full of bristles. Fennel stores best if dry-roasted – it also grinds more easily. Store the spice in a dry jar away from light.

Fennel seeds are collected just before they become ripe

Fennel seeds

MEDICINAL AND OTHER USES

The use of fennel as a digestive aid is well-known. It relieves flatulence and stimulates the appetite. It is one of the safest medicines for colic in babies and in India, infants are given a daily drink of fennel water. This infusion also makes a good eye-bath. Fennel is thought to relieve wheezing, catarrh and asthma. Fennel is an essential component of *paan*, the betel-leaf quid that many Indians chew after a rich spicy meal. It is sometimes used to scent soaps.

Goan spice stall

Culinary uses

Fennel seems to add richness to meat gravies, sweetness to desserts and a special zest to vegetables. It is used powdered or whole with lamb, potatoes and in crisp golden sweets that are drenched in fennel-flavoured sugar syrup. Fennel is also used in pickles and chutneys in north India and a fennel infusion is a delicious base for refreshing drinks.

Banarasi Aloo
(POTATOES IN SOUR CREAM)

Serves 4
Preparation time 30 minutes
Cooking time 15 minutes

3 tablespoons sunflower oil
1 teaspoon fennel seeds
600g (1¼lb) potatoes, boiled, peeled and cubed
2 teaspoons tamarind pulp, diluted in a little water
4 tablespoons tomato purée
1 teaspoon chilli powder
1 teaspoon turmeric powder
1 teaspoon garam masala powder
Salt
4 tablespoons single cream
4 tablespoons coriander leaves, chopped

1 Heat the oil in a wok or kadai. Add the fennel. When the seeds change colour, drop in the potatoes. Stir-fry for a minute or so.

2 Add the tamarind pulp, tomato purée, powder spices and salt. Stirring until well-blended. The potatoes should be coated with a thick sauce.

3 Serve hot, garnished with swirls of cream and coriander leaves.

Malpuri
(SWEET, CRISP CRUNCHIES)

Serves 4
Preparation time 2 hours
Cooking time 30 minutes

300g (10oz) self-raising flour
3 tablespoons semolina
150ml (5fl oz) yoghurt
½ teaspoon bicarbonate of soda
Ghee as needed

For the syrup:
150g (5oz) sugar
150ml (5fl oz) water
1 teaspoon fennel seeds
1 teaspoon cardamom powder
4 tablespoons double cream

1 Mix the flour, semolina, yoghurt and bicarbonate of soda, adding a little water to make a thick batter. Then cover and leave in a warm place for about 2 hours.

2 In the meantime, mix the sugar, water and fennel seeds. Cook to a light syrup. Take off the heat, add the cardamom powder and reserve.

3 Heat the ghee for frying in a kadai or wok. When it begins to smoke, lower the heat and pour in a ladleful of the batter. Fry, turning over once, until golden. Drain and arrange on a platter. The discs should be spongy in the centre and crisp around the edges.

4 When all the discs or *poories* are fried, pour over the warm fennel syrup. Serve warm with a drizzle of cream.

Market scene, Jaipur

Illicium verum
STAR ANISE
(ANASPHAL)

One of the most beautiful spices available, star anise is not as commonly used in India as it is in China. As well as adding a decorative touch, it lends its delicate fragrance to north Indian dishes although it is not grown in India at all. It is imported from China where it is an essential spice, used whole as well as crushed into the blend of Chinese 5-spice powder. It is likely that star anise found its way to India along the silk route from China.

HOW IT GROWS

Star anise is the fruit of a tree of the magnolia family which grows up to a height of 8–15m (25–45ft). Star anise is native to tropical and subtropical east Asia and grows mainly in Kwangsi in southern China and Vietnam.

APPEARANCE AND TASTE

Dried star anise is mahogany in colour, hard and has eight hollow, boat-shaped petals which form a perfect star. Each point of the star contains a shiny, bead-like, oval seed. Though star anise is not related to aniseed, the spice is similar in flavour, but the aromatic, sweet taste is more pronounced.

BUYING AND STORING

In India, star anise is almost always sold whole though in other countries, it is available ground or broken into pieces. It is sometimes adulterated with the fruit of a Japanese tree, also called 'poison bay' or 'bastard star anise' which is poisonous, so make sure to buy pre-packed bags of the spice. Being dried and whole, it keeps well for up to a year.

MEDICINAL AND OTHER USES

In some places, star anise is chewed to freshen breath and to help digestion. It is soothing to the stomach and carminative and is an essential flavouring in cough mixtures. Its oil relieves rheumatism and is used as an antiseptic. The oil from star anise contains anethole which flavours confectionery, chewing gum, liqueurs and pharmaceutical preparations like syrups.

CULINARY USES

The Chinese claim that the addition of 1 or 2 carpels of star anise greatly improves the flavour of roast chicken. They also use it in tea. In India, it is used mainly in rice dishes like biryani and in succulent meat curries.

Star anise is native to southern China and Vietnam

Star anise is considered an exotic spice and its addition to any food makes the dish slightly more special. The following recipes are for two dishes that are as rich as you can get in Indian cookery and a plethora of spices join forces to give them their appeal.

HYDERABADI GOSHT BIRYANI
(HYDERABADI LAMB AND RICE)

Serves 4
Preparation time 40 minutes
Cooking time 1 hour

For the marinade:
150ml (5fl oz) yoghurt
2 teaspoons ginger paste
2 teaspoons garlic paste
3 teaspoons tomato purée
3 onions, chopped finely
2 teaspoons turmeric powder
2 teaspoons chilli powder

2 teaspoons garam masala powder
2 teaspoons raisins
2 tablespoons flaked almonds
Salt

600g (1¼lb) boneless lamb, trimmed and cubed
6 tablespoons sunflower oil
15 black peppercorns
6 cloves
6 cardamom
5–6 strips mace, broken
5 star anise
4cm (1½in) stick cinnamon
2 bay leaves
300g (10oz) basmati rice, washed and drained

To garnish:
3 tablespoons ghee
1 large onion, sliced
2 teaspoons raisins
2 teaspoons flaked almonds
6 tablespoons coriander leaves, chopped
½ teaspoon saffron strands
2 teaspoons milk

1 Mix all the marinade ingredients together. Add the lamb and marinate for 30 minutes.

2 Heat 4 tablespoons of the oil in a heavy pan. Add all the whole spices and fry for a minute.

3 Add the drained, marinated lamb and fry well. When browned, add 650ml (1¼pt) of hot water and any remaining marinade, cover and cook on a low heat until the meat is tender.

4 In a separate pan, heat the remaining oil and add the rice. Stir-fry until translucent. Add 600ml (1pt) of hot water, cover and cook on a low heat until it is fluffy.

5 Make the garnishes by heating 1 tablespoon ghee in a small pan. Fry the onion until dark golden.

6 Add the raisins and almonds and fry for a minute. Reserve.

7 In a separate, large, heavy pan, arrange a layer of rice, then one of the meat along with its sauce. Repeat until all the rice and meat is layered. The top layer should be rice.

8 Sprinkle the fried onions, raisins, almonds, and coriander on top. Mix the saffron into the milk and pour over. Pour the remaining ghee over the biryani, cover tightly and place in a hot oven to warm through.

9 Serve in the same pan or transfer to another dish and lightly mix. Serve with a green salad.

Kheema Mutter is especially popular with Punjabi and Sindhi communities. This dish could be served with rice, rotis or even pasta.

KHEEMA MUTTER
(MINCED LAMB WITH GREEN PEAS)

Serves 4
Preparation time 30 minutes
Cooking time 30 minutes

1 teaspoon sugar
6 tablespoons sunflower oil
10 black peppercorns
4 star anise
2 medium onions, chopped finely
2 teaspoons ginger, minced
2 teaspoons garlic, minced
8 tablespoons tomato purée
300g (10oz) lamb, minced
150g (5oz) green peas, shelled if fresh, or frozen
1 teaspoon chilli powder
1 teaspoon turmeric powder
1 teaspoon garam masala powder
Salt
2 tablespoons coriander leaves, chopped

1 Heat a kadai or wok and add the sugar. Allow it to caramelise, then add the oil. When the oil is hot, add the pepper and star anise and fry for a minute. Add the onions. Fry until golden, then add the ginger and garlic.

2 Stir a few times and add the tomato purée. Cook until the oil separates.

3 Then add the mince, green peas, powder spices and salt. Cover and cook on a low heat until the lamb is done.

4 This dish should be served hot, garnished with the chopped coriander.

Laurus nobilis/Cinnamomum tamala

BAY LEAF

(TEJ·PATTA)

Although the Indian bay leaf comes from the Indian cassia tree, its properties are quite different. It grows in the hill stations of India, little townships situated at high altitudes, developed by the British to recreate the cool land they had left behind. The use of bay

Dried Indian bay leaves

leaves in cookery had been introduced by the Mughals to India and as the British spent more and more time at their hill resorts, they too became familiar with the spice and introduced it into the Raj cuisine.

Fresh European bay leaves

HOW IT GROWS

Indian bay leaves come from a moderately sized evergreen tree which grows to a height of up to 8m (25ft). The leaves are ready for harvesting when the trees are 10 years old and they continue to bear leaves for a century. The leaves are collected each year from young plants and every alternate year from the older ones. Small branches with leaves are dried in the rare mountain sun for 3–4 days and tied into bundles to be sent to the markets. Sometimes the leaves are separated and packed in cylindrical bamboo nets called *bora* or *gungra*. Bay leaves found in the West are similar to the Indian variety and can be used instead.

APPEARANCE AND TASTE

Dried Indian bay leaves are dull sage-green in colour and quite brittle. They range in size from 4–10cm (1½–4ins). They have a sweet, woody aroma, quite like that of cinnamon and a neutral, slightly pungent flavour. They are added to food to scent rather than flavour it.

BUYING AND STORING

Bay leaves are available dried, either whole or in pieces. Look for leaves that are green and free of mould. Store in an airtight container for up to 6 months.

MEDICINAL AND OTHER USES

The leaves are carminative and used to treat colic and diarrhoea. Bay leaves are used in the clarifying process of many dyes. They are also put into some potpourri mixtures, into pickles and bottled fruits.

CULINARY USES

Used chiefly in the meat and rice cookery of north India, bay leaves are usually removed from a dish before serving. They are added to hot oil before the main ingredient, as frying releases their sweet perfume. In the West, they are used to flavour stuffings, roast meats and sauces. In India, they constitute a part of garam masala.

WARNING!
ALWAYS REMOVE EUROPEAN BAY LEAVES BEFORE SERVING AS THEY ARE POISONOUS; INDIAN BAY LEAVES ARE NOT.

There is a little, nondescript restaurant in Bombay whose specialities are a chicken dish called *rashida* and a spicy dal. They are so tasty that die-hard food addicts threaten to kill for them. *Laurus nobilis*

MURG RASHIDA
(CHICKEN IN EGG SAUCE)

Serves 4
Preparation time 45 minutes
Cooking time 30 minutes

For the marinade:
1 teaspoon chilli powder
Salt
1 teaspoon turmeric powder
2 teaspoons ginger paste
2 teaspoons garlic paste
4 tablespoons vinegar

600g (1¼lb) boneless chicken, cubed
5 tablespoons sunflower oil
1 teaspoon caraway seeds
2 bay leaves
2 large onions, grated and squeezed to remove the water
10 tablespoons tomato purée
2 teaspoons garam masala powder
2 eggs, size 1, beaten
2 tablespoons double cream
4 tablespoons unsalted cashew nuts, coarsely crushed
2 tablespoons coriander leaves, chopped

1 Mix all the marinade ingredients and drop the chicken in. Coat evenly and reserve for 30 minutes.

2 Heat the oil in a heavy pan and add the caraway seeds and bay leaf. Stir a few times. Then add the onion and fry until golden, stirring to

prevent it from sticking. Add the tomato purée and blend well.

3 Add the chicken and garam masala powder and fry until the chicken is brown.

4 Pour in a little water, cover and cook on a low heat until the chicken is tender. Keep checking the dish while it is cooking – if the curry dries keep adding a little water.

5 Move the chicken pieces to one side of the pan and beat the egg into the sauce with a fork so that it cooks in tiny shreds.

6 Stir in the cream and the cashew nuts, simmer for a minute and take off the heat. Sprinkle with coriander and serve hot with naan and a green salad.

TARKA DAL
(SPICED GRAM LENTILS)

Serves 4
Preparation time 30 minutes
Cooking time 1 hour

220g (8oz) split gram lentils (channa dal), soaked for 15 minutes
4 tablespoons sunflower oil
4 cloves
16 black peppercorns
6 cardamom
2 bay leaves
2 teaspoons panch phoron
1 teaspoon turmeric powder
1 teaspoon chilli powder
1 teaspoon mango powder
Salt
1 teaspoon sugar

1 Bring the lentils to the boil in 750ml (1¼pt) water and simmer until soft but whole. Reserve. Have all the other ingredients to hand.

2 Heat the oil in a separate pan and drop in all the ingredients, except the salt and sugar, one after the other. Fry for a minute until the spices crackle.

3 Pour the whole lot over the cooked dal, add the salt and sugar and blend well. Serve hot with rotis or rice and a meat curry.

Murg Rashida

Ripe mangoes packed in straw

Mangifera indica

MANGO POWDER

(AMCHOOR)

The mango season in India is a much-awaited one. As the warm April spring heralds the summer months, fruit stalls begin to sell plump, juicy mangoes that start off green and gradually turn a rich gold-pink. Mango is native to India and is highly valued. Considered romantic since ancient times, Sanskrit literature is full of lovers meeting under a mango tree in full, fragrant blossom. There are hundreds of varieties of mango, the Alphonso or Aapoos being the most desired and therefore the most expensive. The fruit is a versatile one – it is used green in savoury curries and pickles and ripe in puddings or as a dessert fruit. One of the treats of an Indian summer is the baskets of scented mangoes that friends and well-wishers send each other as a gesture of friendship and goodwill. Being such a prized fruit, the mango motif is used in Indian textiles, paintings, and jewellery as an everlasting symbol of desire and plenty.

Mango powder

MANUFACTURE

Mango powder is made from raw, sour, green mangoes, especially windfalls or mangoes that grow wild. The unripe fruits are peeled and cut into thin slices. The slices are then dried in the sun, powdered or left whole and packed in jute bags for sale.

APPEARANCE AND TASTE

Dried mango slices look like fine slices of shrivelled wood, light brown in colour. The powder is camel-coloured, fine and full of lumps which crumble easily when touched. Mango powder has a tangy sour taste.

Popular textile mango motif

BUYING AND STORING

It is available as dried slices or as powder. In Hindi, *aam* means mango and *choor* is powder. Mango powder will keep up to a year in a clean, dry jar. The slices need to be used within 4 to 5 months. Make sure that the stored powder does not come into contact with water.

CULINARY USES

Mango powder is used as a souring agent in north India. Chutneys, soups, vegetables, stuffings and lentil dishes are made with this spice. It is especially used in tangy potato fillings for samosas and savoury pasties. It can be added to a dish either before or after the main ingredient is dropped into hot oil. If added before, it gives a deep taste; if added after, the flavour is more subtle. It is also used in pickles.

The first of the following recipes uses mango powder as a marinade while the second uses it as a flavouring for a stuffing. Both the dishes can be served as a starter.

KHATTI MACCHI
(BAKED SOUR FISH)

Serves 4
Preparation time 20 minutes
Cooking time 20 minutes

8 boneless portions cod (or any firm white fish)
1 teaspoon chilli powder
1 teaspoon tandoori masala
1 teaspoon ginger paste
1 teaspoon garlic paste
Salt
1 teaspoon mango powder
4 tablespoons dried breadcrumbs
4 tablespoons sunflower oil

1 Marinate the fish in the chilli powder, tandoori masala, ginger and garlic pastes and salt for 5 minutes.

2 Mix the mango powder and breadcrumbs. Then arrange the fish on a greased baking tray. Sprinkle with the breadcrumbs and drizzle the sunflower oil over.

3 Bake in a moderate oven (180°C, 350°F, gas mark 4) for about 20 minutes or until the fish can be flaked.

4 Serve hot with a salad.

Mangoes are native to India

Khatti Macchi

PHOOLGOBI KE PAKODE
(CAULIFLOWER PUFFS)

Serves 4
Preparation time 20 minutes
Cooking time 30 minutes

4 tablespoons sunflower oil
1 teaspoon cumin seeds
2 green chillies, minced
½ teaspoon turmeric
1 teaspoon mango powder
300g (10oz) cauliflower, cut into small florets
2 tablespoons coriander leaves, chopped
Salt
300g (10oz) plain flour
2 teaspoons sunflower oil
Salt
Water as needed
Sunflower oil for deep-frying

1 Heat the oil in a pan and add the cumin. When it changes colour add the green chilli, turmeric and mango powder.

2 Stir a few times and add the cauliflower, coriander leaves and salt. Pour in a little water, cover, cook until crunchy.

3 Remove the cover and stir-fry to dry up any water. Take off the heat.

4 Make a stiff dough with the flour, oil, salt and water. Make into balls about the size of a cherry.

5 Roll out each ball to a thin disc 6cm (2½in) in diameter. Place a little of the cauliflower mixture in the middle and fold over one half to meet the other, like a half moon. Pinch shut.

6 Heat the oil in a deep kadai or wok. When nearly smoking, reduce the heat and deep-fry the puffs until pale gold in colour, a few at a time.

7 Serve warm with tamarind chutney.

Myristica fragrans

NUTMEG/MACE

(JAIPHAL/JAVITRI)

Nutmeg

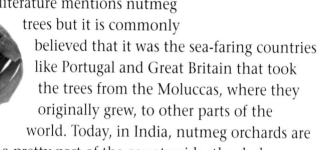

Nutmeg and mace both come from the fruit of the same plant – *Myristica fragans*. Indians have always prized these spices for their medicinal value. Ancient Indian literature mentions nutmeg trees but it is commonly believed that it was the sea-faring countries like Portugal and Great Britain that took the trees from the Moluccas, where they originally grew, to other parts of the world. Today, in India, nutmeg orchards are a pretty part of the countryside, the dark green trees a sure sign that one is in the tropics.

Mace

BUYING AND STORING

Nutmeg is sold whole or ground. There's nothing quite like the aroma of a few fresh shavings of nutmeg to liven up a dish. Mace is available whole as aril, cut into slivers, or ground into a powder. Buy whole nutmeg and grate it as needed. Powdered nutmeg loses its flavour quickly. Mace, on the other hand, keeps well in its ground form. Beware of adulteration – buy reputed brands or buy whole mace blades.

HOW THEY GROW

Nutmeg and mace come from an evergreen tree that is usually 10–12m (30–36ft) high with dark leaves and fruits that look like apricots. When the ripe fruit bursts open, the mace is seen as a lacy scarlet filigree closely enveloping the hard kernel inside which is the nutmeg. The mace or aril is carefully removed, pressed flat and dried. On drying the colour changes from a bright red to a warm orange. The kernel within is also dried. It is then cracked open and the seed removed. Nutmeg and mace are cultivated in the Moluccas, Sri Lanka, the West Indies and India.

APPEARANCE AND TASTE

Dried mace is yellowish-red to pale yellow depending on its origin and the lacy blades are brittle. Nutmegs are oval with a dusty brown, rough exterior. The inside is lighter brown and patterned. Nutmegs are sometimes sold in their shells which are egg-shaped, shiny and the colour of dark chocolate. Nutmeg and mace are similar in flavour but mace tastes cleaner. The aroma of both is perfumed, sweet and distinctive. The taste of nutmeg tends to be bittersweet and mace bitter. Nutmeg and mace are not interchangeable.

Although nutmeg and mace come from the same plant they are not interchangeable

Freshly picked nutmeg fruit

MEDICINAL AND OTHER USES

Nutmeg is widely used in Indian medicine. It is a sure cure for digestive disorders, insomnia and rheumatism. The external application of nutmeg in a paste made from powder and water is said to improve skin conditions like eczema and ringworm. It is also an aphrodisiac. Nutmeg butter, obtained by cooking and pressing any low quality seeds, is used in toothpaste, candles and perfumes.

Nutmeg butter is used to make candles

CULINARY USES

In India, both the spices are used to enhance meats, rice and desserts. Rice pudding swirled with nutmeg is a delicacy. Powdered nutmeg is often sprinkled on creamy, set milk desserts for a decorative and aromatic touch. In other countries, nutmeg and mace are added to vegetables, sauces, cheese dishes and soups. In Malaysia, the ripe fruit, which is high in the jelling agent pectin, is used to make jellies and jam, and the rind is candied.

This is a recipe for a halwa which is one of the many delicious ways of preserving fruits. This dish makes a good dessert or an instant energy snack.

KELE KA HALWA
(BANANA FUDGE)

Serves 4
Preparation time 10 minutes
Cooking time 1 hour

150ml (5fl oz) ghee
600g (1¼lb) banana, peeled and chopped
220g (8oz) sugar
½ teaspoon nutmeg powder
½ teaspoon cardamom powder

1 Heat 2 tablespoons of the ghee in a heavy pan. Add the banana and the sugar and cook on a low heat, stirring all the while to prevent it from sticking.

2 Keep drizzling in a little of the ghee from time to time until all the moisture evaporates and the mixture becomes sticky and brown.

Ground nutmeg

This drink is served especially on a festive night called *Kojagiri Purnima* when the autumn full moon heralds the beginning of the harvesting season.

Kele ka Halwa

3 Add the powdered spices and stir. Remove from the heat when the mixture leaves the sides of the pan. Do not overcook as the halwa will turn hard.

MASALA DOODH
(SWEET MILK FIESTA)

Serves 4
Preparation time 10 minutes
Cooking time 0

1 litre (1¾pt) milk
½ teaspoon nutmeg powder
½ teaspoon cardamom powder
A few strands of saffron
2 tablespoons almonds, chopped finely
2 tablespoons pistachio nuts, chopped finely
Sugar to taste

1 Mix all the ingredients together and chill well.

2 Serve in decorative glasses with a cube of ice if desired.

4 Pat the halwa into a deep platter, cool and cut into squares or slices.

Nigella sativa

NIGELLA

(KALONJI)

Often confused with black cumin, nigella comes from a completely different plant. This plant is a relative of the delicate 'love-in-a-mist' which decorates many gardens world-wide. Though the consumption of nigella in India is mostly limited to the north, it is cultivated over vast areas, its pale blue flowers creating a sea of colour in the lush landscape. Nigella is usually known as black onion seed, a misnomer really, as the seeds have nothing to do with onions.

Charminar, Hyderabad

HOW IT GROWS

Nigella is the dried seed-like fruit of a small herb about 45cm (18in) in height. The plant has wispy sage-coloured leaves and graceful flowers which ripen into seed capsules. These are collected when ripe. They are then dried, crushed whole and sieved to separate the seeds. Nigella grows in the Middle East, southern Europe, and most extensively in India.

APPEARANCE AND TASTE

The seeds of nigella are 2–3mm (⅛in) long and jet black with a matte finish. They closely resemble tiny chips of coal and have five distinct points. Nigella has a faint nutty, but bitter taste due to the presence of nigellin.

BUYING AND STORING

Nigella is almost always sold whole. The seeds can be powdered at home, after roasting them to develop their flavour and make them brittle. The seeds are best bought whole to save the risk of adulterated ground nigella. The spice stores well in a cool, dry place.

MEDICINAL AND OTHER USES

Nigella is considered carminative, a stimulant, and diuretic. A paste of the seeds is applied for skin eruptions and is sure to relieve scorpion stings. The seeds are often scattered between folds of clothes as an effective insect repellent. Alcoholic extracts of the seeds are used as stabilising agents for some edible fats.

CULINARY USES

Even in India, nigella is a mysterious spice. Many people are not aware of its flavour and therefore tend to be sceptical about its use. However, nigella goes beautifully with fish, in naan bread and in salads. In west Bengal the most prolific spice blend is panch phoron, a mixture of 5 spices including nigella, and this gives vegetables, pulses and lentils a distinctive Bengali taste. In the Middle East it is used to flavour bread.

Most nigella is grown in India

The following recipes are very easy to make. The prawns can be served as a starter or main course. The nigella gives them an unusual flavour which is relished in the town of Hyderabad, from where this dish comes.

TALEY HUE JHINGE
(SPICY FRIED PRAWNS)

Serves 4
Preparation time 25 minutes
Cooking time 20 minutes

1 teaspoon turmeric powder
1 teaspoon chilli powder
Salt
4 tablespoons distilled vinegar
600g (1¼lb) large raw prawns, shelled
5 tablespoons sunflower oil
2 teaspoons nigella seeds
2 teaspoons garlic, sliced
4 small dried red chillies, deseeded
10 curry leaves

1 Mix the powder spices and salt with the vinegar. Marinate the prawns in this mixture for 10 minutes.

2 Heat the oil in a kadai or wok. Add the nigella, garlic, red chillies and curry leaves. Reduce the heat and stir-fry for a minute.

3 Add the prawns, stirring continuously until they are completely cooked.

4 Remove the chillies and curry leaves.

5 Serve hot with a bland accompaniment, like rice or rotis, to balance the spicy heat of the prawns.

This salad is an exotic accompaniment to grilled or fried meats.

MOOLI KA SALAAD
(WHITE RADISH SALAD)

Serves 4
Preparation time 15 minutes
Cooking time 0

300g (10oz) Indian white radish (mooli), grated
Salt and pepper
2 tablespoons distilled vinegar
Large pinch of sugar
2 tablespoons sunflower oil
½ teaspoon black mustard seeds
½ teaspoon nigella seeds
½ teaspoon cumin seeds

1 Mix the radish with the salt, pepper, vinegar and sugar.

2 Heat the oil in a small pan. When it is hot, drop in all the seeds. As soon as they finish crackling pour the oil and the seeds onto the radish mixture. Mix lightly.

3 Serve at room temperature.

Papaver somniferum

POPPY SEEDS

(KHUS KHUS)

White poppy seeds

The word poppy instantly brings to mind opium which is obtained from the poppy plant. In fact it is this narcotic that gives the poppy its botanical name *Papaver somniferum*, which refers to its ability to promote sleep. Opium contains compounds from which morphine and codeine are extracted and these are responsible for the heady effect of the drug. The use of poppy was known to the ancient Greeks and it reached India and China by the 8th century. By and by it became an important ingredient in the Indian kitchen. Today, though the drug opium is banned in many countries, poppy seeds are eaten all over the world.

HOW THEY GROW

Poppies grow widely in China, Turkey, Iran, Holland, Canada and France. India is a major producer. Poppy the spice is the seed of an annual plant which bears large leaves and bright red flowers with a dark purple centre. As the flowers die away, they leave behind a seed capsule which is oval and is crowned by a spiky stigma. These capsules are dried then cracked to reveal vertical chambers containing thousands of seeds.

APPEARANCE AND TASTE

Indian and European poppy seeds vary greatly in appearance. Both are very tiny and light but the Indian variety are ivory to beige and the European variety called Maw is dark grey. There is also a Turkish variety which is tobacco-brown. Contrary to belief, poppy seeds do not

Papaver somniferum

give you a high. When cooked they have a distinct nutty aroma. Their graininess is often used to give texture to Indian dishes.

BUYING AND STORING

Poppy seeds are always sold whole. They are simple to grind at home and dry-roasting them makes this task easier. Indian cookery uses only the cream-coloured seeds as the grey ones affect the colour of the final product. Store the seeds in a clean jar taking care not to spill any.

MEDICINAL AND OTHER USES

Poppy seeds are effective for fever, inflammation and irritation of the stomach. Powdered and mixed with honey, they are a recommended cure for dysentery. The oil is used in soaps and in artists' paints.

Opium is the reddish-brown addictive drug prepared from the juices of the unripe seed pods of the poppy

CULINARY USES

In India, poppy seeds are usually ground with other spices and used to thicken curries for meat, fish and vegetables. Poppy seeds are cooked with jaggery and coconut, enveloped in a case of flaky pastry and deep fried to make a delicious sweet called *karanji*. They are also sprinkled over naan bread and cooked in a clay oven called a *tandoor*. In Turkey, poppy seeds are made into sweet halva and in the Middle East they flavour bread and desserts.

In Delhi there is a famous street entirely devoted to kababs of every size, shape and flavour. As you walk through it you are enveloped by the fragrance of spicy roasting meat and the sound of sizzling. People flock to the 'kabab street' at night and eat their way from one end to the other. Seekh kababs are one of the most popular dishes served there.

Khus Khus Poorie

SEEKH KABABS
(MINCE KABABS)

Serves 4
Preparation time 40 minutes
Cooking time 40 minutes
You will also need 4 skewers

300g (10oz) lean minced lamb
2 teaspoons ginger paste
2 teaspoons garlic paste
1 large onion, chopped very finely
2 teaspoons white poppy seeds
1 teaspoon chilli powder
1 teaspoon garam masala powder
1 teaspoon turmeric powder
2 tablespoons mint leaves, chopped
2 tablespoons coriander leaves, chopped

Salt
2 tablespoons lemon juice
2 tablespoons sunflower oil

1 Knead all the ingredients except the oil together.

2 Take a small amount at a time and pat into a sausage-like shape about 5cm (2in) long around a skewer. Make only one per skewer.

3 Brush each kabab with a little oil and grill under medium heat or barbecue until well browned and cooked. Serve very hot. To serve, slide the kabab off the skewer and arrange on a plate with a generous salad and mint chutney (page 103).

This recipe is for a banana-flavoured, puffed bread. It can be served with any dry vegetable or curry.

KHUS KHUS POORIE
(FRIED POPPY SEED BREAD)

Serves 4
Preparation time 20 minutes
Cooking time 30 minutes

300g (10oz) plain flour
150g (5oz) banana, mashed
1 teaspoon lemon juice
Pinch of bicarbonate of soda
Salt
2 teaspoons caster sugar
2 tablespoons white poppy seeds
Sunflower oil for deep frying

1 Knead the flour, banana, lemon juice, bicarbonate of soda, salt and sugar with just enough water to make a stiff dough. Cover and leave for 10 minutes.

2 Make equal-sized balls of the dough (1.5cm (¾in) diameter). Roll each ball in a plate of poppy seeds.

3 Heat the oil in a kadai or wok. Roll out each ball to a thin, even disc.

4 Gently slide the poorie into the oil and fry until puffed up and golden. Take care not to overheat the oil. Drain on a slotted spoon and remove onto absorbent paper. Serve hot.

Pimenta officinalis

ALLSPICE

(KABABCHINI)

Allspice berries

This spice is probably called allspice because it has the flavour of cloves, nutmeg, cinnamon and black pepper all rolled into one. Allspice is indigenous to the West Indies but it is used in some regional Indian cookery. It is one of the spices that seldom comes out of the pantry, but it is sometimes the secret, magic ingredient that gives such a scent of heaven to north Indian curries and biryanis. Although south Indian food has no use for allspice, it takes its special place alongside garam masala, cardamom and bay leaves on the north Indian housewife's kitchen shelf.

Shikaras in Kashmir where allspice grows

HOW IT GROWS

Allspice is the dried, unripe berries of a bushy, evergreen tree which grows to about 9m (30ft) in height. The berries are green when unripe and become dark purple when ripe. The spice is cultivated in the West Indies, Central and South America, in Kashmir and other parts of India.

APPEARANCE AND TASTE

The whole berries are 4–7mm (¼–⅓in) in diameter, reddish brown, with a textured surface. The ground spice is fine and rust coloured. Allspice has a warm, highly perfumed odour. The taste is sharp and mildly sweet.

BUYING AND STORING

Allspice is sold whole or ground to a powder. It is easy to grind, so it is best to buy the berries and grind at home as required, in a processor. Store in an airtight jar and use within 6 months.

MEDICINAL AND OTHER USES

Allspice is used to relieve diarrhoea, dyspepsia and flatulence. In the West, allspice is used as a traditional ingredient of potpourri. It is also added to tea to make a warm, fragrant drink. Many men's perfumes owe their spicy overtones to allspice, and several liquors and soaps are scented with it.

CULINARY USES

Though allspice features in rich north Indian curries, its main use is in ketchup, preserves and relishes. Around the world, it is used in cakes, pies, canned meats, and stews. It also adds a spicy note to mulled wine.

Allspice adds a warm note to the following recipes. The first dish is from north India and is ideal for a summer brunch or barbecue. As an added extra, leftovers can be made into sandwiches.

BHOONI MURG
(OVEN-BAKED SPICY CHICKEN)

Serves 4
Preparation time 20 minutes
Cooking time 45 minutes

4 large chicken drumsticks, skinned
1 teaspoon chilli powder
1 teaspoon turmeric powder
1 teaspoon allspice powder
½ teaspoon garam masala powder
1 teaspoon ginger paste
1 teaspoon garlic paste
2 teaspoons lemon juice
Salt
4 tablespoons sunflower oil

1 Mix together all the ingredients except the oil. Reserve for 15 minutes.

2 Place the chicken in a foil-lined baking dish, drizzle the oil over and fold the foil to seal. Bake in a moderate oven (190°C, 375°F, gas mark 5) for 40 minutes or until done.

3 Open the foil carefully to allow the steam to escape. Transfer the chicken to a flameproof dish and brown under a hot grill, turning as required. Serve hot.

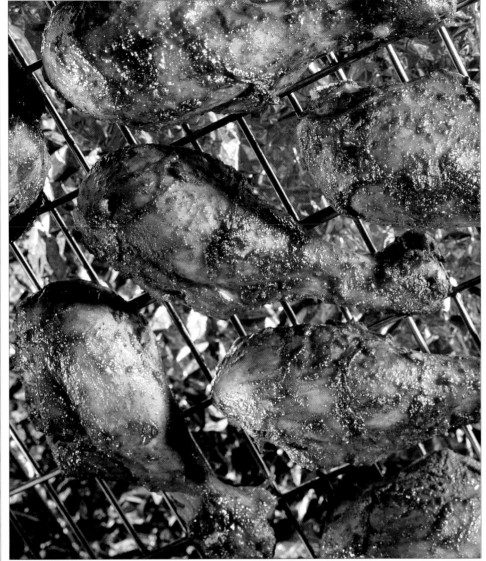

Bhooni Murg

This recipe also comes from the north, from the state of Kashmir.

KHEEMA TIKKI
(MINCED LAMB PATTIES)

Serves 4
Preparation time 40 minutes
Cooking time 40 minutes

300g (10oz) lean lamb mince, stir-fried and drained
300g (10oz) potatoes, boiled, peeled and mashed
2 teaspoons turmeric powder
1 teaspoon chilli powder
1 teaspoon allspice powder
4 tablespoons coriander leaves, chopped finely
2 tablespoons mint leaves, chopped finely
1 large onion, chopped finely
2 teaspoons ginger paste
2 teaspoons garlic paste
2 teaspoons lemon juice
Salt
Sunflower oil for deep frying
300g (10oz) fresh breadcrumbs

1 Make a soft dough with all the ingredients except the breadcrumbs and oil. Make 8 equal-sized balls of the mixture. Shape each ball into a heart and reserve.

2 Heat the oil in a wok or kadai. When it is nearly smoking, reduce the heat. Press each heart into the breadcrumbs and deep fry 1 or 2 at a time, until golden. Alternatively, shallow-fry them in a little oil until crisp. Serve with tomato ketchup.

Ground allspice

Pimpinella anisum

ANISEED

(VILAYATI SAUNF)

Flavoured and sweetened, aniseed is eaten on its own or blended with nuts or spices and served as the ideal Indian 'after-dinner mint'. Anise or aniseed is native to the Middle East and is a close relative of fennel, caraway and cumin. In India both fennel and aniseed are called *saunf* because of their similarity in appearance and flavour. Children are often given multi-coloured, sugar-coated aniseed as a special treat, the sweet, brittle shell complementing the sharp, aromatic flavour of the spice within.

Aniseed is often sold in *supari* mixtures

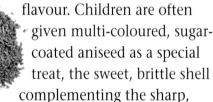

HOW IT GROWS

Aniseed is an annual herbaceous plant. It bears vivid green leaves and clusters of white flowers. Before the seeds ripen, the entire plant is pulled up and dried. The seeds are then threshed by beating the dried plants. Aniseed is grown in Bulgaria, Cyprus, France, Germany, the former USSR, Mexico, Italy, South America, Syria and India.

APPEARANCE AND TASTE

The spice aniseed consists of small, oval seeds 3–5mm (⅛–¼in) long and sage to ochre in colour. Aniseed is aromatic and sweet. The flavour is strong with a fresh and bitter, green zest. Aniseed can be dry-roasted which heightens the smell and changes the taste to bitter sweet.

BUYING AND STORING

It is best to buy whole seeds as the ground powder easily loses its flavour. Lightly roasting the seeds makes them brittle and crushing them becomes extremely easy. Store in a clean, dry jar and use within six months.

MEDICINAL AND OTHER USES

Aniseed is esteemed in medicine as an expectorant, digestive and diuretic. Gripe water given to babies to relieve colic contains aniseed extract. Aniseed tea is considered a soporific and should be drunk just before going to bed. Caution: over-boiling the seeds destroys their digestive properties and essential oil, so simmer for only 3 minutes. It is used as a

Ground aniseed

flavouring for sweets and cough lozenges. It is also used as an insecticide and fungicide. The spice is responsible for the unique flavour of some aperitifs and liqueurs like Pernod and anisette.

CULINARY USES

Aniseed is one of the 20-odd spices that can flavour a rich meat curry. It is also thrown into hot oil and poured over vegetables and lentils as a sizzling, fragrant garnish. Powdered aniseed is added to sweets and beverages.

Aniseed grows all over India

In a country like India where alcohol is not as much a part of life as it is in the West, other drinks like tea and coffee are popular. Tea is drunk in great quantities throughout the day and is often embellished with different spices to create variety. This recipe is a great summer drink.

SAUNF KI CHAI
(COLD ANISEED TEA)

Serves 4
Preparation time 5 minutes
Chilling time 15 minutes

600ml (1pt) water
2 Indian teabags
4 teaspoons whole aniseed
Honey to taste
12 ice cubes

1 Make the tea in the normal way ensuring that it is not too strong.

2 Stir in the aniseed and honey while it is very hot and leave to infuse.

3 When cool, strain and put it into the refrigerator to chill well. Serve poured over ice.

This recipe is a delicate vegetable dish from the northern state of Uttar Pradesh.

MATHURA KI KADDU KI SUBZI
(RED PUMPKIN STIR-FRY)

Serves 4
Preparation time 15 minutes
Cooking time 20 minutes

6 teaspoons sunflower oil
1 teaspoon cumin seeds
1 teaspoon whole aniseed
4 dried red chillies, deseeded
  and broken
600g (1¼lb) red pumpkin,
  peeled and cubed
Salt
1 teaspoon sugar

1 Heat the oil in a kadai or wok. Add the cumin seeds and aniseed. Just as they begin to change colour, drop in the red chillies.

2 Stir 2 or 3 times then add the pumpkin. Sprinkle in the salt and sugar.

3 Cover and cook on a low heat until the pumpkin is easily mashable.

4 Serve very hot with poories.

Saunf ki Chai

Piper nigrum/ Piper longum

PEPPER

(KALI MIRCH)

On the 20th of May 1498, Vasco da Gama stepped on Indian soil and cried, 'For Christ and for spices!' His arrival marked the end of a long sea-voyage in search of, primarily, pepper. Until he showed the world the way to India, the spice used to be carried overland by Arab traders who kept the route a secret. In the 15th century, the West valued pepper as much as gold and ship-loads of the spice would journey through tropical oceans ensuring a hefty profit for the traders. Demand was huge, supply could never be enough. Happily, today, pepper is freely available around the world and is used in almost every cuisine. It is rightly known as the 'king of the spices' and accounts for the lion's share of the spice exports from India. The name pepper is from the Sanskrit *pippali* for long pepper and it is believed that ancient Aryans used it as a medicine and aphrodisiac. A popular pepper story relates how a Tamil chef once served an Englishman a dish made of lentils and spices. When asked the name of the soup, he replied that it was *'Molaga-tanni'*, pepper-water in Tamil. 'Splendid!' remarked the Englishman. 'Let's have this mulligatawny more often, shall we?' And a legend was born.

19th-century
English spice traders

Pepper flowers give way to green and red fruit

HOW IT GROWS

Pepper is the fruit of a perennial vine with large leaves and white flowers. The flowers give way to berries which are first a green then a red fruit and become the familiar black spice after it is sun–dried for many days. The vine continues to bear fruit for up to 20 years. The plants are trained to climb up trees in the hot rain forests of south India where more than 24 varieties of pepper are grown. In the spring, the fruits are yellowish-red and ready for harvest. The entire spike of berries is plucked and dried whole. Alternatively, the berries are rubbed, threshed or trampled off the root-like spike and dried until black. Long pepper, another distinct variety, is also grown and dried similarly. White peppercorns are simply ripe berries which are softened in water, divested of their outer skin and dried until biscuit-coloured. The main producers of pepper are Malaysia, Indonesia, Brazil and India.

APPEARANCE AND TASTE

The most commonly used pepper is round, black, shrivelled and hard. White peppercorns are smooth and creamy, while fresh pepper-corns look like garlands of plump, green berries. The taste of pepper is just spicy hot. The aroma is woody, penetrating, pungent and aromatic and is good enough to rustle up a healthy appetite. White pepper is sharper and less pungent whereas green pepper is mild and has a flavour that is fresh and aromatic. Long pepper is 2-3cm (1-1¼in) long, grey and scaly.

White peppercorns

Green
peppercorns

BUYING AND STORING

Green peppercorns are sold fresh, pickled in vinegar, bottled in brine or dried. Dried black peppercorns are used whole, powdered or crushed. White peppercorns are available whole or powdered. *Schinus molle* berries are called pink peppercorns but they come from a completely different plant. Chinese shops sell Szechwan peppercorns which resemble tiny flower buds. Fresh green peppercorns should be bought plump and juicy. In the black, dried variety, look for large berries, the bigger the better. Ground pepper loses its flavour quickly, so powder your own at home. Commercially crushed pepper is not as tasty or as strong. Store dried peppercorns in a clean, dry jar, and fresh ones in the refrigerator.

MEDICINAL AND OTHER USES

Black pepper is a stimulant, digestive and diuretic. It is believed to relieve flatulence, colds, amnesia and even impotency. The external application of crushed pepper is often used to counteract muscular pains and tooth-ache. The essential oil of pepper is used in flavouring and perfumery, where it imparts spicy, oriental notes.

CULINARY USES

In India, pepper is used in every type of regional cookery. In the north it flavours meat, in the south, lentils, in the east, fish and in the west, vegetables. It is thrown whole into hot oil, roasted and ground with coconut and spices, and made into paste and applied to meats. It is also used to make herbal tea. Green pepper is usually pickled. In view of the preservative qualities of pepper, it is used extensively in canning and pickling. Several spice blends like garam masala feature pepper as a key ingredient. Around the world, pepper-corns are used to flavour sauces, meats and marinades.

This dish is from the state of Uttar Pradesh. The curry goes well with rice or rotis and evokes the feel of a state that produces some of India's finest saris – the Benarasi, made of shimmer-ing silk in jewel colours and embroidered with fine filaments of pure 22 carat gold.

PAKODEWALI KADHI
(CREAMY DUMPLING CURRY)

Serves 4
Preparation time 10 minutes
Cooking time 30 minutes

300ml (½pt) yoghurt
8 tablespoons gram flour
½ teaspoon green chilli, chopped finely
½ teaspoon turmeric powder
2 teaspoons sugar
Salt
4 tablespoons sunflower oil
2 teaspoons cumin seeds
10 black peppercorns
6 cloves

'Pink peppercorns'
in brine

Powdered white
peppercorns

Green peppercorns
in brine

For the dumplings:
150g (5oz) gram flour
Pinch of bicarbonate of soda
1 medium onion, chopped finely
½ teaspoon fenugreek seeds
½ teaspoon cumin seeds
2 teaspoons dried fenugreek leaves
Salt
Sunflower oil for deep frying

For the garnish:
2 tablespoons coriander leaves, chopped
2 tablespoons ghee
½ teaspoon chilli powder

1 Beat the yoghurt with the gram flour, green chilli, turmeric, sugar and salt.

2 Heat the oil in a heavy pan and add the cumin, pepper-corns and cloves.

3 Give the yoghurt mixture a good stir ensuring that there are no lumps left and add to the pan. Reduce the heat and cook until the consistency resembles that of a thick batter and the raw flour aroma is replaced by a fragrant one. Take off the heat.

4 To make the dumplings, make a thick batter of all the ingredients except the oil, adding water as necessary.

5 Heat the oil in a heavy pan. When it starts smoking, lower the heat and drop in 2 to 3 teaspoonsful of the batter at a time. Fry until golden, drain and dip into a bowl of water to soften a bit. Remove immediately, squeeze out the water and add to the yoghurt curry. Make all the dumplings in this manner.

6 To garnish, sprinkle over the coriander leaves. Heat the ghee in a small pan and add the chilli powder. Take off the heat at once and pour over the curry. Do not stir. Serve hot.

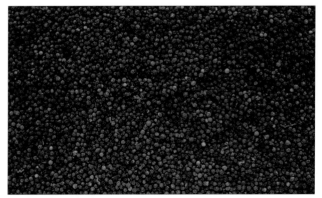

Black peppercorns

The recipe given below comes from the coastal, coconut-laden strip of India where the sharp taste of pepper and the creamy sweetness of coconut are combined to create fire-works of flavour.

PHOOLGOBI RASSA
(CAULIFLOWER IN COCONUT AND PEPPER SAUCE)

Serves 4
Preparation time 30 minutes
Cooking time 30 minutes

The masala for the sauce:
2 tablespoons sunflower oil
10 black peppercorns
2cm (1in) stick cinnamon
6 cloves
2 teaspoons coriander seeds
1 large onion, sliced finely
220g (8oz) coconut, grated if fresh, or desiccated

4 tablespoons sunflower oil
2 teaspoons cumin seeds
600g (1¼lbs) cauliflower, cut into small florets
150g (5oz) peas, shelled
4 tablespoons unsalted cashew nuts

150g (5oz) tomatoes, chopped
1 teaspoon chilli powder
1 teaspoon turmeric powder
Salt

1 First cook the masala. Heat the oil in a kadai or wok. Add the whole spices. Fry for a minute. Then drop in the onion and stir-fry until golden and add the coconut and stir-fry until brown. Remove from the heat and cool the mixture.

2 Add a little water and grind to a coarse paste in a blender.

3 In a separate kadai or wok heat the oil and add the cumin seeds. When they change colour, add the cauliflower, peas and cashew nuts. Mix well.

4 Add the tomatoes, powder spices and salt. Mix. Add a little water, cover and cook until the cauliflower is nearly done.

5 Gently stir in the ground masala, season with salt and simmer for 3 minutes. Serve with rotis and sweet chutney.

ROCK SALT

Sodium chloride

(KALA NAMAK)

Rock salt

Walk through the streets of any Indian city and you will be treated to an endless vision of colour and bustle and to the mouthwatering fragrance of a special cuisine. This is the street food of India, or *chaat*, which consists of a multitude of snacks, fried, soaked in yoghurt, stuffed or tossed in spices and smothered in various hot, sweet and tangy chutneys. These instant snacks are eaten at any time of day or night. The one flavour that all these snacks rely on for their zip is *kala namak* or rock salt. This salt is procured from the earth and not the sea. It is also called black salt or *saindhav*.

Ground rock salt

MANUFACTURE

Rock salt is mined from the soft-stone quarries of the fertile Gangetic plains in central India.

APPEARANCE AND TASTE

Irregular, but beautiful in appearance, crystals of rock salt range from translucent amber and deep brown to grey-brown. They have smooth, glossy surfaces where cleaved. Powdered rock salt is fine and brown or smoke-grey. Rock salt has a peculiar, unpleasant aroma akin to pickled eggs and a salty taste that is less powerful than common salt. The strange flavour seems to acquire a personality when added to cold foods like yoghurt and salads. Well worth a try.

BUYING AND STORING

Crystals of rock salt as well as the powder can be found in Indian shops. Powdered rock salt is ready for use but is not as flavourful as the crystals. However, it is sometimes a bit gravelly because of the earth that gets crushed with it. Rock salt lasts for ever if stored in dry containers. The crystals are dissolved in liquid or crushed before use.

MEDICINAL USES

Ayurvedic texts record the benefits of rock salt. Even today, Indian doctors recommend it over ordinary salt. If on a low salt diet, consult your doctor before use. It is also a sure cure for flatulence and heartburn.

CULINARY USES

It is an essential ingredient in many snacks, salads and drinks. In fact, in north India where the Indian summer is at its hottest, fresh lemonade spiked with rock salt is served everywhere, even at airports. It is considered a very good antidote to dehydration in conditions of extreme dry heat.

NIMBU SHERBET
(SPICY LEMONADE)

Serves 4
Preparation time 15 minutes
Cooking time 0

Nimbu Sherbet

900ml (1½pt) cold water
4 teaspoons sugar
6 tablespoons lemon juice
2 teaspoons rock salt
20 mint leaves
12 ice cubes
4 lemon wedges

1 Mix the water with the sugar and stir until it dissolves.

2 Add the lemon juice, rock salt, mint leaves and ice cubes. Chill thoroughly.

3 Serve with a lemon wedge on the edge of each glass.

BEETROOT RAITA
(SWEET AND SOUR BEETROOT SALAD)

Serves 4
Preparation time 10 minutes
Cooking time 0

300g (10oz) beetroot, boiled, skinned and sliced thinly
900ml (1½pt) yoghurt, beaten
2 teaspoons caster sugar
1 teaspoon rock salt
2 tablespoons coriander leaves, chopped
2 teaspoons mint leaves, chopped

1 Mix the beetroot with the yoghurt. Add the sugar and the salt.

2 Place in a glass bowl and decorate with coriander and mint leaves. Serve chilled.

Punica granatum

POMEGRANATE SEEDS

(ANARDANA)

Fresh pomegranate seeds

The pomegranate is an ancient fruit and has been a symbol of plenty and prosperity from the earliest times. Pomegranate trees and the fruit itself adorn miniature paintings from India's Mughal era. Native to Iran, Afghanistan and Baluchistan, it now grows throughout the tropics and subtropics. The pomegranate season in India is a gourmet's delight. Rows of shiny, red fruit, some as big as a grapefruit, fill stalls and chilled, ruby-red pomegranate juice is served as an aperitif in the burnished autumn evenings. As with many other Indian fruits, the pomegranate is used in its entirety, the skin, seeds and flesh being all eaten in one way or another.

Dried pomegranate seeds or *anardana*

BUYING AND STORING

Available as whole seeds or in powdered form, *anardana* is used so sparingly that it is not worth buying large amounts. Buy dark, wine-coloured seeds or branded powder.

MEDICINAL AND OTHER USES

The seeds are supposed to be soothing to the stomach while the pulp is good for the heart and stomach. The rind and the skin of the fruit are sun-dried, powdered and mixed with honey to cure diarrhoea and dysentery. Pomegranate juice is a natural face mask, its astringency and acidity being beneficial for oily skin.

HOW THEY GROW

The deciduous pomegranate tree grows to a height of 5–8m (15–24ft) and bears glossy leaves, vivid, scarlet flowers and fruits, shiny red to pink in colour, crowned by a calyx. When opened, angular seeds can be seen inside the translucent red or pink flesh. It is these seeds that are eaten. The fruits are hand picked towards the middle of October when they are ripe and burnt red in colour. The seeds with the flesh are separated by hand from the rind and are sun-dried for 10–15 days to make *anardana*.

Pomegranate fruits

APPEARANCE AND TASTE

Although they are called pomegranate seeds in English, *anardana* actually comprises the dried seeds with the flesh of the pomegranate. Reddish-brown, sticky and hard, *anardana* tends to form clumps when whole, but when powdered it assumes the texture of dried tea leaves. *Anardana* has a sour smell and a dry taste with a note of astringency.

Indian women use pomegranate potions to promote their beauty

CULINARY USES

Used in north Indian cookery, *anardana* adds tang to chutneys, curries, stuffings, vegetables and lentils. Punjabi cookery relies on anardana for flavouring pulses like chickpeas. In India pomegranate seeds are sprinkled on yoghurt raitas and sprouted pulses as a pretty garnish.

The following recipe for chickpea salad is easy and quick to turn out. It can be served as a light lunch with some crusty bread and soup.

CHANNE KI MISAL
(CHICKPEA SALAD)

Serves 4
Preparation time 30 minutes + overnight soaking
Cooking time 1 hour

150g (5oz) dried chickpeas, soaked overnight in plenty of water (alternatively you can use canned chickpeas)
4 tablespoons onion, chopped finely
4 tablespoons red pepper, chopped finely
4 tablespoons potato, peeled, boiled and cubed
1 teaspoon pomegranate seeds (anardana), coarsely ground
½ teaspoon ground black pepper
1 teaspoon lemon juice
Salt and sugar

1 Bring the chickpeas to the boil in plenty of water and simmer until they are soft but not mushy, drain and cool (alternatively, drain canned chickpeas).

2 Mix with all the other ingredients. Serve at room temperature.

This dish, a rich lamb curry, makes a wonderful Sunday lunch after which a snooze is a must! Eat it with rotis or rice and a green salad with lemon dressing.

SHAHI GOSHT
(ROYAL LAMB CURRY)

Serves 4
Preparation time 40 minutes
Cooking time 1 hour

600g (1¼lb) lean lamb, cubed
1 teaspoon turmeric powder
2 teaspoons coriander powder
1 teaspoon salt
6 tablespoons sunflower oil
2 onions, chopped finely
1 teaspoon green chillies, minced
1 teaspoon cumin seeds
1 teaspoon black mustard seeds
2 teaspoons white poppy seeds
2 teaspoons pomegranate seeds (anardana)
2 teaspoons ginger paste
2 teaspoons garlic paste
300ml (10fl oz) yoghurt
4 tablespoons coriander leaves, chopped

1 Marinate the lamb in the powder spices and salt for 15 minutes.

2 Heat the oil in a heavy pan and add the onions. Fry until golden and add the green chillies.

3 Grind the cumin, mustard and poppy seeds with the pomegranate seeds, ginger and garlic and a little water to make a coarse paste.

4 Stir the onions and the chillies a few times and add the paste. Fry for a minute and add the lamb. Brown well.

5 Add the yoghurt, enough water to make a thick sauce and more salt if needed.

6 Cover and cook on a low heat until the meat is tender. Serve hot, sprinkled with coriander.

Chane ki Misal

Sesamum indicum

SESAME

(TIL)

Based on the Hindu belief that foods can produce either heat or cold in the body, certain traditional festive dishes are made to mark the onset of winter or summer in India. Thus as the winter mists swirl in, sweets made of sesame seeds, known for their warming energy, are eaten in every part of the country to celebrate the festival of *Sankranti*. Children fly multi-coloured kites and exchange little sugared grains of sesame or sesame fudge saying, 'Eat sweet sesame and speak sweetly'. In the southern states, young, newly married women are decorated with jewellery made of sweetened sesame and the day is one of great feasting and laughter. Women make ropes of candied sesame pearls to wear as necklaces, bracelets and hair ornaments.

Kite making

HOW IT GROWS

The sesame plant is an annual which grows up to 1.5m (4ft) high, with large leaves and pretty pinkish-white flowers. Sesame comes from India, China, Mexico, Guatemala and the USA.

APPEARANCE AND TASTE

Sesame seeds differ in appearance according to variety. The most common type used in India is cream-coloured, small and glossy. Chinese sesame is black. On cooking, the flavour of sesame is distinctly nutty and sweet. Black seeds are stronger in flavour than the cream ones.

BUYING AND STORING

Sesame seeds are always sold whole. It is a good idea to dry-roast the seeds for a couple of minutes before storing. This helps sesame to keep and taste better. As always, store in a dry jar away from strong sunlight. Moisture will cause the seeds to stick together and form clumps. A popular cooking medium, sesame oil is very stable and does not turn rancid even in hot climates.

MEDICINAL AND OTHER USES

Sesame seeds and sesame oil are thought to be laxative. A hot poultice of sesame seeds is used to relieve aches and pains. In north India where the winters are intense, sesame oil is rubbed into the skin for warmth and to keep it supple. It is also massaged into the scalp to promote luxuriant hair growth, and is used to make soap and cosmetics

CULINARY USES

Sesame seeds are used in several sweets including *laddoos* or jaggery and sesame balls flavoured with cardamom, *revdi* or discs of sugared sesame and *tilgul* or drops of sugar-coated sesame grains. The spice is also made into a coarse, nutty chutney served as an accompaniment to rice pancakes or sprinkled over bread before baking to give texture and taste. In other cuisines, sesame is made into sweet halva in the Middle East, flavours Japanese rice and is ground with garlic and lemon juice in the Mediterranean dip tahini.

This is a chutney that can be used as a sandwich filling or served with any fried snack like samosas or crisps.

KHUS KHUS KI CHUTNEY
(SESAME SEED CHUTNEY)

Serves 4
Preparation time 10 minutes
Cooking time 10 minutes

2 tablespoons sunflower oil
8 tablespoons sesame seeds
8 tablespoons unsalted peanuts
2 tablespoons garlic, chopped finely
8 tablespoons desiccated coconut
Salt
1 teaspoon tamarind paste

1 Heat the oil in a pan and gently fry all the ingredients except the salt and tamarind, until brown.

2 Mix in the salt and tamarind, cool and grind to a coarse powder in a blender.

3 Store in an airtight jar and use as required, within 3 weeks.

Til laddoos

This recipe is for a bread that goes well with a meat curry. It is a bread made on special occasions.

KHASTA ROTI
(CRISP SESAME BREAD)

Serves 4
Preparation time 10 minutes
Cooking time 30 minutes (to cook all the rotis)

300g (10oz) wholemeal wheatflour
2 tablespoons hot ghee for dough
Salt
2 tablespoons sesame seeds
Extra ghee as needed

1 Make a stiff dough with the flour, ghee, salt, sesame seeds and water as needed.

2 Make equal sized balls, 3cm (1in) in diameter. Then roll out each ball to a flat disc, 12cm (5ins) in diameter.

3 Heat a griddle and gently place the roti on it. Lower the heat and dot the roti with ghee.

4 Turn over once and cook until both the sides are crisp. Serve hot (immediately if possible).

*Trachyspermum ammi/Carum ajowan/
Carum copticum*

AJOWAN

(AJWAIN)

Ajowan is a close relative of dill, caraway and cumin and belongs to a family called *Umbelliferae* which has 2700 species. In India it is also called bishop's weed, carom or omum, and is particularly found in the delicate vegetarian fare from the state of Gujarat.

Ajowan seeds

HOW IT GROWS

Ajowan is an annual, herbaceous plant which bears feathery leaves, red flowers and tiny seeds which are the spice. When the seeds are ripe, they are dried and threshed. Ajowan grows in Iran, Egypt, Afghanistan, Pakistan and widely in India.

APPEARANCE AND TASTE

Ajowan is tiny, oval and ridged. The greyish-green seeds are curved and look like miniature cumin seeds, with a fine stalk attached. The fragrance of the spice is very similar to that of cumin. Chewed on their own for their medicinal value, the seeds taste bitingly hot and bitter. They can leave the tongue numb for a while. When cooked with other ingredients, the flavour mellows a bit.

BUYING AND STORING

Ajowan is usually sold whole though some shops may also stock the ground form. It is used sparingly in cooking so don't buy too much. Ajowan will keep up to a year if stored in a clean, dry jar.

MEDICINAL AND OTHER USES

A sure cure for stomachache or over-eating is to chew a spoonful of ajowan. The seeds are also useful for flatulence, diarrhoea, cholera and colic. Ajowan poultices relieve rheumatism and asthma. The essential oil of ajowan is used in toothpastes and in perfumery.

CULINARY USES

Ajowan goes particularly well with green beans, root vegetables and in dishes that are flour based, all of which form an important part of India's vast vegetarian cuisine. Snacks like Bombay mix and potato balls depend on spices like ajowan for a special zing. Breads are also flavoured with the spice. It is often added to lentils and pulses as they are difficult to digest.

Amritsar is a sacred town in Punjab where the Sikh Golden Temple stands, proud and radiant. Its dome covered with pure gold leaf, this monument stands for universal brotherhood and peace. The first recipe that follows is from this town.

MACCHI AMRITSARI
(FRIED FISH AMRITSARI)

Serves 4
Preparation time 30 minutes
Cooking time 10 minutes

8 *pieces cod (or any firm, white, boneless fish)*
2 *teaspoons lemon juice*

For the batter:
1 *teaspoon ginger paste*
1 *teaspoon garlic paste*
1 *teaspoon ajowan seeds*
1 *teaspoon chilli powder*
150g (5oz) *gram flour*
Large pinch of bicarbonate of soda
Salt
4 drops orange food colouring
Sunflower oil for frying

1 Marinate the fish in the lemon juice for 15 minutes.

2 Make a thick batter with all the other ingredients except the oil, adding water as necessary, ensuring that there are no lumps.

3 Heat the oil in a deep kadai or wok. Dip each piece of fish in the batter and deep fry until crisp. Drain on a slotted spoon and remove onto absorbent paper.

4 Serve hot with coriander chutney and a fresh salad.

The Golden Temple at Amritsar

This recipe comes from the state of Gujarat. It has been simplified, keeping the non-availability of some of the ingredients outside India in mind.

OONDHIYOON
(MIXED GUJARATI VEGETABLES)

Serves 4
Preparation time 1 hour
Cooking time 1 hour

4 tablespoons sunflower oil
1 teaspoon cumin seeds
½ teaspoon ajowan seeds
150g (5oz) small aubergines
  (available at Indian grocers),
  quartered

150g (6oz) small potatoes,
  peeled and quartered
150g (6oz) sweet potatoes,
  peeled and cut into 3cm (1in)
  long pieces
90g (3oz) peas
90g (3oz) carrot, cut into 3cm
  (1in) pieces
90g (3oz) yam, peeled and cut
  into 3cm (1in) pieces

For the masala:
1 teaspoon ginger paste
1 teaspoon garlic paste
1 teaspoon green chilli, minced
150g (5oz) coriander leaves,
  chopped
150g (5oz) fresh fenugreek
  leaves, chopped
150g (5oz) fresh coconut, grated
½ teaspoon turmeric powder

1 teaspoon sugar
Salt

For the garnish:
120g (4oz) fresh fenugreek
  leaves, chopped
4 tablespoons gram flour
Pinch of bicarbonate of soda
Pinch of ajowan seeds
Salt
Water as needed
Sunflower oil for frying

1 Heat the oil in a large pan. Add the cumin and ajowan. When they change colour, add all the vegetables. Stir-fry and mix well.

2 Add all the masala ingredients one after the other and mix. Pour in a little water, cover and cook on a low heat until the vegetables are done but not mushy.

3 In the meantime, make the garnish. Knead to a soft dough all the ingredients except the oil.

4 Heat the oil in a deep kadai or wok. Make small, cherry-sized balls of the dough and deep-fry until golden. Drain and remove onto absorbent paper. Check that the centres are cooked. If not, reduce heat and refry.

5 Serve very hot with the garnish on top.

Trigonella foenum-graecum

FENUGREEK

(METHI)

Food and social custom are interwoven in India as in no other country. There are special foods for weddings, deaths, festivals and even eclipses. These are chosen for their medicinal or religious significance and vary from region to region depending on availability and local custom. Fenugreek seeds are associated with childbirth and a new mother is given sugared balls, or *laddoos*, of nuts, seeds and dried fruits flavoured with fenugreek for a period of 40 days after the birth. Fenugreek is an ancient spice. Papyri from the Egyptian tombs reveal that it was used as a food as well as a medicine.

Fenugreek seeds

Ground fenugreek

MEDICINAL AND OTHER USES

Ancient herbalists believed that fenugreek aided digestion. Even today the seeds are eaten to relieve flatulence, diarrhoea, chronic cough and diabetes. Fenugreek contains a steroidal substance called diosgenin which is used in the synthesis of sex hormones and oral contraceptives. The seeds promote lactation. They are crushed and fed to cows to increase their supply of milk. They are also used to keep horses' coats glossy. Fenugreek is used in hair tonic and during the Middle Ages, it was believed to be a cure for baldness. The powdered seeds yield a yellow dye.

CULINARY USES

Fenugreek is used to flavour all sorts of Indian savouries and some sweets like *laddoos*. It is an essential ingredient of curry powder and is widely used in southern Indian cookery in breads, batters, chutneys and lentils. The leaves are eaten in a number of ways.

HOW IT GROWS

Fenugreek is an annual that grows 30–60cm (1–2ft) tall and is very easy to grow in mild climates. It produces thin oval leaves and slender pods which contain about 20 seeds each. The leaves are eaten as a popular vegetable all over India. Even in the West, a hot summer is enough to harvest a good crop of fenugreek leaves. Just sow the seeds, cover lightly with soil, water regularly and let nature take its course. Fenugreek is grown around the Mediterranean, Argentina, Egypt, France and all over India.

APPEARANCE AND TASTE

Fenugreek the spice consists of small, hard, ochre, oblong seeds. They have a diagonal groove across one side and are about 3mm (⅛in) long. The whole plant has a pronounced, aromatic odour and the seeds smell of curry. Fenugreek is one of the most powerful Indian spices. The taste is bitter and lingering. Cooking the seeds subdues the flavour.

BUYING AND STORING

The seeds are available whole, crushed or powdered. The fresh stalks with leaves are sold in every Indian food shop and the dried leaves, called *kasuri methi* are sold in packs, either whole or powdered. Fenugreek seeds store well and are easy to crush if roasted. As they are usually used whole, crush them as and when needed at home. It is well worth buying kasuri methi – it is used as a flavouring and adds a very wholesome touch to meats, vegetables and onion-based curries. Store the seeds as well as kasuri methi in dry jars. Use the seeds in 6 months, the leaves in 4.

Fenugreek grows all over India

The addition of fenugreek adds a sweetness of aroma to this yoghurt curry. It is served with rice and a savoury pickle. It is supposed to be sweet so don't be surprised at the amount of sugar in the recipe.

GUJARATI KADHI
(GUJARATI YOGHURT CURRY)

Serves 4
Preparation time 15 minutes
Cooking time 15 minutes

300ml (10fl oz) yoghurt
6 tablespoons gram flour
750ml (1¼pt) water
Salt
3 teaspoons sugar
3 teaspoons sunflower oil
1 teaspoon black mustard seeds
1 teaspoon cumin seeds
16 curry leaves
½ teaspoon fenugreek seeds
15 black peppercorns
6 cloves
*4 small dried red chillies,
   deseeded and broken up*

1 Blend the yoghurt, flour, water, salt and sugar to a smooth mixture and cook on a low heat to prevent the yoghurt from curdling, stirring until the curry is creamy and done. The test is in the aroma which should be fragrant and not 'raw'.

2 Heat the oil in a small pan and add the mustard seeds. When they crackle add all the other ingredients. Stir for a minute and pour the oil and the spices over the yoghurt curry.

3 Do not boil the curry but serve hot.

This is a quick pickle that goes with anything. Try it as an unusual sandwich spread.

SUBZION KA ACHAR
(QUICK VEGETABLE PICKLE)

Serves 4
Preparation time 30 minutes
Cooking time 10 minutes

150g (5oz) carrots, cut into strips
*150g (5oz) French beans,
   halved lengthways*
*150g (5oz) cauliflower, cut into
   florets*
1 teaspoon turmeric powder
1 teaspoon chilli powder
Large pinch of asafoetida
1 teaspoon sugar
Salt
4 teaspoons lemon juice
1 tablespoon sunflower oil
1 teaspoon black mustard seeds
1 teaspoon fenugreek seeds

1 Mix the vegetables with the turmeric, chilli powder, asafoetida, sugar, salt and lemon juice.

2 Heat the oil in a small pan and add the mustard seeds. When they crackle, add the fenugreek seeds and fry until they turn dark.

3 Remove, cool and grind coarsely in a coffee mill.

4 Add to the vegetable mixture and mix well.

5 Store in an airtight bottle, refrigerate and use within a month.

Zanthoxylum rhetsa

TIRPHAL

Tirphal buds

Deep in the rain forests of western India grow clusters of old, gnarled trees. They produce a spice called tirphal not known to the rest of India. In fact, even after searching carefully I have been unable to find an English name for it, so exclusive is it to this particular region. Tirphal is quite a festive spice. In the monsoon, at the time of *Janmashtami* or the birthday of the Hindu god Krishna, as part of the festivities, little children fill the nearly ripe fruits of tirphal into piston-like cylinders called *petnoli*. The piston is pushed to 'pop' each berry and this game excites all the little ones around.

BUYING AND STORING

Tirphal is always used whole in Indian cookery. As it is used only in one part of India, it may be difficult to obtain. Store in an airtight jar. It will keep for about 6 months.

MEDICINAL USES

A decoction of tirphal is a good cure for dysentery. The spice is known for its anti-flatulent properties.

HOW IT GROWS

Tirphal trees are only found wild in the states of Maharashtra and Karnataka. The tree bears fruits in the monsoon which are picked by October. They are then laid out to dry in the strong autumn sun until they split open and dry completely. The berries contain seeds that are discarded.

APPEARANCE AND TASTE

The berries dry to a dark brown colour and split to reveal a creamy-white interior. They look like tiny opened flower buds. The berries are hollow and have a rough, spiny exterior. They sometimes have a fine stalk attached. Tirphal has a strong woody aroma that is quite pungent. The taste is sharp and biting with a marginally bitter after-taste.

Fishing along the Goan coastline

Aurey Bendi

CULINARY USES

The berries are always added after the main ingredient. They may be dry-roasted before use to release their aromatic oils but they heat quickly and start smoking, so remove to another pan as soon as their aroma develops. Tirphal is used mainly with fish or pulses. In India, foods that are difficult to digest like peas and beans are cooked with spices like tirphal.

The recipes that follow are eaten regularly in the beautiful region of Goa. The aroma of these dishes conjures up visions of Goan beaches at dusk, when the notes of the guitar fill the air and curry and rice stalls start their trade.

GOA MACCHI KADHI
(GOA FISH CURRY)

Serves 4
Preparation time 20 minutes
Cooking time 30 minutes

4 dried red chillies, deseeded and stems removed
1 teaspoon coriander seeds, roasted slightly
2 teaspoons tamarind pulp diluted in a little water
Salt
8 pieces cod or any firm white fish
300g (10oz) fresh coconut, grated
1 tablespoon sunflower oil
6 tirphal

1 Grind the red chillies, coriander seeds and tamarind to a fine paste in a blender.

2 Add salt and smear the paste onto the fish.

3 Liquidise the coconut with 300ml (½pt) water in a blender and extract the thick milk by squeezing it hard through a sieve or muslin cloth. Repeat with 150ml (¼pt) water to get a second, thin milk.

4 Heat the oil in a pan and gently fry the fish along with its marinade.

5 Turn it over and add the thin coconut milk. Simmer until the fish is cooked.

6 Add the tirphal and thick milk, bring to the boil once and remove from the heat.

7 Serve hot with boiled rice.

AUREY BENDI
(BUTTER BEANS IN GARLIC AND COCONUT)

Serves 4
Preparation time 20 minutes + overnight soaking
Cooking time 20 minutes

300g (10oz) butter beans, soaked overnight in water
300g (10oz) coconut, grated if fresh, or desiccated
4 dried red chillies, deseeded, stems removed, soaked in a little water
2 teaspoons tamarind pulp, diluted in 1 teaspoon of water
Salt
6 tirphal
2 teaspoons sunflower oil
2 teaspoons garlic, sliced

1 Boil the beans in 600ml (1pt) water until soft.

2 Grind the coconut, red chillies and tamarind to a paste in a blender, adding water as needed from the cooked beans.

3 Stir the blended paste into the beans very gently and add enough water to make a thick sauce. Add the salt and tirphal.

4 Bring to the boil only once. Remove from the heat.

5 In a separate pan, heat the oil. Add the garlic and fry for a minute until the aroma fills the air.

6 Pour over the curry. Stir and serve with rotis or rice.

FROM THE GRINDING STONE

SPICE MIXTURES

GARAM MASALA

Every Indian dish, whether eaten under the swaying coconut palms of Tamil Nadu or in the fiery deserts of Rajasthan, is flavoured with a distinct blend of spices. Some simple vegetarian curries may have just a sprinkling of mustard seeds and turmeric but a rich north Indian meat curry simmers for hours in a mixture of up to 15 different spices. Good Indian cookery depends wholly on using the right blend of spices. That is why traditional combinations are home-ground and kept ready for use. The term for those mixtures is *masala*. Each region of India has its own special blend depending on availability, climate and methods of cooking. In the north, where the winters are bitterly cold, a blend called *garam masala*, meaning hot spice, is preferred to chillies which cool the body by promoting perspiration. Some of the most expensive spices go into the making of garam masala and there are as many recipes for it as there are households in India. Depending on individual taste, the proportions of the various ingredients can be adjusted.

Winter in Uttar Pradesh

Garam masala powder

Garam masala ingredients

BUYING AND STORING

Commercially produced garam masala is not aromatic enough, and does not seem to retain its flavour for very long. The blend is easy to grind at home, so it is best to buy whole, plump spices and crush them in an electric grinder or coffee mill. This mixture can then be stored for up to 6 months.

CULINARY USES

Indian cooks use garam masala in small amounts. It can be added at different stages of cooking for different degrees of flavour. It can be dropped into hot oil to give a spicy, fried taste, added along with the main ingredient to create an aromatic warmth, or sprinkled on top of cold salads or yoghurt for a gentle hint of spicy flavour.

Every Indian household has its own recipe for garam masala. Here is a guide but you can vary the quantity of any spice according to taste.

APPEARANCE AND TASTE

Garam masala is used whole or ground depending on what's cooking. The basic blend includes cloves, cinnamon, cardamom, peppercorns, bay leaf, mace, cumin and coriander seeds. When ground, the powder is slightly coarse and tobacco-brown in colour. Garam masala has a rich, warm fragrance and tastes hot and aromatic.

1 teaspoon black peppercorns
2 teaspoons cumin seeds
2cm (¾in) stick cinnamon
1 teaspoon cardamom seeds
  (removed from their husks)
1 teaspoon cloves
3 bay leaves

Grind all the spices in a small electric grinder (a coffee mill is perfect) and store in an airtight jar.

Garam masala is the main flavouring in the following recipes. The first one is a festive rice dish from Maharashtra and is often served at weddings.

VANGI BHAAT
(AUBERGINE-FLAVOURED RICE)

Serves 4
Preparation time 30 minutes
Cooking time 30 minutes

4 tablespoons sunflower oil
1 teaspoon cumin seeds
1 large onion, chopped
12 curry leaves

300g (10oz) aubergines, cubed
300g (10oz) basmati rice
1 teaspoon turmeric powder
1 teaspoon chilli powder
1 teaspoon garam masala
  powder
Salt
4 tablespoons coriander leaves,
  chopped
4 wedges of lemon

1 Heat the oil in a heavy-bottomed pan, and add the cumin seeds. Stir for a minute and add the onion and curry leaves. When the onion is golden, add the aubergines and stir-fry for a couple of minutes.

2 Add the rice, spices and salt. Mix and fry until the rice becomes translucent.

3 Add 600ml (1pt) hot water, stir and bring to the boil. Then reduce the heat, cover and simmer until the rice is cooked and fluffy.

4 Remove from the heat and serve hot, garnished with coriander and lemon wedges.

Garam masala spices on sale

BHOONI HUI SIMLA MIRCH
(GREEN PEPPER STIR-FRY)

Serves 4
Preparation time 20 minutes
Cooking time 15 minutes

4 tablespoons gram flour
4 tablespoons sunflower oil
1 teaspoon cumin seeds
Large pinch asafoetida
2 onions, chopped
600g (1¼lb) green pepper,
  deseeded and cubed
4 tablespoons unsalted peanuts,
  coarsely crushed
1 teaspoon chilli powder
1 teaspoon turmeric powder
1 teaspoon coriander powder
1 teaspoon garam masala
  powder
Salt

1 Heat a heavy pan and dry-roast the gram flour, stirring until it is brown and fragrant.

2 Heat the oil in a separate pan. Add the cumin and asafoetida. Stir a few times, then add the onion and fry until golden.

3 Add the green pepper, peanuts, powder spices and salt. Cover and cook until the pepper is crunchy.

4 Sprinkle the gram flour over and stir well to break up the lumps. Cook for 5 more minutes, then remove from the heat. Serve hot with rotis.

SAMBHAR POWDER

In Tamil Nadu most people are vegetarian, and the cuisine exudes simplicity, cleanliness of flavour and freshness. Traditional meals are served on fresh green banana leaves and the fragrance of new butter and succulent vegetables permeates every house. The special spice blend of this region of India is sambhar powder. This masala or mix is so-called because it is used to flavour a *dal* of the same name which is popular in this region. *Sambhar* is a preparation of lentils and vegetables that is spiked with different spices and laced with coriander. *Sambhar* is eaten every day in Tamil Nadu as the lentils provide protein in a meat-free diet.

Ingredients for
sambhar powder

CULINARY USES

It goes into sambhar or south Indian dal, or into vegetable dishes. It is best added before the lentils or vegetables so that it then has a chance to cook and develop its flavour. As the powder is a blend of spices and lentils, it acts as both a flavouring and a thickening agent.

One recipe for sambhar powder is given below:

1 teaspoon black mustard seeds
1 teaspoon fenugreek seeds
2 teaspoons cumin seeds
12 dried red chillies (or your personal preference), stalks removed and deseeded
1 teaspoon black peppercorns
1 teaspoon coriander seeds
1 teaspoon turmeric powder

¼ teaspoon asafoetida
3 teaspoons sunflower oil
3 teaspoons split gram lentils (channa dal)
3 teaspoons split black lentils (urad dal)
3 teaspoons split yellow lentils (toor dal)

Heat a heavy pan and dry-roast all the whole spices. Keep the heat low and stir constantly to stop them burning. The seeds will crackle and fly out so beware! Add the turmeric and asafoetida, give the mixture a good stir and take off the heat. Transfer it to a dry bowl and in the same pan, heat the oil and fry the three lentils. When they turn dark, add to the roasted spices. Cool the mixture and grind in an electric blender until fine.

A typical south Indian meal

APPEARANCE AND TASTE

Sambhar powder is fine and rust-coloured. It has a strong, earthy, dry smell of roasted spices and lentils. The taste is warm and acid.

BUYING AND STORING

Ready-made sambhar powder is available but it is never quite the same as home-made. However, if you get an authentic south Indian brand, it may well be good. Make a good quantity – it will store for up to a year in a dry, airtight jar.

The aroma of *sambhar* reminds me of the Temple of Meenakshi, the goddess with the fish-shaped eyes, in south India. After the ritual worship, streams of devotees are served a simple meal of rice, *sambhar*, ghee and sweets.

VENGAI SAMBHAR
(SOUTH INDIAN LENTILS WITH SHALLOTS)

Serves 4
Preparation time 45 minutes + soaking for 30 minutes
Cooking time 30 minutes

300g (10oz) split yellow lentils (toor dal), soaked in water for 30 minutes and drained
750ml (1¼pt) water
12 shallots, peeled
Salt
1 teaspoon turmeric powder
1 teaspoon chilli powder
3 tablespoons sunflower oil
1 teaspoon black mustard seeds
1 teaspoon cumin seeds
12 curry leaves
Large pinch of asafoetida

1 teaspoon tamarind paste, diluted in 2 teaspoons of water
2 teaspoons sambhar powder
2 tablespoons coriander leaves, chopped

1 Simmer the lentils in the water. When nearly done, add the shallots and simmer until cooked.

2 Add the salt, turmeric and chilli powder. Mix well, take off the heat and reserve.

3 Heat the oil in a small pan and add the mustard seeds. When they crackle, add the cumin, curry leaves and asafoetida. Stir for a minute.

4 Add the tamarind and cook until thick and bubbly.

5 Add the sambhar powder and cook for a couple of minutes. Pour the mixture over the lentils and stir. Serve hot, garnished with coriander.

Rasam

Meenakshi Temple at Madurai, southern India

Rasam is a close relative of **sambhar** but it is thinner and is therefore often served as a spicy soup. Try it on cold winter nights!

RASAM
(SOUTH INDIAN TAMARIND SOUP)

Serves 4
Preparation time 15 minutes + 15 minutes soaking
Cooking time 30 minutes

4 tablespoons split yellow lentils (toor dal), soaked for 15 minutes and drained
750ml (1¼pt) water
Salt
1 teaspoon jaggery, grated
2 tablespoons sunflower oil
1 teaspoon black mustard seeds
1 teaspoon cumin seeds
Large pinch asafoetida
10 curry leaves
4 whole cloves garlic, peeled
1 teaspoon tamarind paste diluted in 2 tablespoons water

1 teaspoon sambhar powder
1 teaspoon turmeric powder
1 teaspoon chilli powder
2 tablespoons coriander leaves, chopped

1 Bring the lentils to the boil in the water and simmer until soft. Add the salt and the jaggery, mixing until they dissolve.

2 Heat the oil in a separate pan and add the mustard seeds. When they crackle, add the cumin, asafoetida, curry leaves and the whole garlic. Fry for a minute.

3 Then add the tamarind and cook until it becomes thick and bubbly. Stir in the powder spices.

4 Pour the lentils into the tamarind mixture, bring to the boil and remove from the heat immediately. Serve hot with fresh coriander.

GODA MASALA

The state of Maharashtra, of which the capital is Bombay, is on the west coast of India and has a tropical climate. Richly verdant, it enjoys a good monsoon and hot, languid summers. Maharashtra is an agricultural state which provides plenty of fresh vegetables, rice, mangoes, coconuts, jaggery, peanuts and cashew nuts. The cuisine includes hot, aromatic meat and fish dishes, vegetables in coconut sauce or flavoured with spice blends like *goda masala*, savoury tidbits and crisp, crunchy sweets made of rice and jaggery.

Ingredients for goda masala

CULINARY USES

As with most spice blends, goda masala flavours a variety of lentils, vegetables and pulses. It can be added before or after the main ingredient to vary the taste from strong to subtle.

Goda masala can be made in the following way:

5 cardamom
1cm (½in) stick cinnamon
5 cloves
2 bay leaves
1 teaspoon sunflower oil
2 teaspoons white sesame seeds
2 teaspoons coriander seeds
4 teaspoons desiccated coconut
10 black peppercorns
5 cassia buds
2 tablespoons white poppy seeds

Remove the cardamom seeds from their husks. Fry the cinnamon, cloves, cardamom and bay leaves in the oil until the cloves swell. Dry-roast the rest of the ingredients over a low heat until the coconut is dark brown. Cool and grind with the fried spices until fine. Store in an airtight container for up to 4 months.

APPEARANCE AND TASTE

The masala is a black, aromatic powder with a burnt sweetness which comes from the coconut in the mixture.

BUYING AND STORING

Goda masala is not readily available in shops as it is made by just a few communities in Maharashtra. It is almost always made at home so just store a little at a time.

Scraping coconut

Pune, one of the most culturally alive cities of Maharashtra, has a special cuisine of its own. Created and perfected by a community called the Puneri Brahmins, it is delicate and fragrant. Goda masala is used a great deal in their cooking and the following two recipes come from there.

Modern Pune

PUNERI DAL
(YELLOW LENTILS PUNE-STYLE)

Serves 4
Preparation time 30 minutes
Cooking time 40 minutes

220g (8oz) split yellow lentils (toor dal), washed
2 teaspoons goda masala powder
1 teaspoon turmeric powder
1 teaspoon chilli powder
6 kokum
2 teaspoons jaggery, grated
4 tablespoons coconut, grated if fresh, or desiccated
Salt
1 tablespoon sunflower oil
1 teaspoon black mustard seeds
1 teaspoon cumin seeds
Large pinch of asafoetida
12 curry leaves
2 tablespoons coriander leaves, chopped

1 Simmer the lentils in double their quantity of water until soft.

2 Add the powder spices, kokum, jaggery, coconut and salt. Simmer for just a minute. Take off the heat.

3 In a separate pan, heat the oil and add the mustard seeds. When they crackle, add the cumin, asafoetida and curry leaves. Stir once and pour the oil as well as the spices over the lentils.

4 Mix well. Serve very hot, sprinkled with coriander, to accompany boiled rice and a vegetable curry.

Farasbean Bhaji

Maharashtrian food flavoured with goda masala

FARASBEAN BHAJI
(FRENCH BEAN STIR-FRY)

Serves 4
Preparation time 30 minutes
Cooking time 20 minutes

3 tablespoons sunflower oil
1 teaspoon black mustard seeds
1 teaspoon cumin seeds
Large pinch asafoetida
1 large onion, chopped finely
150g (5oz) potato, peeled and cut into small cubes
300g (10oz) French beans, chopped finely
1 teaspoon turmeric powder
1 teaspoon chilli powder
1 teaspoon goda masala powder
1 teaspoon coriander powder
Salt

1 Heat the oil in a kadai or wok. Add the mustard seeds. When they crackle, add the cumin and asafoetida. Stir once. Add the onion and stir until translucent.

2 Add the potatoes and fry for a minute.

3 Drop in the French beans, all the powder spices and salt.

4 Add a teaspoon or so of water, cover and cook the vegetables in their own steam until the potatoes and French beans are cooked. Serve hot with rotis.

TANDOORI MASALA

Cooking in a *tandoor*

Aptly called the granary of India, Punjab is an emerald-green vision of rippling wheat and cornfields which are fed by 5 of India's most important rivers. Punjab is famous for its energetic dance and music, and robust food. Its biggest contribution to the food repertoire of India is tandoori cooking. Huge earthen or clay ovens, half-buried in the ground, are made red-hot with a coal fire lit at the bottom. Marinated meat, chicken, fish or cheese is threaded onto skewers and cooked in this *tandoor* until done. Bread or flat rotis are stuck onto its sides until they puff up and come away easily. The food gets flavoured by a mixture of spices and charcoal. Tandoori masala is a versatile blend as it can give a tandoori-like flavour to dishes cooked in a wok!

Red food colouring

Tandoori masala

APPEARANCE AND TASTE

Commercial tandoori masala is bright red due to added colouring. This makes the food to which it is added a deep orange. Tandoori masala has a distinctive aroma, very fragrant and spicy. The taste is hot, salty and sour, with a predominant flavour of cumin and coriander.

BUYING AND STORING

Commercial tandoori masala is very good and gives authentic results, so just buy a good brand. Stored in an airtight container, it will keep for about 6 months.

CULINARY USES

Tandoori masala can be used in marinades or added to hot oil before the main ingredient or along with it. Dry-roast a little over a low heat and mix into mayonnaise for an unusual dip with crisps or chips. Meats are marinated in a mixture of yoghurt and tandoori masala before being baked. Mixed peppers and potatoes go well with it and you can try making tomato- and cream-based curries with a touch of tandoori masala.

Ingredients for tandoori masala

Here is one version of the blend:

2 teaspoons cumin seeds
2 teaspoons coriander seeds
2cm (¾in) stick cinnamon
1 teaspoon cloves
1 teaspoon chilli powder
1 teaspoon ginger powder
1 teaspoon turmeric powder
1 teaspoon garlic powder
1 teaspoon mace powder
1 teaspoon salt
¼ teaspoon red food colouring powder (available from Indian grocers)

Dry-roast all the whole spices until they smoke. Cool and grind with the powder spices, salt and food colouring in an electric grinder.

Nearly every high street Indian restaurant outside India is called a 'tandoori restaurant', though sometimes it does not feature any tandoor-cooked food at all. The first recipe is a hallmark dish of Punjab and is tremendously popular with non-vegetarian Indians. Punjabis make the best *paneer*, or cottage cheese. The second recipe is a rich blend of cottage cheese and spices. Serve it with fresh, hot naan.

MURG TANDOORI
(RED BAKED CHICKEN)

Serves 4
Preparation time 45 minutes
Cooking time 30 minutes

For the marinade:
150ml (5fl oz) yoghurt, beaten
2 teaspoons ginger paste
2 teaspoons garlic paste
1 teaspoon turmeric powder
1 teaspoon chilli powder
2 teaspoons tandoori masala powder

8 chicken legs
3 tablespoons sunflower oil
4 lemon wedges
Onion rings

1 Mix all the ingredients for the marinade. Drop in the chicken and coat well. Reserve for 30 minutes.

2 Line a baking tray with a sheet of cooking foil. Smear 1 tablespoon of the oil over the sheet.

3 Place the chicken on the tray without overlapping the pieces. Pour over any remaining marinade. Drizzle the remaining oil on top and bake in a moderately hot oven (200°C, 400°F, gas mark 6) for 30 minutes or until the chicken is cooked. Then put under a hot grill to dry up the juices and to brown the chicken a bit.

4 Serve hot, garnished with lemon wedges and onion rings.

Alternatively, you can barbecue the marinated chicken legs. (Note: If you can get hold of a tandoor, skewer the chicken and bake at a hot temperature.)

Paneer Makhni

PANEER MAKHNI
(SPICED COTTAGE CHEESE)

Serves 4
Preparation time 30 minutes
Cooking time 30 minutes

3 tablespoons sunflower oil
1 teaspoon ginger paste
1 teaspoon garlic paste
2 onions, chopped, boiled until soft and translucent, and ground to a paste
10 tablespoons tomato purée
1 teaspoon chilli powder
1 teaspoon turmeric powder
1 teaspoon cumin powder
1 teaspoon tandoori masala
Salt
1 teaspoon sugar
300g (10oz) paneer, cubed
6 tablespoons double cream

1 Heat the oil and add the ginger and garlic pastes. Fry for a minute.

2 Add the onion paste and fry until the oil separates. Then add the tomato purée and all the spices. Stir well.

3 Add the salt and the sugar and simmer for 5 minutes.

4 Drop in the paneer gently, without breaking it. Simmer for 1 minute and take off the heat.

5 Serve hot with a generous swirl of cream on top.

NOTE: Paneer is available in most Indian grocery shops. It is also easy to make your own at home. To make 150g (5oz) of paneer, you need:

450ml (¾pt) full cream milk
2 tablespoons fresh lemon juice (or as much as it takes to curdle the milk)

Heat the milk until it boils. Remove from the heat and stir in the lemon juice until the milk separates into paneer (cheese) and whey. Let it stand for a few minutes to coagulate completely, then strain through a piece of muslin or a very fine strainer. The whey can be used in doughs instead of water. Place the paneer on a plate and weigh it down with a heavy object like a pan for a few hours until all the excess whey has drained out and the paneer is set. Then cut and used as required. Refrigerate any leftover paneer and use within 3–4 days.

Ingredients for panch phoron

PANCH PHORON

Bengal lies in the north-east of India. Art, literature, food and festivals are all an inseparable part of every Bengali's life. The people are known for their passion for river fish, rice and sweets made of clotted or burnt milk, flavoured with rose-water or saffron and soaked in sugar syrup or cold, sweet milk. The most popular blend of spices here is *panch phoron* – Bengal's equivalent of the Chinese 5-spice powder. This mixture too has 5 different spices which are used whole or ground, to flavour lentils, pulses or vegetables. The unique aroma of Bengali cuisine is largely due to panch phoron.

APPEARANCE AND TASTE

Panch phoron is a colourful blend of green fennel seeds, black mustard seeds, black nigella, yellow fenugreek seeds and sage-coloured cumin seeds. It is kept whole or ground to a fine powder. The flavour is bittersweet and the aroma is powerful.

BUYING AND STORING

Though panch phoron is available ready-mixed, it is possible to blend it at home. It is best to grind small quantities as and when required.

CULINARY USES

Panch phoron is added to hot oil before adding vegetables, lentils or pulses. As it begins to splutter, the rest of the ingredients are dropped in. Alternatively, it is fried in the ghee which is poured on top of a dish to liven it. As with other blends, you can vary the ingredients according to taste.

The recipe for panch phoron is to mix equal quantities of:

Cumin seeds
Fennel seeds
Fenugreek seeds
Black mustard seeds
Nigella seeds

Ground panch phoron

Bengalis love the good things of life. Academic and artistic by nature, they translate these passions into their cuisine, with a rich blend of flavours and textures. The following recipes are typical Bengali dishes made to accompany a meal that is predominantly fish and rice.

CABBAGE CHORCHORI
(BENGALI CABBAGE STIR-FRY)

Serves 4
Preparation time 30 minutes
Cooking time 30 minutes

5 tablespoons mustard oil
1 large onion, sliced finely
600g (1 ¼lb) cabbage, shredded finely

Grind to a coarse paste with 2 teaspoons of water in a blender:
1 teaspoon black mustard seeds
2 teaspoons ginger, shredded
4 dried red chillies, deseeded, soaked in water
1 teaspoon turmeric powder

Salt
2 teaspoons panch phoron

1 Heat 4 tablespoons of the oil in a pan and add the onion. Fry until golden and add the cabbage. Stir-fry until translucent, then add the ground mixture and salt.

2 Add 4 tablespoons of water and cook until the cabbage is done but still crisp. Take off the heat.

3 Heat the remaining oil in a separate pan and add the panch phoron.

4 When it crackles, pour the oil and the seeds over the cabbage. Stir well.

5 Heat through to blend the vegetable and spices. Serve hot.

BENGALI DAL
(SWEET-AND-SOUR BENGALI LENTILS)

Serves 4
Preparation time 20 minutes +
  1 hour soaking
Cooking time 1 hour

*300g (10oz) split gram lentils
  (channa dal)*
750ml (1¼pt) water

1 teaspoon turmeric powder
Salt
2 teaspoons sugar
3 tablespoons sunflower oil
2 tablespoons panch phoron
*4 dried red chillies, deseeded
  and crumbled*
2 bay leaves
1 teaspoon mango powder
2 teaspoons raisins

1 Simmer the lentils in the water until soft and mushy.

2 Add the turmeric, salt and sugar. Blend well.

3 Heat the oil in a small pan and add the panch phoron. When it crackles, add the red chillies, bay leaves, mango powder and raisins. Reduce the heat.

4 Fry for a minute and pour the oil and the spices over the lentils.

5 Add water if required to adjust the consistency which should be that of a thick soup. Bring to the boil once and serve hot.

Whole panch phoron

KHOLOMBO POWDER

In the states of Maharashtra, Karnataka and Goa along the western Konkan coast of India lives a community of people called the Konkani Saraswats. Being a coastal people, their cuisine is studded with coconut, fish, rice and mangoes. Saraswat food is fragrant and superbly balanced with complementary textures and flavours. Known for their variety, Saraswat feasts must be seen to be believed. It is not surprising that Saraswat or Konkani food is becoming increasingly popular in restaurants all over India. As it is still relatively unknown gourmets will have the pleasure of discovering its mysterious secrets.

Kholombo powder

Ingredients for kholombo powder

APPEARANCE AND TASTE

The mixture is a light brown fine powder with an aroma reminiscent of wood smoke that enhances the flavour of food, as grilling does to meat on a barbecue. The taste is hot with a slightly bitter aftertaste. It is always used in conjunction with tamarind.

Coconut scraper

BUYING AND STORING

Kholombo powder is only available in very select Konkani shops and there are few if any outside India. Therefore it is necessary to make the blend at home. Make small quantities and store in a dry, airtight container.

CULINARY USE

It is used to flavour pulses, rice and vegetables and is added along with the main ingredient.

One of the best recipes I have found for kholombo powder is:

2 teaspoons coriander seeds
8 dried curry leaves
2 teaspoons cumin seeds
4 cloves
1 teaspoon black peppercorns
2cm (¾in) stick cinnamon
3 tablespoons desiccated coconut
2 tablespoons split gram lentils (channa dal)
2 tablespoons split black lentils (urad dal)
1 tablespoon sunflower oil

Fry all the ingredients in hot oil until the lentils are dark brown and the aroma is rich, like distant wood smoke. Cool and grind to a powder. Use within 3 months.

VAINGAN KHOLOMBO
(SMOKY LENTILS)

Serves 4
Preparation time 20 minutes
Cooking time 30 minutes

220g (8oz) split red lentils
  (masoor dal)
220g (8oz) aubergine, cubed
750ml (1¼pt) water
Salt
1 teaspoon tamarind pulp,
  diluted in 2 teaspoons water
1 teaspoon kholombo powder
4 teaspoons peanut oil
1 teaspoon black mustard seeds
4 dried red chillies, deseeded
  and crumbled
Large pinch of asafoetida
12 curry leaves

1 Simmer the lentils and the aubergines in the water until soft.

2 Add the salt, tamarind and kholombo powder and bring to the boil. Take off the heat.

3 In another pan, heat the oil and add the mustard seeds. When they crackle, add the chillies, asafoetida and curry leaves.

4 Fry for a minute and pour over the lentils. Mix well and serve with rice and a hot pickle.

VATANA USAL
(STIR-FRIED SMOKY PEAS)

Serves 4
Preparation time 15 minutes
Cooking time 20 minutes

4 tablespoons peanut oil
1 teaspoon cumin seeds
12 curry leaves
Large pinch asafoetida
1 teaspoon ginger, shredded
1 teaspoon turmeric powder
1 teaspoon chilli powder
1 teaspoon kholombo powder
600g (1¼lb) green peas, shelled,
  or frozen

Vaingan Kholombo

Salt
6 tablespoons coconut, grated if
  fresh, or desiccated

1 Heat the oil in a pan and add the cumin.

2 When it changes colour, add the curry leaves and asafoetida.

3 Stir once and add the ginger and powder spices. Fry for a minute.

4 Add the peas, salt and 4 teaspoons of water and cook until tender (you may need to add more water for fresh peas).

5 The cooked peas should be dry. Sprinkle the coconut over the peas, toss the mixture to blend and serve warm. Do not reheat on a high heat as the taste of the coconut will be affected.

FROM THE GARDEN

DRIED HERBS

Cymbopogon citratus

LEMON GRASS

(BHUSTRINA)

Ground lemon grass

Fragrant lemon grass grows in gardens all over India. Its special bouquet is a favourite of 2 Indian communities – the Gujaratis and the Parsees. The Parsees were Persians who migrated to India in the first century BC and made it their home. Their cuisine is a blend of Indian, Iranian and Continental. Even though lemon grass grows widely in India, its use in cookery is limited and it flavours only drinks and soups.

Fresh lemon grass

Dried lemon grass

HOW IT GROWS

Lemon grass is a perennial, aromatic, tall grass with rhizomes and densely tufted fibrous roots. Narrow leaves with sharp edges grow in clusters and are up to 90cm (3ft) long. Lemon grass likes a hot climate with sunshine and rain, so most of India is perfect for it. Many people grow it in their gardens and pinch off a leaf to add to the morning pot of tea. Native to Asia, it is also cultivated in the USA, Africa and Australia.

APPEARANCE AND TASTE

The long blades of grass are cut to a manageable size, dried if desired and tied into bundles for sale. They look like little parcels of green hay and are quite sharp to touch. The fresh stalks and leaves have a clean, lemon-like odour as they contain an essential oil which is also present in lemon peel. The taste of fresh lemon grass is vibrant, that of dried is less so.

The essential oil of lemon grass is used in Indian perfumery

BUYING AND STORING

Lemon grass is available fresh or dried. Buy fresh lemon grass with unbruised leaves and make sure that if you buy dried it is free from mildew. You can tear off a tiny piece of leaf to check the aroma. Fresh grass can be stored for up to a week in the refriger-ator, dried for up to two.

Lemon grass is a popular flavouring for tea in India

MEDICINAL AND OTHER USES

The grass is considered a diuretic, tonic and stimulant. It promotes good digestion and induces perspiration in a fever which cools the body down. The essential oil, which is the colour of sherry, is used in perfumery.

CULINARY USES

Add it to the water you boil for tea for a subtle, exotic flavour. It goes well in clear, vegetable soups. In south-east Asia, it is used extensively with onions and garlic, to enhance meat and fish. Lemon grass is a staple of most Thai dishes.

There is nothing like the fragrance of fresh lemon grass but you could use dried in the following recipes. The tea is sure to refresh if served in the afternoon along with a savoury snack.

PATTI KI CHAI
(LEMON GRASS TEA)

Serves 4
Preparation time 0
Cooking time 10 minutes

*8–9 lemon grass blades, 4cm
  (1½in) long
600ml (1pt) water
2 Indian teabags
Milk and sugar*

1 Boil the lemon grass in the water and simmer for 3 minutes.

2 Add the teabags and take pan off the heat. Cover and allow to steep for 3 minutes.

3 Add milk and sugar to taste. Serve hot.

This soup is a good starter for a light, summery meal.

SUBZION KA SHORBA
(SPRING VEGETABLE SOUP)

Serves 4
Preparation time 30 minutes
Cooking time 15 minutes

*1 tablespoon sunflower oil
4 tablespoons carrots, grated
120g (4oz) peas
60g (2oz) French beans,
  chopped finely
150g (5oz) mushrooms, sliced
1 teaspoon tamarind paste,
  diluted in 4 teaspoons water
900ml (1½pt) water
1 teaspoon ginger, grated
1 teaspoon sugar
Salt
12 blades lemon grass, 4cm
  (1½in) long
12 Holy Basil leaves*

1 Heat the oil and add the vegetables. Stir-fry for 5 minutes then add the tamarind paste and stir well for a minute.

2 Pour in the water. Stir. Add all the other ingredients and bring to the boil. Then reduce the heat and simmer until all the vegetables are cooked but crunchy.

3 Pick out and discard the lemon grass. Serve warm.

Mentha

MINT

(PUDINA)

Mint displayed on a fresh lemonade stall

Most Indians associate mint with chutneys and the snacks that are served with them. Crisp samosas, soft lentil cakes called *dhoklas*, little flour dumplings in yoghurt… the list is endless. Mint is used more in north India than in the south. It was probably introduced into Indian cookery by the Muslim rulers of Delhi. They used mint to perfume their meats and, after settling down in the fertile rice-rich land of India, developed their cuisine to include many mint-flavoured biryanis and pulaos.

Dried mint

HOW IT GROWS

Mint belongs to the genus *Mentha* which has about 40 species of aromatic, perennial herbs growing mainly in the northern hemisphere. In India 8 of these varieties grow, both wild and culti-vated. Mint is a bushy shrub which grows up to 60cm (2ft) high, has textured leaves and thick stalks. It grows easily in climates with moderate rainfall.

APPEARANCE AND TASTE

The herb leaves are small with uneven surfaces and edges. The stalks vary from green to deep purple and get rather woody as the plant matures. Mint has a fresh, clean aroma all its own. If chewed, the leaves are rather peppery, but added to food they lend a distinct, green note that goes well with sweets or savouries.

BUYING AND STORING

Mint is sold fresh and is also available dried and crushed to a fine olive-green powder. Fresh mint should be selected on the basis of its vitality and colour. Avoid bruised, blackened or wilted leaves. Fresh mint stores for a week in the refrigerator. It is also easily frozen. Wash the leaves, dry well and put into a freezer bag. Seal tightly or everything else in your freezer will smell minty. Dried mint has a subtle fragrance but loses its flavour after 3 to 4 months.

MEDICINAL AND OTHER USES

It is often used to ease stomach disorders, kidney problems and bronchitis. An infusion of mint sweetened with honey is a good expectorant. Mint oil is used in throat lozenges and ointments for headaches. Mint is used to flavour toothpaste, mouthwash, tobacco in menthol ciga-rettes, confectionery and in perfumery.

CULINARY USES

Chutneys and relishes made with mint complement a wide range of savouries. Mint tea is popular in India and several home-made drinks get their cooling flavour from this herb. Ice-creams, sauces and stuffings flavoured with mint are made the world over and a few sprigs of the herb are used as a fresh garnish on many dishes. Rich Indian meat or chicken curries are embellished with mint.

Mint is native to Europe but now grows freely in India

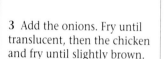

Fresh mint

Mint always adds freshness to a dish and it is the main flavouring in the recipes given below. The first one is a chicken dish that makes a refreshing change from the rich, red curries that are normally served in Indian restaurants.

MURG HARIYALI
(GREEN CHICKEN)

Serves 4
Preparation time 1 hour
Cooking time 30 minutes

For the marinade:
300ml (½pt) yoghurt
300g (10oz) mint leaves
300g (10oz) coriander leaves
2 teaspoons ginger, chopped
2 teaspoons garlic, chopped
1 teaspoon green chillies, chopped
1 teaspoon turmeric powder
Salt

8 large chicken drumsticks
6 tablespoons sunflower oil
6 cloves
10 black peppercorns
4cm (1½in) stick cinnamon
6 cardamom
2 large onions, sliced finely
2 tablespoons flaked almonds
1 teaspoon dried mint powder

1 Grind all the marinade ingredients in a blender until smooth and creamy. Then marinate the chicken for 30 minutes.

2 Heat the oil in a pan and add the cloves, peppercorns, cinnamon and cardamom. Fry for a minute.

3 Add the onions. Fry until translucent, then the chicken and fry until slightly brown.

4 Add any remaining marinade, cover and cook on a low heat until the chicken is tender.

5 Serve hot, sprinkled with almonds and dried mint powder.

Pudine ki Chutney

This recipe is a tangy, cooling chutney that tempers the effect of fiery dishes like kababs and spicy samosas.

PUDINE KI CHUTNEY
(MINT CHUTNEY)

Serves 4
Preparation time 10 minutes
Cooking time 0

4 tablespoons natural yoghurt
2 tablespoons fresh mint, chopped or 2 teaspoons dried mint
2 small green chillies, minced
1 teaspoon sugar
Salt

1 Grind all the ingredients in a blender until smooth and creamy.

2 Serve at room temperature or slightly chilled.

Murraya koenigii

CURRY LEAVES

(KADHI PATTA)

Northern India relies on mint whereas the south uses the powerful-smelling curry leaves. No south Indian savoury is complete without this herb. It lends its lingering aroma to a dish but is not eaten. In fact, an old Indian saying likens a person who is only wanted for a particular use and is discarded after this end is met, to a curry leaf, which enhances a dish but is eventually discarded.

Fresh curry leaves

Selling herbs in Bombay

HOW THEY GROW

Curry leaves come from a shrub which grows to 0.9m (3ft) or a beautiful tree up to 6m (20ft) in height. The tree is native to India and Sri Lanka and thrives in tropical climates. When young it is grown on kitchen window sills so that a few leaves can easily be plucked when needed. As the plant is so widely grown, the herb is cheap and vegetable vendors often toss a few fresh sprigs into your shopping basket free of charge, as a little extra.

APPEARANCE AND TASTE

The dark green leaves are almond-shaped. The whole plant has a strong curry-like odour. The taste is slightly bitter but pleasant and aromatic.

BUYING AND STORING

Curry leaves are available fresh or dried. Buy fresh curry leaves that are unbruised and have springy stalks. Dried leaves are greyish-green and brittle.

MEDICINAL AND OTHER USES

The ancient Hindu practice of Ayurvedic medicine relies heavily on curry leaves for many of its cures. The leaves and the stem are used as a tonic, stimulant and carminative. They can also be made into a paste to cure eruptions and bites. Fresh juice of the leaves mixed with lemon juice and sugar is prescribed for digestive disorders and eating 10 curry leaves every morning for 3 months is said to cure hereditary diabetes. A few drops of the juice are said to keep eyes bright. A liberal intake of curry leaves impedes premature greying of the hair. The leaves, boiled in coconut oil, are massaged into the scalp to promote hair growth and retain colour. The wood of the curry tree is hard, even, close-grained and durable, which makes it suitable for agricultural implements.

CULINARY USES

In south India curry leaves are used to flavour meats, vegetables, lentils, breads and fish. The herb is used in Gujarat to embellish vegetarian delicacies. The leaves are ground with coconut and spices to make a superlative chutney which is a good accompaniment to any meal. Curry leaves are dropped into hot oil before adding the main ingredient or used to scent the oil that is poured on top of many dishes to add richness and flavour.

South Indian vegetarian meal served on a banana leaf

As most homes in south India have a curry leaf plant, the leaves are only picked when needed to ensure maximum freshness. However, dried leaves can be used in the following recipes.

This recipe is for a snack that is sold in little stalls along the motorway in the state of Maharashtra. It makes a wonderful addition to a picnic hamper and is ideal for long journeys.

BATATA VADA
(POTATO AND GARLIC FRITTERS)

Serves 4
Preparation time 30 minutes
Cooking time 15 minutes

600g (1¼lb) potatoes, boiled,
*   peeled and mashed*
Salt
½ teaspoon turmeric powder
2 tablespoons coriander leaves,
*   chopped*
1 teaspoon green chilli, chopped
*   finely*
1 teaspoon garlic, chopped
*   finely*
2 tablespoons sunflower oil
1 teaspoon black mustard seeds
Large pinch of asafoetida
1 teaspoon cumin seeds
16–20 curry leaves

For the batter:
220g (8oz) gram flour
Large pinch of bicarbonate of
*   soda*
Salt
Sunflower oil for deep frying

1 Combine the potatoes, salt, turmeric, coriander leaves, green chilli and garlic.

2 Heat 2 tablespoons of oil in a small pan and add the mustard seeds. When they crackle add the asafoetida and cumin. Stir once and add the curry leaves.

3 Take off the heat after a minute and pour over the potato mixture. Mix well and make into small balls 3cm (1in) in diameter.

4 Make a batter of pouring consistency with the gram flour, bicarbonate of soda and salt and as much water as needed.

5 Heat the oil in a deep wok or kadai.

6 Dip each ball in the batter and deep fry until golden. Reduce the heat to prevent burning. Serve hot with tomato ketchup or coriander chutney. If taking on a picnic, wrap the fritters in aluminium foil to keep warm.

This dish comes from southern India and is a happy blend of coconut, tomatoes and spices. It can also be served as an unusual version of tomato soup.

TOMATOCHI KADHI
(TOMATO AND COCONUT CURRY)

Serves 4
Preparation time 15 minutes
Cooking time 10 minutes

300g (10oz) coconut, grated
2 tablespoons sunflower oil
1 teaspoon black mustard seeds
1 teaspoon cumin seeds
Large pinch of asafoetida
10 curry leaves
300g (10oz) tomatoes, chopped
*   finely*
1 teaspoon chilli powder
1 teaspoon turmeric powder
1 teaspoon sugar
Salt
2 tablespoons coriander leaves,
*   chopped*

1 Add a little water to the coconut and grind to a coarse paste in the blender.

2 Heat the oil in a kadai or wok. Add the mustard seeds. When they crackle, add the cumin, asafoetida and curry leaves. Stir 2 or 3 times and add the tomatoes, powder spices, sugar and salt and mix well.

3 Cook until the tomatoes can easily be mashed to a pulp. Reduce the heat.

4 Stir in the coconut paste, simmer for 2 minutes taking care not to boil the curry and take off the heat.

5 Serve hot, sprinkled with coriander.

Batata Vada

Ocimum sanctum

HOLY BASIL

(TULSI)

Holy basil is considered one of the most sacred plants of India and is native to the Indian subcontinent. It is an integral part of Hindu ceremonies and sacraments. Holy basil forms an essential part of worship in thousands of homes and temples in India, where it is associated with the Hindu god Vishnu who wears a garland of basil leaves. According to ancient custom, a gift is considered to be truly given away when a basil leaf is given with it. In a Hindu wedding, therefore, the parents of a bride give her away by presenting a basil leaf to the groom. Wealthy Hindus have this leaf made of solid gold, intricately carved or studded with precious gems. This is later set into an ornament for the bride.

HOW IT GROWS

Holy basil is a herb which is extremely easy to grow in the right climate. Most people grow it at home, often in tall, square pots which are decorated with images of gods and goddesses. The branched, erect plant grows up to 75cm (2½ft) high and has small, fragrant leaves. It bears spikes of tiny purple or scarlet flowers. Several species of basil are widely grown.

Holy basil plant

APPEARANCE AND TASTE

Holy basil leaves range from dark green to almost purple and have uneven edges. They are small and quite ornamental. The whole plant has a green, woodland perfume and the leaves taste peppery, almost like a cross between ginger and mint.

BUYING AND STORING

Holy basil plants need sunlight so they should be kept on a sunny windowsill and watered regularly. As Holy basil is so seasonal outside India, the best way of preserving it for use in the colder months is to dry the leaves and seeds.

This can be done by wiping them gently and then spreading them thinly on a plate to dry in a warm, shady place. The leaves are delicate so do not crush them or leave them to dry in the sun as they will turn black. Store the dried leaves in a clean, dry jar. Any trace of water will produce a fine, cottony fungus on the herb. Dried Holy basil is too fragile to sustain long periods in the store cupboard, so use up what you have within 2 to 3 months.

MEDICINAL USES

Holy basil has wonderful medicinal properties. An infusion of the leaves is a quick home remedy for bronchitis and colds, whereas an infusion of the seeds is an excellent diuretic. A decoction of the roots is said to relieve malarial fever.

Holy basil in a sacred planter

CULINARY USES

Although the plant grows so easily in India it is hardly used in food. Instead, it is used to make refreshing, herbal drinks. Experiment with it in soups, fish dishes and sweets. Dried basil leaves should ideally be boiled or steamed in the recipe and not fried as this destroys the delicate fragrance.

Holy basil leaves used in a Hindu marriage ceremony

This first recipe is the surest cure for a persistent sore throat and also makes a refreshing herbal drink.

TULSI KADHA
(HOT BASIL TEA)

Serves 4
Preparation time 5 minutes
Cooking time 5 minutes

2 cardamom
2 cloves
1 teaspoon cumin seeds
1 teaspoon fennel seeds
600ml (1pt) water
2 teaspoons Holy basil leaves,
dried
Honey to taste

1 Remove the cardamom seeds from their husks then roughly crush with the cloves.

2 In a heavy-bottomed pan, dry-roast the cloves, cardamom, cumin and fennel. As soon as they start smoking, add the water and then the holy basil. Bring to the boil, reduce the heat and simmer for 2 to 3 minutes. Remove from the heat.

3 Sweeten to taste with honey. Serve hot.

Here is an unusual drink to enjoy on balmy, summer evenings. Served in tall, frosted glasses over nibs of crushed ice, this makes a really special change from the more common iced tea. Iced basil tea tastes even better with fresh Holy basil leaves, but the dried ones are definitely more handy.

TULSI KA SHERBET
(ICED BASIL TEA)

Serves 4
Preparation time 5 minutes
Cooking time 5 minutes

Tulsi Kadha and Tulsi ka Sherbet

2 tablespoons Indian tea
leaves
600ml (1pt) water
2 teaspoons dried, Holy basil
leaves
Sugar to taste
2 teaspoons lemon juice

Crushed ice
4 lemon slices to garnish

1 Make the tea by adding the tea leaves to boiling water. Drop in the Holy basil and remove from the heat. Allow to cool, then strain.

2 Mix the tea infusion, sugar and lemon juice.

3 Serve in tall glasses over lots of crushed ice. Garnish with lemon slices and a fresh Holy basil leaf if available.

FROM THE
FIELDS BEYOND

Vegetables and Fruit

Allium cepa

ONION

(PIYAZ)

Onion is one of the oldest cultivated vegetables. It was popular in ancient Egypt and is depicted on Egyptian tombs dating back to 3200 BC. It was first discussed in ancient Indian treatises as early as AD 600 and the mythical doctor to the gods, Dhanvantari, is supposed to have described the use of onions in great detail. Today they are used extensively in India for their flavour and medicinal value and every kitchen maintains a stock of onions.

HOW IT GROWS

Onions are believed to have originated in Central Asia but are now cultivated practically all over the world. Different varieties of onions are grown in different countries; Indian onions are white, pink or purple and range from small to large. Onion is perhaps the most widely eaten vegetable in India and is grown on farms and in kitchen gardens. It is a biennial herb with a short, flattened stem at the base which increases in diameter as it grows. The leaves are long, linear and hollow. The onion bulb, which grows underground, is

Harvesting red onions

formed by the thickening of the leaf base. After being dug from the earth, onions are left to dry until the skin is brittle.

APPEARANCE AND TASTE

Onions are rotund with a little pointed end on the top. They have white or pink layers which can be easily separated and a thin, brittle skin. They contain an essential oil and organic sulphides which give them a peculiar, sulphurous smell. This smell is released when the tissues of the onion are cut. The taste of raw onions is quite pungent with a hint of sweetness. When cooked, onions have a wholesome aroma and sweetish taste.

BUYING AND STORING

They are available fresh, dried, powdered or flaked. Onion flakes and powder are made by dehydrating fine slices of the vegetable. Buy firm, fresh-looking onions that do not have any grey mildew. Store them in a cool, dry, airy place as any moisture will cause them to rot. They are available all year round.

Small onions are used whole in curries

Powdered onion

Flaked onion

Red onions

White onion

MEDICINAL USES

Onions have diuretic properties and are often used to relieve catarrh in the bronchial tubes. A teaspoon of onion juice mixed with honey is even given to babies for this purpose. Onions' iron content is easily assimilated and therefore they are prescribed for anaemia. They also help reduce blood cholesterol and their consumption is recommended for people with heart complaints.

CULINARY USES

Onions are used in every kind of Indian cookery to flavour, thicken, colour, garnish or accompany dishes. They can be boiled or fried and ground to a paste as a base for curries, fried until dark brown as a garnish or simply sliced and served as a salad. They go well with tomatoes, ginger, garlic, meat and potatoes. Onions are high in minerals and vitamins.

Typical Gujarati farmer's lunch

Kandyachi Bhaji

Onions are used in a thousand and one ways in Indian cookery. Here are 2 easy-to-make dishes that are well-loved the world over. The first is an all-purpose chutney that can accompany kababs, samosas or any snack.

PIYAZ KI CHUTNEY
(ONION CHUTNEY)

Serves 4
Preparation time 10 minutes
Cooking time 0

4 large onions, chopped
2 teaspoons ginger, shredded
2 teaspoons garlic, shredded
150g (5oz) mint leaves, chopped
300g (10oz) coriander leaves, chopped
1 teaspoon sugar
1 teaspoon lemon juice
Salt

1 Combine all the ingredients, add a little water and grind to a smooth, thick purée in a blender.

2 Stir well before serving. Store in the refrigerator for up to 3 days until needed but serve at room temperature.

This dish really needs no explanation. Under the name 'onion bhaji', it is sold worldwide.

KANDYACHI BHAJI
(ONION FRITTERS)

Serves 4
Preparation time 25 minutes
Cooking time 20 minutes

2 large onions, sliced finely
½ teaspoon salt

For the batter:
300g (10oz) gram flour
½ teaspoon chilli powder
½ teaspoon turmeric powder
1 teaspoon cumin seeds
½ teaspoon ajowan seeds
Salt
A little water
Sunflower oil for deep frying

1 Sprinkle the onions with the salt and put them aside for 15 minutes.

2 Make a thick batter with all the other ingredients and water as needed.

3 Squeeze out all the water from the onions and stir them into the batter.

4 Heat the oil in a deep wok or kadai. When it begins to smoke, drop in spoonfuls of the onion batter and fry until dark gold in colour. These fritters are uneven in shape and should be fried on a low heat to prevent them from breaking up and burning. Serve hot with onion chutney.

Garlic cloves

Garlic bulbs

Allium sativum

GARLIC

(LAHSUN)

Flaked garlic

Hailed as the 'bulb of life', garlic was known to ancient physicians as an incomparable medicine. Susruta (c. AD 350), one of the earliest Indian surgeons, wrote a treatise on its therapeutic properties. In India, garlic is considered to have special powers and in rural India strings of garlic bulbs are hung up to ward off insects, snakes and evil. In Egypt, Khnoum Khoufouf, the builder of one of the oldest pyramids (4500 BC) also realised its virtues and decided that all his workers should eat a clove of garlic a day to maintain their health and strength. Hippocrates, the father of modern medicine, (460–357 BC) recommended garlic to guard against infectious diseases and intestinal disorders.

Garlic originates from India

HOW IT GROWS

Garlic is a hardy, bulbous perennial herb of the onion family with narrow, flat leaves and small white flowers. The bulb consists of 6–30 individual bulbils called 'cloves'. Garlic is ready for harvesting when the tops turn yellowish-brown, about a month after the seed stalks emerge. The bulbs are lifted, the earth is shaken off and the leaves are tied at the top. The bulbs are then dried for 3 to 4 days in the shade. The leaves are removed before the product is marketed.

APPEARANCE AND TASTE

Bulbs of garlic are onion-shaped and are made up of individual half-moon-shaped cloves encased in a thin white or pinkish papery sheath that is easy to remove.

The whole bulb is also surrounded by a glossy white or pink sheath with a pointed top. The aroma of garlic is unmistakable and pungent. It has a flavour that is much stronger than that of onion. The smell has an undernote of sulphur which is either loved or hated, as some people find its lingering aroma distasteful. The taste can be quite sharp and biting and can increase the heat of a dish.

BUYING AND STORING

Dried bulbs are the most common but the fresh green herb is also available, especially in winter. Garlic oil, flaked garlic and garlic powder can be bought too. Old garlic can sometimes have a blackish-green, powdery fungus in the folds of its covering and if it dries up it becomes hard and hollow. Look for plump, firm bulbs that are brightly coloured and unbroken. Store in an airy, dry place at room temperature. Ropes of strung garlic can be hung up.

MEDICINAL AND OTHER USES

Garlic has been used to treat asthma, deafness, leprosy, bronchial congestion, arteriosclerosis, worms and countless other ailments. Modern medicine also attributes great curative powers to garlic. Doctors believe that garlic oil capsules, commonly known as 'garlic pearls', can check high cholesterol, aid digestion, or control blood pressure, rheumatism, cancerous growths and whooping cough. Garlic

Garlic paste

is also considered a wonderful aphrodisiac and has the power to boost the libido. It is good for treating skin conditions like spots. Try rubbing the cut surface of a garlic clove on an eye sty – it will sting but the sty will disappear in no time.

CULINARY USES

Garlic is one of the most widely used ingredients in the world. In India it is used in curries, marinades, chutneys, vegetable dishes, barbecued meats, pickles and countless other preparations. Each clove of garlic is first peeled, then the flesh can be chopped, grated or made into paste. Garlic can be eaten raw or cooked; when frying make sure that the oil is not too hot or the garlic will burn and taste acrid. Garlic and ginger complement each other and are often used together.

Garlic powder

The recipe for garlic chutney given below comes from coastal India where coconut is the base for nearly everything. It adds a lift to any meal and leftover chutney can be used as a sandwich filling.

LAHSUN CHUTNEY
(GARLIC CHUTNEY)

Serves 4
Preparation time 15 minutes
Cooking time 0

4 teaspoons garlic, chopped
150g (5oz) coconut, grated if fresh, or desiccated
Salt
½ teaspoon tamarind pulp, diluted in 2 teaspoons of water
2 small dried red chillies, deseeded, broken up and soaked for 5 minutes

1 Combine all the ingredients, add a little water and blend to a semi-solid chutney in a food processor. If the taste is too sharp, add more coconut. Serve with hot rotis and a vegetable curry.

This recipe comes from north India where bread-making is almost an art and the repertoire of breads is varied and endless.

LAHSUN PARATHAS
(GARLIC BREAD)

Serves 4 (16 parathas)
Preparation time 35 minutes
Cooking time 25 minutes

450g (1lb) wholewheat flour
Water, as needed
6 tablespoons melted ghee
1 teaspoon garlic, minced finely
2 teaspoons coriander leaves, chopped finely
½ teaspoon turmeric powder
½ teaspoon salt
Extra ghee for rolling and serving

1 Mix all the ingredients except the extra ghee, and knead for a couple of minutes to blend completely and form a soft dough.

2 Cover with a damp cloth and reserve for 15 minutes.

3 Divide the dough into 16 equal-sized balls. Roll each ball into a flat disc about 8cm (3in) in diameter.

4 Smear each one with a little ghee and roll into a hollow cylindrical shape, then flatten with your palm, dust with a little flour and roll out again.

5 Heat a griddle or frying pan and place one of the parathas on it. As soon as tiny bubbles appear on the surface, turn it over. Press down the edges with a clean cloth to ensure even cooking.

6 When the paratha is done, it should appear slightly puffed with brown patches. Remove it from the pan and set on a warm plate. Smear with ghee and serve immediately or keep warm to serve later. Cook the remaining parathas in the same way.

Lahsun Parathas

Cocos nucifera

COCONUT

(NARIAL)

The coconut is aptly called *shrifal* or the fruit of the gods. The coconut tree is called the *kalpavriksha* or the tree that grants boons. This is because every part of the tree is used in various ways, making it one of the most useful trees in existence. The fruit is used widely in Hindu religious ceremonies, where it features with a full pot and mango leaves as a constant reminder that we should make our life a full, rich experience. In south India no gift is complete without a coconut, and it is given to honour elders, women and expectant mothers. In the absence of idols, coconuts often represent gods and goddesses of the Hindu pantheon, the 3 black spots of the coconut symbolising the eyes and the sacred forehead dot of the deity.

At the beginning of any auspicious event, a coconut is broken as an offering to the gods, and the creamy kernel is eaten as a blessing.

Desiccated coconut

HOW IT GROWS

Coconut trees grow in salty, sandy soil to a height of up to 20m (70ft). The straight, smooth trunk is crowned by a spray of large leafy fronds that are quite sharp to touch. The tree bears fruit that starts off being green and tender and matures to a streaky brown. Coconut trees love a hot, tropical climate and grow all over Asia and Africa. Climbing a coconut tree is a skill in itself as the smoothness of the trunk is a great deterrent. A rope is looped around the trunk and shifted upwards as the climber ascends. Coconuts are picked when they are mature and dried until hard.

APPEARANCE AND TASTE

Coconuts used in cookery are large, brown, hairy fruits with a hard, woody shell and a creamy-white kernel. The shell has to be broken to get to the flesh and this is best done by placing a newspaper on the floor and banging the coconut against it. The water inside the coconut makes a refreshing drink. Coconut water, which is transparent and slightly cloudy, should not be confused with coconut milk which is the juice of the kernel and is white. Coconut has a subtle, oily aroma and a sweet, nutty flavour. The texture is crisp and crunchy and enhances both savoury and sweet dishes. It is delicious eaten on its own.

BUYING AND STORING

Coconut is available fresh, desiccated, as milk or creamed. Coconut water is also sold in cartons. There are several brands of dehydrated coconut milk on the market. You will also find hard, dried halved kernels called copra. When buying fresh coconut, shake it to establish that it has water. If there is no sound of water, the kernel is probably dry and tough. Coconuts keep for up to a week. The flesh can be grated and frozen for up to 3 months. Desiccated or powdered coconut should not smell oily. Cartons of coconut water are best drunk chilled. Refrigerate coconut milk or cream. Creamed coconut will keep for up to 6 months in the refrigerator. If you are buying copra, watch out for a black mildew that sometimes grows on old kernels.

A coconut tree bears up to 100 fruits a year

OTHER USES

In southern India, the wide, strong-stemmed leaves of the coconut palm are woven skilfully into green sheets used for thatching cottages. They are also dried to make brooms and scrapers. The outer hairy coir of the fruit is used as fuel, for making mats, mattresses, ropes and several artistic and functional objects. It also makes a good scourer. The shell is cleaned, polished and used as a bowl, or, with a handle attached, as a large spoon. The bark of the tree is used in the construction of rural huts. Coconut oil, extracted from copra, is excellent for the hair and the skin and is used as a cooking medium.

Set
coconut oil

CULINARY USES

The creamy kernel has inspired a very special cuisine in the many states of south India, especially along the west coast. The milk of the kernel or creamed coconut is the base for many curries. Goa's famed fish curries, Kerala's mixed vegetable *avial*, Karnataka's coconut and green mango chutneys are all becoming popular the world over. The milk is also sweetened with jaggery and served as a dessert with rice cakes. Grated coconut makes a pretty, snow-white garnish for many dishes. Creamed coconut is used as a base for curries whereas desiccated coconut is used in garnishes,

Coconut used in a Hindu religious ceremony

chutneys, desserts or in curries where it is often fried until golden and blended to a paste before being added. It is also sweetened and used as a stuffing between layers of crisp pastry. In India, coconut water is drunk straight from the fruit. A little portion from the top of a tender, green coconut is lopped off, a straw is inserted and one of the world's purest and most refreshing drinks is instantly available.

The following recipes are from the southern coast of India. They are so delicious that they make the effort of grating the coconut a most rewarding one. This is a lovely salad that can be made with any firm fruit. I've suggested mango here, but you can use bananas, pears, pineapple, oranges or seasonal fruit like peaches, cherries and grapes. The salad is compar- able to the north Indian raita which has a yoghurt base, but here the creaminess of the yoghurt is replaced by that of coconut.

AAM KA SASAM
(MANGO AND COCONUT SALAD)

Serves 4
Preparation time 20 minutes
Cooking time 0

300g (10oz) coconut, grated
2 dried red chillies, deseeded, broken into small pieces and soaked in water for 5 minutes
4 teaspoons jaggery, grated
Salt
½ teaspoon coriander seeds
½ teaspoon black mustard seeds
300g (10oz) ripe mango, peeled and cubed

Blend the coconut, chilli, jaggery, salt, coriander seeds and mustard seeds with a little water to a coarse paste in a food processor. Mix this paste with the mango pieces and chill. Serve cold.

The first dish is the Indian version of the European pancake and was a break-fast treat during my childhood.

NARIAL KE DOSEY
(SWEET COCONUT PANCAKES)

Serves 4
Preparation time 30 minutes
Cooking time 30 minutes

300g (10oz) rice flour
Salt
Water, as necessary

150g (5oz) jaggery, grated
220g (8oz) coconut, grated if fresh, or desiccated
½ teaspoon cardamom powder
½ teaspoon nutmeg powder
4 tablespoons ghee

1 Make a batter with the flour, salt and as much water as necessary to create a pouring consistency.

2 Heat a heavy pan and melt the jaggery. Add the coconut and cook until the mixture thickens. Then take off the heat and stir in the spices.

3 In a griddle or a non-stick frying pan heat a few drops of ghee.

4 Reduce the heat and pour a ladleful of batter in the centre, spreading it with the back of the ladle to a thin disc. Cover and cook for a minute on a low heat.

5 When the edges start to curl up and the pancake is cooked, arrange some of the coconut mixture along the centre of pancake and roll it up into a cylindrical shape. Serve warm.

Narial ke Dosey

Cucumis melo

MELON SEEDS

(CHOR MAGAZ)

Melon seeds

Indian melons come in a variety of colours, from cool coral to a translucent pistachio green. Tall frosted glasses of sweet melon juice are served on the rocks, and wedges of fruit are used to embellish many salads and sweets. After the juicy flesh of the melon is eaten, the seeds as well as the hard flesh closest to the rind are put to use. The hard flesh is grated and added to seasoned and sweetened flour to make melon bread which is popular on the western coast of India. The seeds go into many sweets and snacks.

Countless varieties of melon grow in India

Slice of melon showing seeds in centre of fruit

HOW THEY GROW

Although melons grow in many countries around the world, in India their cultivation is particularly unusual. As the winter gives way to summer, countless small rivers in India begin to dry up, creating for the farmer a fertile river-bed. It is here that myriad varieties of melons are grown. The melon vine, which grows along the ground, has the unique power of drawing water from deep within the earth. In the summer one can see melon seeds laid out to dry like ivory carpets on the thatched roofs of rural cottages. The seeds are cleaned and spread out on jute sheets until they are completely dry. They are then packed and sold.

APPEARANCE AND TASTE

Only white melon seeds are used in Indian cookery (therefore not the seeds of the water melon). The outer, greyish-white, hard shell is opened to reveal the ivory-white kernel. This is slightly soft and oval. Melon seeds have no smell but are nutty and sweet in flavour.

BUYING AND STORING

Melon seeds are sold in the shell or peeled. However, you can collect your own after eating a melon. Just wash them in a sieve to remove all the pulp or fibres and spread them out to dry. Shell them by breaking off the tapered end then discard the shells. Lay out the kernels to dry off completely, then store in an airtight jar.

CULINARY USES

They are primarily used roasted in snacks like Bombay mix. The seeds are sprinkled on top of sweets like sticky halwas and fruit fudge. They are also added to mouthfresheners which are a mixture of nuts and spices and are eaten after meals. North Indian meat curries, especially those that are white in colour, are thickened with a paste of melon seeds. Try them in salads, with breakfast cereals and on top of fruit puddings.

Melon juice

Unusual sweet fruit halwas like banana, jackfruit, chikoo, mango or potato are very popular in India. This recipe is for bottle gourd halwa. This pale green, bottle-shaped or long vegetable is easily available from Indian grocery shops and is called lauki or doodhi. It is usually cooked as a savoury with lentils, but here it makes an interesting sweet.

LAUKI KA HALWA
(BOTTLE GOURD SWEET)

Serves 4
Preparation time 30 minutes
Cooking time 30 minutes

600g (1¼lb) bottle gourd (lauki or doodhi), peeled and cut into tiny cubes
220ml (8fl oz) milk
150g (5oz) jaggery, grated
1 teaspoon cardamom powder
2 teaspoons melon seeds

1 Cook the bottle gourd in the milk until soft.

2 Add the jaggery and stir until all the liquid is absorbed and the mixture thickens.

3 Take off the heat and add the cardamom powder. Mix well.

4 Cool, spoon into dishes and serve sprinkled with melon seeds.

This recipe is for one of the many snack mixes stored in every Indian home.

CHIWDA
(SAVOURY SNACK MIX)

Serves 4
Preparation time 10 minutes
Cooking time 30 minutes

300g (10oz) flaked rice
4 tablespoons sunflower oil
1 teaspoon black mustard seeds
Large pinch asafoetida
16 curry leaves
1 teaspoon green chillies, minced
1 teaspoon turmeric powder
1 teaspoon coriander powder
1 teaspoon cumin powder
6 tablespoons roasted peanuts
4 tablespoons melon seeds
4 tablespoons raisins
6 tablespoons dry coconut (copra), sliced
2 teaspoons sugar
Salt

1 Dry-roast the flaked rice in a kadai or wok until crisp. Set aside.

2 Heat the oil in a pan and add the mustard seeds. When they crackle, add all the other ingredients except the sugar and salt.

3 Fry for a minute, stirring all the while. Add the roasted rice, sugar and salt and mix well.

4 Stir a couple of times, take off the heat and cool completely. Store in an airtight jar and use as required. Consume within a month as it loses its crunch with keeping.

Emblica officinalis

AMLA

(EMBLICA)

Sometimes known as the Indian gooseberry, this tangy fruit is considered to be the elixir of good health. Several thousand years ago when the Indian herbal system of medicine, Ayurveda, was already developed, sages would go deep into the forests looking for newer and more effective remedies. One such sage, Chyavan, blended together certain energising herbs, fruits and spices based on a secret recipe. The principal fruit used in his mixture, *Chyavanprash*, was amla, to which are attributed near magical powers. This dark brown tonic is still sold and consumed in India and is believed to increase vitality and stamina.

Fresh amla fruit

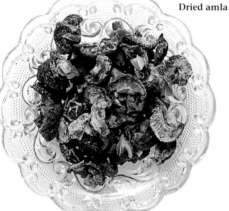

Dried amla

HOW IT GROWS

Amla is the fruit of a small, deciduous tree grown all over India. The pale green flowers grow in clusters below the leaves and give way to the fruit around winter.

APPEARANCE AND TASTE

Amla fruits are between 1.5–2.5cm (½–1in) in diameter, pale green and translucent. They have a fine, glossy skin and crunchy, crisp flesh. The skin is faintly divided into 6 lobes and there is 1 seed within each lobe. The fruit can be round or slightly ridged. The aroma is sour. The fruit tastes acidic and leaves the teeth tingling if bitten into. Mature fruits are sweeter.

BUYING AND STORING

The fruits can be used fresh or dried. Dried amlas are sometimes ground into a powder and are also available stoned and chopped so they are easy to reconstitute. Store the dried pieces or powder in an airtight container for up to a year. If buying fresh, look for fruits that are green and have a tight, smooth skin. The fresh fruits need to be put into the refrigerator and will keep for 2 weeks.

MEDICINAL AND OTHER USES

Amla is the major ingredient in several herbal tonics which are good for the liver, eyes and stomach. A fermented liquor is made of the fruits to relieve indigestion, anaemia, jaundice, heart ailments, piles and constipation. Amla is a very rich source of Vitamin C and is used to cure the common cold, scurvy and pulmonary tuberculosis. Indian beauticians have used amla in various hair preparations for centuries. Amla hair oil (coconut oil in which amla has been boiled) is excellent for hair growth and nourishment. Even the water in which dried amla has been boiled makes a good finishing rinse and adds gloss and bounce to hair. Amla is also used in shampoos, dyes and inks. The timber from the amla tree is used for furniture and the leaves are used in cardamom plantations as manure.

CULINARY USES

Though it is an ideal souring agent, amla is not widely used in Indian cookery. However, it is often made into chutneys and preserves. Fresh amla can be added to salads or used as a garnish. Ripe fruit can be chopped into a fruit salad.

Fresh amla adds to the taste and nutritive value of these recipes but as it is difficult to find, I've used dried. In India these preserves are made seasonally, but with dried amlas they can be

AMLA CHHUNDA
(SWEET AMLA PRESERVE)

Serves 4
Preparation time 25 minutes +
  2 hours soaking
Cooking time 1 hour

Amla chutney

Amla is used in Ayurvedic herbal remedies

*150g (5oz) dried amla pieces,
  soaked for 2 hours
2 teaspoons ginger, grated
220g (8oz) sugar
½ teaspoon chilli powder
Large pinch salt*

Chyavanprash

1 Boil the amla in plenty of water until soft, drain and dry thoroughly.

2 Combine all the ingredients and cook on a low heat until the mixture is thick and sticky.

3 Store in a clean, airtight jar and use within a fortnight.

AMLA CHUTNEY
(EMBLICA CHUTNEY)

Serves 4
Preparation time 20 minutes +
  2 hours soaking
Cooking time 0

*150g (5oz) dried amla pieces,
  soaked for 2 hours
8 tablespoons water
4 teaspoons sugar
Salt
1 teaspoon ginger paste
Large pinch chilli powder
2 teaspoons distilled vinegar*

1 Simmer the soaked amla in the water until soft.

2 Add all the other ingredients and grind to a paste in a blender. The chutney should be quite thick. Any leftover chutney can be stored in the refrigerator for up to a week.

Garcinia indica

KOKUM

The kokum is native to India and has no English name. Even in India it is used only in the regional cookery of Gujarat, Maharashtra and a few southern states where big glasses of kokum sherbet are drunk throughout the parched summer months. Along the ribbon-like west coast of India lies an area called Malvan, known for its coconut-dominated cuisine. In this region, where the sweltering heat demands cooling food and drink, recipes need ingredients like kokum, which is well known for its ability to counteract the heat. People from Malvan swear by the fruit which grows in their area and, should they migrate, they make sure that they have a regular supply from their families back home.

HOW IT GROWS

Kokum is a slender, evergreen tree with sloping branches and oblong leaves. The kokum fruit is round and about 2.5cm (1in) in diameter. It is deep purple when ripe and contains 5–8 large seeds. The fruits are picked when ripe, the rind is then removed, soaked repeatedly in the juice of the pulp and then sun-dried. The rind is used as a food flavouring.

APPEARANCE AND TASTE

Kokum is dark purple to black, rather sticky with curled edges. Sometimes the entire fruit is halved and dried, so that the dried seeds are visible in their chambers, like a halved orange. When added to food, it imparts a beautiful pinkish-purple colour. As kokum contains malic and tartaric acids, it smells and tastes sour, but pleasantly fruity.

Kokum is eaten on the west coast of India

BUYING AND STORING

Kokum is available as a dried rind or fruit. The deeper the colour the better the kokum. It will keep well in an airtight jar for up to a year. Kokum butter, which is sold in pale grey or yellow slabs, is used for cooking in some regions.

MEDICINAL AND OTHER USES

The fruit is an excellent anti-histamine and an infusion can either be drunk or applied locally to relieve skin allergies. It is also used to treat piles and tumours. The fruits are steeped in sugar syrup to make *amrutkokum* which is diluted with water and drunk to relieve sun-stroke. Kokum butter is used in ointments, candles and soaps.

CULINARY USES

Kokum enhances coconut-based curries and is added to vegetables like okra and potatoes and to lentils. It will colour everything it touches so if you want to preserve the colour of a dish, use lemon instead. It may also stain your clothes, so handle with care.

This recipe is a refreshing, light curry that is sometimes served as a starter and is a classic accompaniment to rice and fried fish.

SOLKADHI
(LIGHT KOKUM CURRY)

Serves 4
Preparation time 40 minutes
Cooking time 0

600g (1¼lb) fresh coconut, grated , or 600ml (1pt) ready-made coconut milk
6 kokum
Salt
1 teaspoon garlic paste
2 tablespoons coriander leaves, chopped finely

1 Add 600ml (1pt) of water to the fresh coconut and grind in a blender. Squeeze out the thick coconut milk and repeat the process with 300ml (½pt) of water. Add the second milk to the first and discard the residue.

2 Add the rest of the ingredients to the coconut milk, mix well and allow to stand for 20 minutes.

3 Remove the kokum, squeeze the juice from it into the curry and discard if the curry is pink and fairly sour. If it is not, leave the kokum in for longer.

4 Stir well before serving cold with rice.

This recipe is for a creamy prawn curry that comes from the warm, emerald region of the Malabar, along India's southern coast.

Kokum dye

MALABAR JHINGA KADHI
(KERALA PRAWN CURRY)

Serves 4
Preparation time 35 minutes
Cooking time 20 minutes

5 tablespoons sunflower oil
2 large onions, chopped finely

Masala to be dry-roasted and ground to a powder in a coffee mill:
2 teaspoons cumin seeds
2 teaspoons black mustard
    seeds
1 teaspoon fenugreek seeds
1 teaspoon chilli powder
1 teaspoon turmeric powder

2 teaspoons ginger paste
2 teaspoons garlic paste
300g (10oz) raw prawns,
    shelled and cleaned
6 kokum
Salt
150g (5oz) coconut, fresh,
    ground to a paste with some
    water in a liquidiser

1 Heat the oil in a pan and add the onions. Fry until golden.

2 Add the ground masala powder, ginger and garlic pastes, and prawns. Fry well.

3 Add a little water and cook until the prawns are pink.

4 Add the kokum, salt, coconut paste and enough water to make a thick curry. Simmer for 3 minutes, without allowing the curry to boil.

5 Serve hot with rice.

Glycyrrhiza glabra

LIQUORICE

(MULETHI)

In India, liquorice is used more as a medicine than a food, but it is found in all Indian kitchens. Followers of the ancient Indian system of medicine called Ayurveda were convinced that nature had a cure for all medical problems. One of the greatest finds of these early pharmacists was liquorice – a sweet root that is in use even today because of its miraculous, curative properties. Ancient Chinese herbalists also knew of the drug and its rejuvenating properties. They distilled the essence of the herb and its root, prescribing it for a wide range of conditions, a practice that is followed even in modern medicine.

Liquorice plant

Spices on sale, Ahmedabad

HOW IT GROWS

A tall, erect herb up to 1.5m (5ft) high, the plant bears small spikes of lilac-coloured flowers. The flat fruits of the herb grow up to 3cm (1⅛in) long. Liquorice is cultivated in southern Europe, Syria, Iraq, Turkey, Greece, Russia and all over India.

APPEARANCE AND TASTE

The dried roots and underground stems of the plant are the useful parts. These look like dried pieces of wood, very hard and fibrous. They are ridged and dark on the outside. The smell of liquorice is medicinal and highly aromatic. It tastes sweet with a slightly bitter aftertaste, similar to the flavour of saccharine. When liquorice is chewed on its own, it seems to get sweeter and sweeter.

BUYING AND STORING

Liquorice is available as dried, woody pieces of root, as powder or as solid sticks of concentrated essence. These are black in colour, glossy, sweet, slightly bitter and partly soluble in water when pure. If stored in a dry container, liquorice will keep for several years.

MEDICINAL USES

Liquorice is chewed to relieve a sore throat. Gargling with an infusion of the root relieves a dry cough and oral inflammations. As it soothes irritation caused by acids, it is prescribed for gastric ulcers. Liquorice powder is mixed with butter and honey and applied to cuts and wounds. A paste of liquorice and mustard oil heals corns. Patchy baldness and dandruff is treated with a local application of a paste of liquorice, milk and saffron. Liquorice is used to flavour medicinal syrups and pills. However, it is contra-indicated in pregnancy, heart conditions and kidney problems.

CULINARY USES

Liquorice is not used in everyday Indian cookery, but is stored in the pantry for use as a household medicine.

Liquorice root

The following preparations are more medicinal than refreshing but they make a pleasant alternative to many remedies. Of course, you can always include them in your daily fare.

MULETHIWALI CHAI
(LIQUORICE TEA)

Serves 4
Preparation time 5 minutes
Cooking time 10 minutes

2 small pieces liquorice root
2cm (¾in) piece ginger, bruised
750ml (1¼pt) water
2 Indian teabags
Sugar
Milk

1 Add the liquorice and the ginger to the water and bring to the boil.

2 Simmer for 3 minutes and add the teabags.

3 Turn off the heat, cover and allow to stand for 5 minutes.

4 Strain and discard the roots. Serve with sugar and milk to taste.

MULETHI KA KADHA
(LIQUORICE TONIC)

Serves 4
Preparation time 10 minutes
Cooking time 15 minutes

6 black peppercorns
6 cloves
4cm (1½in) stick cinnamon
1 teaspoon cumin seeds
1 teaspoon coriander seeds
750ml (1¼pt) water
2cm (¾in) piece ginger, bruised
2 small pieces liquorice root
Honey to taste
4 teaspoons milk

1 Heat a pan and add the peppercorns, cloves, cinnamon, cumin and coriander. Dry-roast until they begin to smoke.

2 Add the water and bring to the boil. Add the ginger and liquorice. Reduce the heat and simmer for 5 minutes.

3 Take off the heat, strain to remove the whole spices and stir in the honey and the milk and serve piping hot.

Mulethi ka Kadha

Tamarindus indica

TAMARIND

(IMLI)

Tamarind pods

Most Indians remember eating tamarind pulp with childhood friends, hidden away from disapproving adults, on hot, lazy afternoons. Its sour sweetness is all the more tasty with a sprinkling of coarse salt. Children mercilessly stone the tree to get the fruit. In the hot summer months, balls of tamarind are laid out to dry in the sun, especially in central and southern India, where the fruit is grown. The dried balls are stored for use through the year in earthen jars and bits are broken off as and when required. Tamarind

Tamarind paste

is sometimes known as the Indian date. In Hindu mythology, tamarind is associated with the wedding of the Hindu god Krishna which is celebrated by a feast in November.

Tamarind is an excellent brass polisher

HOW IT GROWS

The tamarind tree is an evergreen which grows to a height of 20m (70ft). It has small oval leaves and bears pods which are runner-bean shaped, with flowers in May and fruits in October to November. India exports a few thousand tonnes of tamarind to West Asia, Europe and the USA each year.

APPEARANCE AND TASTE

The tamarind pod is crescent-shaped and brown with a thin, brittle shell. It grows up to 10cm (4in) long and contains a fleshy pulp held together by a fibrous husk. Within this pulp are squarish, dark brown, shiny seeds. It is the pulp that is used as a flavouring for its sweet, sour, fruity aroma and taste.

BUYING AND STORING

It is available as a pressed, fibrous slab, or as a jam-like bottled concentrate. To make tamarind extract, soak a little of the tamarind slab in warm water. Once it gets mushy, mix it into a paste and pass it through a sieve. The fine pulp and juice will go through, leaving behind the fibrous husk. If all this seems too time consuming, just buy a jar of the concentrate. Tamarind slabs and paste store well and will last for up to a year. The pods are also available in some Indian shops.

MEDICINAL AND OTHER USES

According to Ayurvedic beliefs, tamarind is considered a mild laxative and digestive. It is used to treat bronchial disorders and gargling with tamarind water is recommended for a sore throat. The seeds are crushed to produce a starch used for jute and cotton yarns. The leaves are used to produce red and yellow dyes. Tamarind is an excellent brass polisher. Take a handful of tamarind, sprinkle on some salt, wet it, and rub the object to be polished. The brass will gleam like gold.

CULINARY USES

Yoghurt and tamarind are the 2 main souring agents used in Indian cookery. Tamarind is used a lot in south Indian and Gujarati lentil dishes, in sweet chutneys and in curries. The extract is also used to flavour rice. Tamarind contains pectin which is used in the manufacturing process of commercially produced jams.

Shelled tamarind

The following recipes are for sweet and sour dishes that provide a change of taste in a simple meal. The chutney goes with virtually anything from samosas to dumplings in yoghurt. It is made in every part of India to accompany different dishes. The lentil dish comes from Gujarat.

MEETHI CHUTNEY
(SWEET TAMARIND CHUTNEY)

Serves 4
Preparation time 10 minutes
Cooking time 10 minutes

150g (5oz) jaggery, grated
60g (2oz) tamarind pulp, diluted in 3 tablespoons of water
4 tablespoons dried dates, chopped
Large pinch chilli powder
½ teaspoon cumin powder
½ teaspoon rock salt
Extra salt if needed

1 Bring the jaggery and tamarind to a boil and simmer over a low heat until the mixture turns shiny and the jaggery is completely melted. If the mixture starts to get too dry and sticky add more water.

2 Add all the rest of the ingredients. Simmer for 5 minutes.

3 Cool and serve at room temperature.

Tamarind pods on the tree

OSAMAN
(GUJARATI DAL)

Serves 4
Preparation time 10 minutes
Cooking time 20 minutes

150g (5oz) split red lentils
½ teaspoon turmeric powder
2 tablespoons tamarind pulp, diluted in 4 tablespoons of water and lumps removed
4 green chillies, sliced
2 tablespoons jaggery, grated
2 tablespoons peanuts, roasted
Salt
2 tablespoons sunflower oil
1 teaspoon black mustard seeds
1 teaspoon cumin seeds
Large pinch asafoetida
½ teaspoon fenugreek seeds
12 curry leaves
2 tablespoons coriander leaves, chopped

1 Wash the lentils and bring them to the boil in 200ml (scant ½pt) water then simmer. When nearly done, add the turmeric, tamarind, green chillies, jaggery, peanuts and salt.

2 Simmer until the lentils are completely cooked.

3 Heat the oil in a small pan. Drop in the mustard seeds. When they crackle, add the cumin, asafoetida, fenugreek seeds and curry leaves. Reduce the heat to prevent burning. Take off the heat after a minute and pour the oil and spices into the lentil mixture. Stir well.

4 Serve very hot, garnished with fresh coriander leaves. This dal goes best with plain, boiled rice, a vegetable and a savoury pickle.

Prunus armeniaca

APRICOTS

(KHUBANI)

The Maharajas of India were known for their gorgeous palaces, their ravishing jewels and their rich, elaborate cuisine. The Nizam of Hyderabad, reputedly the richest man in the world in his time, was a lover of good food and his favourite sweet, made of apricots and cream, is still a speciality of that city. As they are grown in only a tiny area of India, apricots are expensive and have come to symbolise extravagance and wealth. They are used to embellish festive food and always form a part of the assortment of dry fruits served after special meals.

Dried Indian apricots

chewy and rich. Fresh or tinned apricots cannot be substituted for dried Indian ones but Hunza apricots are very similar.

BUYING AND STORING

Buy apricots that are large, bright and firm but yielding to the touch. Store in the refrigerator for up to 6 months, taking care not to get them wet.

CULINARY USES

Apricots are used in several sweet and savoury dishes, especially by the Muslim and Parsee communities. Lamb, chicken and rich vegetable curries are studded with the fruit. They absorb the cooking juices and become juicy and plump. Try poaching or frying apricots as a garnish or with meats.

HOW THEY GROW

Apricots grow on large, leafy trees in orchards. In India the fruit ripen during the monsoon time when the weather is clement. The ripe fruits are plucked and dried in the sun or mechanically. In India, apricots are dried with the stone inside.

APPEARANCE AND TASTE

Dried apricots are tan-coloured, shrivelled and hard. They are the size of a large cherry and are matte and opaque. The dried apricots of India and those of the West look completely different. Dried Indian apricots have a fruity, sweet perfume like that of honey. Their taste is sweet,

Apricots are rare and therefore expensive in India, symbolising extravagance and wealth

Hill station, Darjeeling, where apricots thrive in cooler climes

This dish comes from Hyderabad and is reputed to be from the erstwhile ruler, the Nizam's, kitchen.

KHUBANI KA MEETHA
(APRICOT DELIGHT)

Serves 4
Preparation time 15 minutes
Cooking time 15 minutes

300g (10oz) dried Indian apricots
750ml (1¼pt) water
150g (5oz) sugar
2 tablespoons almonds, chopped
4 tablespoons double cream
2 sheets edible silver foil (varq) – optional

1 Combine the apricots and water and stew them on a low heat until soft and pulpy.

2 Make a syrup by boiling the sugar and some of the water from the cooked apricots. The syrup should be fairly thick.

3 Remove the stones from the apricots and discard. Mix the fruit into the syrup and spoon into individual bowls.

4 Sprinkle the almonds and drizzle the cream over each serving.

5 Place a piece of silver foil on top of each bowl and serve well chilled.

This is a speciality of the Parsee community and one that is served on many special days.

JARDALOO MA GOSHT
(LAMB WITH APRICOTS)

Serves 4
Preparation time 1 hour
Cooking time 40 minutes

600g (1¼lb) lean, boneless lamb, trimmed and cubed
300ml (½pt) yoghurt
4 onions, ground to a paste
2 teaspoons ginger paste
2 teaspoons garlic paste
5 tablespoons tomato purée
1 teaspoon chilli powder
1 teaspoon turmeric powder
1 teaspoon garam masala powder
4 teaspoons sugar
Salt

2 tablespoons distilled vinegar
6 tablespoons sunflower oil
150g (5oz) dried apricots, soaked for 15 minutes and stoned

1 Mix the lamb with all the other ingredients except the oil and apricots. Reserve for 30 minutes.

2 Remove the lamb from the marinade.

3 Heat the oil in a heavy pan and add the lamb. Stir until well browned.

4 Add the marinade, cover and cook for 15 minutes on a low heat, adding a little water as necessary.

5 Add the apricots, cover and cook until the meat is done. Serve hot with any crisp roti or vegetable pulao.

Vitis vinifera

SULTANAS/RAISINS

(KISHMISH/MANUKA)

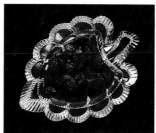

Raisins

Sultanas

Moist and plump, sultanas and raisins seem to hold the very essence of sweetness. Indian grapes come in an array of shapes and colours from apple-green, sunset-orange, through honey-brown to rich purple-black and are sun-dried to prolong their shelf-life. It has been said that the Maharajas of India would insist on having a variety of grapes at every meal, their delicate beauty adding colour and style to the grandest table decor. Black raisins are especially valued in India – their medicinal qualities have been appreciated for centuries and they are still a common home remedy for many ailments.

HOW THEY GROW

Grapes which are dried to form sultanas and raisins grow in the cool orchards of Karnataka and Maharashtra. The fruits hang in bunches from vines which have pretty star-shaped leaves. They are picked when mature, when their sugar content is highest, and laid out to dry in the hazy winter sunshine. They are then sorted, graded and packed for distribution.

APPEARANCE AND TASTE

Sultanas are light in colour, being green or brown, raisins darker, being brown or black. They range in size from 0.5cm to 2cm (¼ to ¾in). Sultanas and raisins have a happy combination of sweetness, perfume and moist flavour. Distinctly grape-like in taste, raisins are slightly richer and fruitier than sultanas.

BUYING AND STORING

Raisins and sultanas are always sold whole, but poor quality fruits are often mixed with the better ones, so look for those that are luscious, even-coloured and relatively stalk-free. Store them for about 3 months at room temperature.

MEDICINAL AND OTHER USES

Black raisins are considered one of nature's best laxatives and even the water in which they are boiled is said to be effective. They are mild enough to be fed to babies. A widely available Indian tonic, *drakshasava*, which is the essence of raisins, is pre-scribed for weakness and lethargy. The high sugar content and astringency of grapes is thought to keep the skin clear and smooth so raisins and sultanas are sometimes made into a paste with water and applied as a rejuvenating face-pack.

Drakshasava

CULINARY USES

Sultanas and raisins are added to rich meat curries and biryanis, yoghurt-based salads called *raitas*, chutneys, fruit salads and a score of traditional sweets like kheer. They can also be tasted in sweet pickles, sweet or savoury stuffings, fried snacks like Bombay mix and in dishes made of paneer or cottage cheese. If lightly fried they become rich and glossy, but if added to cooking liquid, they absorb it and become plump and chewy.

Grapes grow in the cool orchards of Karnataka and Maharashira

Sultanas and raisins add instant glamour to a dish, raising it from everyday fare to something special. The following dishes make a feast of a simple menu. The first is a sweet from Gujarat, similar to a rice pudding but thinner.

DOODHPAK
(SWEET RICE AND MILK)

Serves 4
Preparation time 10 minutes
Cooking time 30 minutes

600ml (1pt) full fat milk
4 tablespoons basmati rice
About 6 teaspoons sugar
½ teaspoon nutmeg powder
2 tablespoons flaked almonds
2 teaspoons sultanas
2 tablespoons cashew nuts, chopped
2 teaspoons chirongi nuts

1 Bring the milk to the boil in a heavy pan and simmer on a low heat until it becomes thick and creamy.

2 In the meantime, cook the rice in a little water until mushy. Drain and reserve.

3 When the milk is done, add all the other ingredients and take off the heat. Chill well and serve.

This recipe is a superb north Indian vegetable medley that is sinfully rich!

NAVRATAN KORMA
(NINE-JEWELS VEGETABLE CURRY)

Serves 4
Preparation time 30 minutes
Cooking time 40 minutes

For the sauce:
6 tablespoons sunflower oil
4 large onions, grated and squeezed to remove juice

Navratan Korma

1 teaspoon ginger paste
1 teaspoon garlic paste
½ teaspoon turmeric powder
1 teaspoon chilli powder
1 teaspoon cumin powder
1 teaspoon coriander powder
1 teaspoon garam masala powder
300g (10oz) tomatoes, chopped
Salt
½ teaspoon sugar
6 tablespoons double cream

6 tablespoons carrots, diced
4 tablespoons peas
6 tablespoons potatoes, peeled and diced

6 tablespoons French beans, chopped finely
4 tablespoons flaked almonds
2 tablespoons sultanas
2 tablespoons pistachio nuts, chopped
2 teaspoons glacé cherries, chopped
2 tablespoons walnuts, chopped roughly
2 teaspoons coriander leaves, chopped

1 Heat the oil and add the onions. Fry until golden and add the ginger and garlic pastes.

2 Fry for a minute and add all the powder spices. Stir well.

3 Stir in the tomatoes and cook until they are pulpy. Add the salt and sugar.

4 Take off the heat and stir in the cream.

5 In the meantime, simmer all the vegetables until they are cooked but crisp.

6 Add the vegetables, nuts and fruit to the sauce. Heat gently then serve with a sprinkling of coriander.

Zingiber officinale

GINGER

(ADRAK)

Dried ginger

Ginger is an ancient herb whose botanical name has its root in its Sanskrit name *singabera*. Ginger has been used as a medicine in India from the Vedic period and is called *maha-aushadhi* which means 'the great medicine'. It is believed to have originated in India and was introduced to China over 3000 years ago. It reached ancient Greece and Rome via the Red Sea and by the 10th century was flourishing in England. Its growth spread quickly to several countries around the world.

Ginger is cultivated all over India

HOW IT GROWS

Ginger is the underground stem or rhizome of a herbaceous plant with long, thin stalks and leaves. The plant grows to a height of 1m (3ft) and bears small, yellow and purple flowers. The rhizomes are dug up while still tender if they are to be used fresh. They are harvested when they are more fibrous and mature if they are to be dried. Dried rhizomes are known as 'hands' or 'races'. India is the largest producer and exporter of ginger.

Ginger rhizome

APPEARANCE AND TASTE

Fresh ginger is bulbous, tan or pale beige in colour, and firm. It has a cream or yellow interior which is fibrous but easy to slice. The skin is very thin and shiny and is quite easy to peel off. Ginger has a warm, fresh aroma with a hint of turmeric. It tastes hot and increases the fieriness of any food it is added to.

BUYING AND STORING

Buy rhizomes that are firm and plump. Avoid those with wrinkled skin, holes or mildew. A knob should snap off easily if the ginger is fresh. Store in the refrigerator for up to 2 weeks. The dried powder can be stored in an airtight container for about 6 months.

MEDICINAL AND OTHER USES

Ancient Indian and Chinese herbalists prescribed ginger for many ailments, especially flatulence, gout and even paralysis. An infusion of ginger is said to relieve sore throats and head colds. In India, a knob of fresh ginger, bruised and added to tea, is believed to have aphrodisiac qualities. Dry ginger mixed with a little water can be applied locally to cure aches and pains. Ginger oil is often used to flavour beers, wines and cordials. It is also used to flavour essences and make perfumes. Dry ginger powder is sprinkled on top of milk before boiling to prevent it from curdling in the tropical climate of India. A mixture of dry ginger and sugar flavoured with cardamom is given to devotees at several Indian temples as *prasad* or blessed food.

CULINARY USES

Meat and vegetable curries are hardly ever made without ginger; it is ground into a paste, chopped or grated and used to flavour the oil before adding the main ingredient. Ginger is sprinkled on top of cooked dishes, used in marinades for meat and fish, and used as an ingredient in many chutneys and preserves. In most Indian cooking, ginger and garlic are used together so cooks often grind them together to make a storable paste. Ginger goes well with vegetables, especially spinach, sweetcorn and cauliflower. Try it raw in green salads with a tangy lemon dressing. Always peel or scrape off the delicate brown skin before use.

Winters in peninsular India are not very cold but the food eaten in this season is warming and nourishing. This is also a time when a succession of festivals bring feasting and fun. The following recipes are chosen from the panorama of festive fare eaten at this time. The first is a drink that is sweet but sharply spicy and the second is a sticky ginger fudge.

SONTH PANAK
(GINGER TINGLER)

Serves 4
Preparation time 15 minutes
Cooking time 0

4 tablespoons jaggery, grated
600ml (1pt) cold water
1 teaspoon lemon juice
1 teaspoon dry ginger powder
4 black peppercorns, crushed
½ teaspoon cardamom powder

1 Stir the jaggery in the water until it dissolves.

2 Add all the other ingredients, stir and serve chilled.

ALEPAK
(GINGER FUDGE)

Serves 4
Preparation time 15 minutes
Cooking time 15 minutes

150g (5oz) coconut, grated
220g (8oz) sugar
6 tablespoons water
4 tablespoons ginger paste
300ml (½pt) full fat milk
1 teaspoon ghee

1 Grind the coconut to a fine paste in a blender.

2 Mix the sugar and water then cook on a low heat until you can take some of the cooled mixture between your thumb and forefinger and separate them to form a single thread.

3 Add the coconut and ginger pastes. Cook for a minute.

4 Add the milk and cook on a very low heat until the mixture is thick and leaves the sides of the pan easily.

5 Grease a deep dish with the ghee and pour in the mixture. Allow it to set. While slightly warm, cut the fudge into squares. You can store this sweet in the refrigerator for a fortnight.

Alepak

FROM THE EARTHEN JARS

NUTS

Anacardium occidentale

CASHEW NUTS

(KAJU)

Cashew fruit

Goa, well-known for its carnival in the early months of the year, welcomes the hundreds of visitors who join in the revelry. Christmas too is celebrated enthusiastically by the largely Roman Catholic population. Traditional Christmas fare, like roast turkey and Christmas pudding, is spiced up with fish and pork curries, coconut cake and meat vindaloo. Every Goan feast is washed down with *feni*, a liquor made of cashew nuts. Strong and heady, this drink is made only in Goa, and the surrounding areas have vast cashew plantations which provide the raw material for this industry. The Indian name *kaju* is derived from the Brazilian term *acajau*. It was the French who converted it to cashew.

HOW THEY GROW

Cashew nuts thrive along the coastline of India. The trees are short and shrubby and bear beautiful, orangey-yellow, bell-shaped fruit. These fruits are fleshy, juicy, sweet but extremely astringent. The cashew nut is the seed, which grows outside the fruit. The nuts are dried and then left in the shell or peeled.

APPEARANCE AND TASTE

Good cashew nuts are about 2cm (¾in) long, creamy-white and kidney-shaped. The seeds have a little nib at one end and can be neatly split in 2 vertically. They have a creamy, nutty taste which is refined and sweet.

BUYING AND STORING

Cashews can be used whole, chopped, broken or powdered. They are also available roasted, fried, salted, spiced or batter-fried. The best Indian cashew nuts come from Goa or Kerala. They are large, smooth and whole. Broken cashews are cheaper and good for curry bases. Store cashews in an airtight jar for up to 6 months. You can get the nuts in the shell, but they require tedious skinning.

MEDICINAL AND OTHER USES

The acrid oil of cashew is used as an anaesthetic in leprosy and as a balm to cure warts and corns. In western and southern India, where cashew trees are common, the cashew fruit has come to mean prosperity and plenty. Therefore the fruit is represented in a wedding necklace called *jod pod*, where tiny replicas of local grains, fruits and nuts like coconut, pineapple and mango are crafted in pure gold and strung into a necklace. This beautiful piece of jewellery is given to every new bride so that she brings good luck and plenty to her new home.

CULINARY USES

Complementary to both savoury and sweet dishes, cashew nuts can be used whole in meat and vegetable curries or ground to a paste for rich gravies. They are often fried until golden and sprinkled over rice or sweets as a garnish. Cashew nuts are also cooked in a sugar syrup which is cooled and cut into hard, golden translucent squares called *chikki*. They are used in stuffings and crisp snacks like Bombay mix.

The first of these recipes is either a drink or a dessert which uses cashew nuts for their texture.

GAJAR KI KHEER
(SWEET CARROT MILK)

Serves 4
Preparation time 30 minutes
Cooking time 1 hour

2 tablespoons ghee
150g (5oz) carrots, grated
900ml (1½pt) milk
5 tablespoons sugar
4 tablespoons cashew nuts
1 teaspoon cardamom powder

1 Heat the ghee in a heavy pan and add the carrots.

2 Fry them well, scraping up any bits that stick to the bottom of the pan. When they are translucent, add the milk, sugar and cashew nuts and bring to the boil.

3 Reduce the heat and simmer until the mixture thickens slightly (about 15 minutes).

4 Take off the heat and add the cardamom powder. Serve cold.

Grading cashew nuts

This recipe uses cashew nuts as the main ingredient and can be eaten as a vegetarian dish or an accompaniment to a meal. Cashew nuts are fattening so if you are on a calorie-controlled diet, be careful!

KAJU KI SUBZI
(SPICY CASHEW NUT STIR-FRY)

Serves 4
Preparation time 10 minutes + 1 hour soaking
Cooking time 15 minutes

1 tablespoon sunflower oil
1 teaspoon black mustard seeds
1 teaspoon cumin seeds
10 curry leaves
300g (10oz) cashew nuts, soaked for an hour
½ teaspoon turmeric powder
½ teaspoon chilli powder
1 teaspoon coriander powder
Salt
2 teaspoons lemon juice
2 tablespoons coriander leaves, chopped

1 Heat the oil in a pan and add the mustard seeds. When they crackle, add the cumin seeds and curry leaves. Stir once.

2 Add the soaked cashew nuts and the powder spices. Stir-fry until all the ingredients are blended.

3 Season with salt and the lemon juice and mix well. Serve hot garnished with fresh coriander.

Arachis hypogaea

PEANUTS

(MOONGPHALI)

Peanuts as an appetizer

Peanuts are widely used in Maharashtrian and Gujarati cookery and are especially significant in religious feasts. Hindus worship the elephant-headed god Ganesha first in every ritual. He signifies perfect balance for although he is plump and loves food, he is an exquisite dancer. The birthday of Ganesha falls around the beginning of September, and is elaborately celebrated with special food. Completely vegetarian, it features ground peanuts, leafy root vegetables, pulses and coconut. Peanuts are also a favourite Indian snack: Bombay's beaches are full of vendors selling small paper cones of warm, roasted peanuts liberally sprinkled with salt.

APPEARANCE AND TASTE

Peanut shells are beige, rough to the touch and fibrous. They contain 2 to 3 peanuts which are oval with a slightly pointed end. Fresh peanuts are moist and pink and turn dark and brittle when dry. Peanuts have an extremely pleasant aroma. They are bland, floury and easily chewed.

BUYING AND STORING

They are available as fresh pods (though these are difficult to find) which can be boiled in salted water and peeled. They are also available in the pod or shelled, roasted, dried, skinned, fried with or without batter. When buying dried, packed ones look for plump, whole nuts. Old peanuts become rancid over a length of time, so finish off all bought stock within 3 months.

CULINARY USES

In western India, they are powdered, crushed or used whole with vegetables and pulses. They complement the flavours of sesame seeds and leafy vegetables. Try them with spinach, potatoes or lentils. Roughly crush them and add to hot oil. Fry until they just begin to change colour, then add the rest of the ingredients. They also add volume and taste to stuffings. Batter-fried peanuts make a good pre-dinner snack, with beer or punch. Peanuts are also used for making sweets. Brittle or *chikki* made of peanuts, jaggery and carda-mom is popular. Peanut oil is the most common cooking medium in India.

HOW THEY GROW

Peanuts grow in little pods under the ground. The pods, which grow in clusters, are dug up, the earth is shaken off and they are dried. Peanuts grow in various countries around the world, most widely in the USA. In India, they grow mainly in the states of Gujarat and Maharashtra.

Peanut seller on the beach, Bombay

The first of the following recipes is a salad from Maharashtra and its name means 'fragrant cucumber'. It combines the juiciness of cucumber with the crunch of peanuts.

KHAMANG KAKDI
(CUCUMBER AND PEANUT SALAD)

Serves 4
Preparation time 30 minutes
Cooking time 0

300g (10oz) cucumber, chopped very finely
½ teaspoon green chilli, minced
4 tablespoons peanuts, coarsely crushed
2 tablespoons coriander leaves, chopped
4 tablespoons coconut, grated if fresh, or desiccated
2 teaspoons sunflower oil
1 teaspoon black mustard seeds
8 curry leaves
Salt
½ teaspoon sugar

1 Mix the cucumber, chilli, peanuts, coriander and coconut.

2 Heat the oil in a small pan and add the mustard seeds.

3 When they pop add the curry leaves and pour over the cucumber mixture.

4 Add the salt and sugar just before serving.

This peanut curry is a sweet and sour dish that complements rice and only needs a savoury pickle to give it a lift.

ANANAS KI SAFED KADHI
(PINEAPPLE AND PEANUT CURRY)

Serves 4
Preparation time 30 minutes + 2 hours soaking
Cooking time 15 minutes

300g (10oz) pineapple, cubed (you can use canned pineapple)
300g (10oz) coconut, grated if fresh, or desiccated
150g (5oz) peanuts, unroasted, soaked for 2 hours in water
1 teaspoon green chillies, chopped
Salt
1 teaspoon sugar
2 teaspoons ghee
1 teaspoon cumin seeds

1 Simmer the pineapple if fresh in a little water until tender. Drain canned pineapple.

2 Grind the coconut, peanuts and chillies to a fine paste in a blender, adding a little water if necessary.

3 Stir into the pineapple cubes and add enough water to make a thick sauce.

4 Add the salt and sugar, bring the mixture to the boil and take off the heat.

5 Meanwhile, heat the ghee in a small pan and add the cumin seeds.

6 When they crackle, pour over the curry.

7 Heat gently before serving, taking care not to boil the curry.

Juglans

WALNUTS

(AKHROT)

A veritable heaven on earth is how emperors and poets have described the flower-laden valley of Kashmir in north India. Walnuts are a speciality of the region – Kashmiri furniture made of polished walnut wood is world-famous and the abundance of the nut has promoted a lavish regional cuisine. Tourists are plied with mounds of walnuts laid out on square cloth sheets in the mild, alpine sunshine.

HOW THEY GROW

Walnuts are the fruit of a tall tree which grows in Europe and India. French walnuts are well known as are Kashmiri walnuts. Before they mature, the fruits are called green walnuts. They have a fleshy casing called the shuck. As the fruits mature, the shuck toughens. In India, walnuts are picked when mature and dried in the sun.

APPEARANCE AND TASTE

Dried walnuts are 2–3cm (1–1¼in) in diameter, round, rough and woody in appearance. The hard, brown shell can be cracked open with a nut-cracker or with a heavy pestle. Inside is the crinkled brown nut which resembles the human brain. It has 5 sections and breaks easily. Walnuts have a distinctive, nutty aroma. Fresh walnuts are pleasant and easily digestible but dried ones are difficult to digest because they have a very high fat content. They also have a slightly bittersweet aftertaste. If kept for a long time, they turn bitter and rancid.

BUYING AND STORING

It is best to buy whole walnuts as they turn rancid quite quickly if exposed to air. Keep them in an airtight container or in the refrigerator for up to 4 months. Look for glossy shells that sound full when shaken.

OTHER USES

Walnuts yield an excellent oil used as a cooking medium and for salad dressings. Pure oil is extracted cold from diced walnuts as heat-pressed oil is inedible. Walnut oil has a pronounced nutty flavour.

Shikaras like these sell walnuts in Kashmir

CULINARY USES

Walnuts are an excellent dietary substitute for meat and are highly regarded by vegetarians. They are not used extensively in Indian cookery due to their bitter flavour. They are ground and used in sweets and rich meat curries. Chopped finely, they are used as a garnish over Kashmiri pulao. Walnuts are used widely in cakes, biscuits, bread and ice cream.

The following recipe is a mixture of East and West. Indian cookery is full of such combinations as many Indian chefs are ingenious at successfully experimenting with European or Far Eastern flavours and giving them a subtle Indian turn.

Akhrot ka Meetha

AKHROT KA MEETHA
(WALNUT COOKIES)

Serves 4
Preparation time 30 minutes
Cooking time 20 minutes

600g (1¼lb) digestive biscuits, crushed
220g (8oz) butter, softened
150g (5oz) sugar
300g (10oz) walnuts, coarsely crushed
4 tablespoons raisins
1 teaspoon cardamom powder
½ teaspoon allspice powder
Single cream to pour over

1 Mix the biscuits and butter and pat into flat discs, 3cm (1in) in diameter. Chill to set.

2 Make a single string syrup (see page 145, *Pista Kichori* step 3) with the sugar and a little water. Add the walnuts and raisins.

3 Cook on a low heat until the mixture is well blended.

Then add the spices.

4 Cool the mixture slightly and place a little on top of each chilled biscuit disc. Serve with single cream poured on top.

This recipe is a feast for vegetarians, cooked in a rich sauce normally used for meat curries.

AKHROT KE KOFTE
(WALNUT BALLS IN CURRY)

Serves 4
Preparation time 30 minutes
Cooking time 30 minutes

For the walnut balls:
4 tablespoons sunflower oil
1 large onion, chopped very finely
150g (5oz) walnuts, coarsely crushed
150g (5oz) bread, soaked in a little milk

4 tablespoons coriander leaves, chopped
Salt
Sunflower oil for frying

For the sauce:
3 tablespoons sunflower oil
1 teaspoon cumin seeds
1 teaspoon ginger paste
1 teaspoon garlic paste
6 tablespoons tomato purée
1 teaspoon turmeric powder
1 teaspoon chilli powder
1 teaspoon garam masala powder
300ml (½pt) single cream
2 tablespoons coriander leaves, chopped

1 Make the walnut balls by heating the oil in pan and adding the onions. Fry until they become translucent and add the walnuts.

2 Fry for a minute and remove from the heat. Add the bread, coriander leaves and salt and knead to make a stiff dough.

3 Make evenly-sized balls the size of large cherries from the dough, pressing firmly to seal the surface.

4 Heat the oil and shallow fry the balls, one or two at a time, until golden. Drain.

5 Heat the oil for the sauce in a pan. Fry the cumin seeds until they pop and add the ginger and garlic.

6 Stir a few times and add the tomato purée and powder spices. Simmer until well blended.

7 Take off the heat, stir in the cream and drop the fried balls into the sauce. Serve hot with coriander leaves.

Shelled walnuts

Pinus pinea

PINE NUTS

(CHILGOZA)

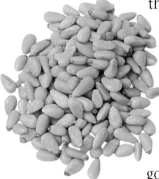

The amphitheatre of Himalayan mountains in the northernmost part of India is thickly forested and virtually untouched by civilisation. Here tall pine trees scent their surroundings, mountain streams twinkle and the entire landscape is suffused with beauty. These pine trees are highly prized for their cones which contain within their flaky depths tiny seeds which are valued by gourmets the world over.

HOW THEY GROW

Pine trees grow all over the Himalayan range of mountains and other cool parts of the world. The large tree bears spiky leaves and cones of tiny, overlapping scales. When the cones are ripe, they are plucked before they open and heated to expand the scales. The seed within can then be easily shaken out. The nuts are used in many cuisines worldwide.

APPEARANCE AND TASTE

Indian pine nuts are about 1.5–2cm (½–¾in) long and slender. They are creamy-white with a thin, dark brown, brittle shell. The nuts get roasted during the process of extraction. Pine nuts resemble almonds in taste and aroma. They are delicate and creamy in flavour.

BUYING AND STORING

As with all dried fruit and nuts, be careful not to buy products that may be old and rancid. If you buy shelled nuts, do not choose any that have gone yellow. Store in an airtight jar for 6 months.

MEDICINAL USES

Since early times medicine has attributed pine nuts with the property of relieving pain and mental distress. They are also considered a stimulant.

Pine cone revealing pine nuts

CULINARY USES

In the region where they grow, pine nuts are a staple food and are used ground or sliced to flavour rice, meat and vegetables. They are shelled and eaten raw as a delicacy and sent as gifts during the festive seasons of Diwali and Christmas. Pine nuts are also used in French and Italian cooking. Slivers of pine nuts are sprinkled as a garnish over confectionery.

Srinagar, Kashmir – an area where pine nuts are harvested

Pine nuts add texture to this easy-to-make, popular snack that can be served with drinks or eaten at teatime. As most of the ingredients are available ready-made, you can rustle it up in just a matter of minutes, provided your pantry is well-stocked.

CORNFLAKE CHIWDA
(CORNFLAKE CRUNCHIE)

Serves 4
Preparation time 15 minutes
Cooking time 0

600g (1¼lb) plain cornflakes
6 tablespoons pine nuts
4 tablespoons chopped dates
150g (5oz) salted crisps, crushed
6 tablespoons cashew nuts
2 tablespoons sunflower oil
Large pinch asafoetida
1 teaspoon turmeric powder
1 teaspoon chilli powder
10 curry leaves
Salt
2 teaspoons sugar

1 Mix the cornflakes, pine nuts, dates, crisps and cashew nuts.

2 Heat the oil and add the asafoetida, turmeric, chilli powder and curry leaves. Pour over the cornflake mixture.

3 Add the sugar and salt and put the whole mixture into a plastic bag. Shake it gently to blend all the ingredients. Store in an airtight jar for up to 3 months and use as required.

This next recipe is for a sweet salad that balances the spice and sizzle of hot curries. Served with cream it can double as a sweet.

Mewa aur Shahed ka Salaad

MEWA AUR SHAHED KA SALAAD
(DRY FRUIT SALAD)

Serves 4
Preparation time 3 hours soaking
Cooking time 5 minutes

Soak in water for 3 hours:
8 tablespoons cashew nuts
4 tablespoons whole almonds
12 dried, Indian apricots
6 tablespoons pine nuts

2 tablespoons ghee
2 tablespoons honey
1 teaspoon lemon juice
1 teaspoon ginger, shredded

1 Drain the fruit and nuts. Then heat the ghee and stir in the fruit and nuts. Add the honey and lemon juice and stir. Then take off the heat and cool.

2 Squeeze the ginger in a garlic press to extract the juice and pour over the fruit salad. Serve in glass bowls.

Areca catechu
BETEL NUTS
(SUPARI)

Chewing betel leaf or *paan* is a concept that is wholly Indian. Chewed after a meal as a mouth freshener and to aid digestion, the nuts of the betel palm are considered sacred and play a part in many religious rituals. In the past, kings would place a betel nut in the open court and ask that anyone willing to take on a particularly difficult task should pick it up. Even today giving a betel nut to someone means that you authorise that person to act on your behalf. Betel nuts are offered to priests who carry out *poojas* or worship on behalf of the *supari*-giver.

Betel/supari

HOW THEY GROW

Betel nuts are fruits of the betel palm which grows up to a height of 20m (70ft). It has wide, leafy fronds at the base of which grow fruits resembling coconuts. When mature, these fruits are picked and dried in the sun until hard and brown. They are then split open and the betel nuts, which can be seen in individual chambers, are removed.

APPEARANCE AND TASTE

Betel nuts are round, about 1–2cm (½in) in diameter and matte, camel-brown in colour. They are variegated on the inside and are extremely hard. They are made into various *suparis* – mixtures of betel nut, spices and sugar which are eaten as a mouth freshener. These mixtures are colourful as the slivers of betel nut which go into them are often dyed red or yellow. Betel nut has no aroma and no particular taste. In fact it is quite woody and astringent.

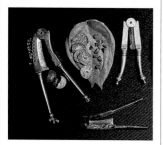

Betel nuts and leaf

BUYING AND STORING

Betel nuts are used in innumerable supari mixtures. On their own, they are finely sliced and eaten by die-hard betel nut enthusiasts. The sweet or fragrant mixtures are widely available in Indian shops and can be stored in an airtight jar for up to 4 months.

Shopkeeper selling *paan*

Shredded betel

MEDICINAL USES

Chewing betel nut chips strengthens the teeth and gums and powdered betel nuts are often added to tooth-cleaning powder in Indian villages. An infusion of betel nut helps a weak digestion and sluggish liver.

CULINARY USES

Tiny chips or curls, scraped off the nut, are included in the *paan quid* which is betel leaf with a filling of sweet, spicy and fragrant ingredients. Although they share a name, the nut and the leaf come from different plants.

Split betel nuts

There are many hundreds of betel nut mixtures that can be bought but here is a recipe for you to make at home. The difficult part is to grate or shred the betel nut. The quantities are just a rough guide to be increased or decreased according to taste.

300g (10oz) betel nuts, grated shredded or split
2 tablespoons ghee
6 tablespoons white poppy seeds
6 tablespoons aniseed
4 tablespoons melon seeds, cracked and kernels extracted
1 teaspoon cardamom powder
2 teaspoons caster sugar

1 Fry the betel nuts in ghee on a low heat until crisp. Add poppy seeds, aniseed and melon seeds and fry until they turn dark. Take off the heat and add the cardamom powder and sugar.

2 Mix well, cool completely and store in a dry, airtight bottle.

Buchanania lanzan

CHIRONGI NUTS

(CHAROLI)

India is a country where those with a sweet tooth will find themselves overwhelmingly indulged. Every whim is catered for in the endless parade of sweet dishes from the richest clotted cream to the most delicate, sugared sweetmeats. Many are sprinkled with petals, silver and gold leaf, and an assortment of nuts. Chirongi nuts are an important garnish for halwas, cakes and creams, and are favoured in Gujarat, Maharashtra and Hyderabad.

Amrakhand

are further dried and then packed for distribution.

APPEARANCE AND TASTE

Chirongi nuts are small, pale and speckled with dark patches. They are slightly flat, and round in shape and are the size of lentils. They have a slightly nutty aroma and a pronounced taste that is between nutty and musky.

HOW THEY GROW

Sometimes called *charooli* or *chirolo*, chirongi nuts have no English name. They are the kernels of a fruit whose shell dries to a brittle hardness. The fruit is cracked open and the nuts are extracted. These

BUYING AND STORING

As they are quite difficult to come by outside India, you will only find them at well-stocked Indian grocery shops. Store them in a dry, airtight jar for up to 6 months.

MEDICINAL AND OTHER USES

Like almonds, chirongi nuts have been credited with the power to sharpen concentration, improve eyesight and provide strength and vigour.

CULINARY USES

Used primarily as a topping for sweets, they go especially well with sweet halwas, where vegetables like carrots and fruits like bananas and sapotas (*chikoo*) are cooked with sugar until smooth and creamy. They are also a must on top of a delightful dessert called *shrikhand*, which is a tantalising combination of thick strained yoghurt, sugar, saffron, cardamom and milk that has been cooked on a slow heat until it resembles condensed cream. Chirongi nuts are used for texture and nuttiness in kababs and kormas. You could be innovative and sprinkle them on fruit salads, soups and chicken or lamb dishes.

This dish is a combination of two traditional sweets: shrikhand (page 38) and pure mango pulp. The combination is out of this world!

AMRAKHAND
(MANGO AND YOGHURT SWEET)

Serves 4
Preparation time 15 minutes + 5 hours draining
Cooking time 0

900ml (1½pt) full fat, set yoghurt
About 6 tablespoons caster sugar, or to taste
300ml (½pt) mango pulp (canned or fresh)
2 tablespoons chirongi nuts

1 Tie the yoghurt in a clean cotton cloth and hang up to drain off the whey.

2 When it is quite dry, untie and place in a bowl. Beat well with a wooden spoon or whisk, adding caster sugar, a little at a time.

3 When the yoghurt is light in texture, stir in the mango pulp and chill.

4 Serve cold, sprinkled with chirongi nuts.

Pistacia vera

PISTACHIO NUTS

(PISTA)

Diwali, the 4-day festival of lights, comes in November. The queen of Indian festivals, its very name – a row of lamps – means radiance and beauty. At this festival gifts and sweets are exchanged and families and friends get together to eat and be merry. Some of the finest sweets are made of pistachio nuts. On their own the nuts make the ultimate gift as they are the most expensive nut available in India. Platters of dry fruits which include pistachios, almonds, figs, dates, cashew nuts and sultanas, make their way across the country during the days leading up to Diwali.

Indian sweets made with pistachio nuts

Pistachio tree with nuts

HOW THEY GROW

Native to Iran, Afghanistan and Turkey, pistachios are imported as they have become an intrinsic part of Indian cookery and enter-taining. Various grades of pistachio nuts are available, the best being large and fat. In India salted pistachios are roasted in their shells in hot sand and then tossed in a thick paste of salt and water to make the salt stick to the shells. During the process, some shells open out and the salt gets to the nut within.

APPEARANCE AND TASTE

Pistachio nuts are available in their shelled or unshelled form. The shells split neatly into two halves, exposing a fresh apple-green nut streaked with violet. Pistachio nuts have virtually no aroma but they possess a rich, smooth, almost creamy taste that complements both sweet and savoury dishes.

BUYING AND STORING

Available whole, chopped, in their shell, salted or roasted. Pistachio nuts are always expensive, but worth the price. Get the largest, greenest nuts. Store in an airtight container. They will keep for up to 8 months. Old pistachio nuts taste rancid. If the weather gets too hot, it is a good idea to store dried fruits and nuts in the refrigerator.

CULINARY USES

Predominantly used in sweets as a garnish or in stuffings, they are powdered, chopped finely or sliced to add colour and flavour to a dish. Try them with ice-cream or in stuffings for poultry. Sprinkle them over soufflés and rice pudding. In India, they are cooked with milk and sugar, set and cut into squares. This sweet is called *pista burfi*.

Pista burfi

There is hardly anything in the culinary world as heavenly as ice-cream and in India exotic and rare flavours transport this much loved dish into the realms of fantasy. Fruit flavours like mango, custard apple, chikoo and melon are eaten seasonally, while nutty *kulfis* enhanced with cream are eaten all through the year. Indians love ice-cream and it is a must at all wedding receptions.

PISTA KULFI
(PISTACHIO ICE CREAM)

Serves 4
Preparation time 20 minutes
Cooking time 30 minutes +
  freezing time

300g (10oz) unsalted pistachio
  nuts
1500ml (2½pt) full fat milk
300g (10oz) caster sugar
300ml (½pt) double cream

1 Soak the nuts in a little of
the milk and boil the
remaining milk in a heavy
pan. Simmer until it is
reduced by half, stirring to
ensure that skin which forms
is well blended into the
milk.

2 Grind the soaked pista-
chios coarsely, reserving a
few for the garnish, and add
with the sugar to the
reduced milk.

3 Simmer for 10 minutes,
stirring constantly. Remove
from the heat and cool.

4 Place in the refrigerator to
chill. When very cold, add
the cream and beat the
mixture with a whisk until
light.

5 Pour into ice-cream trays
and freeze until solid.

6 Turn out to serve and
garnish with the reserved
pistachio nuts.

Shelled pistachio nuts

**This dish is for steamed
puddings that taste even
better if they are cooked in
a fresh turmeric leaf. These
are not commonly available
outside India (unless you
grow your own) so you will
have to rely on ghee for
fragrance.**

PISTA KACHORI
(STEAMED PISTACHIO
DUMPLINGS)

Serves 4
Preparation time 30 minutes
Cooking time 30 minutes (to
  cook all the dumplings)

300ml (½pt) water
Large pinch salt
2 tablespoons sunflower oil
220g (8oz) rice flour
150g (5oz) sugar
*150g (5oz) coconut, grated if
  fresh, or desiccated*

*150g (5oz) unsalted pistachios,
  crushed finely*
1 teaspoon cardamom powder
4 tablespoons ghee

1 Bring the water to the boil
in a pan and add the salt and
the oil. Reduce the heat and
add the rice flour, stirring
constantly until a ball is
formed.

2 Take off the heat, cool
down enough to handle and
knead into a soft, pliant
dough.

3 Make a single-string syrup
with the sugar and a little
water by taking some cooled
syrup between thumb and
forefinger. It is ready when a
single thread is formed when
you separate the thumb and
finger. Add the coconut and
pistachios.

4 Stir for a minute, remove
from the heat and add the
cardamom powder.

5 Make small balls of the
dough and the coconut
mixture.

6 Take a ball of dough in
your palm and flatten it into
a disc. Place a portion of the
coconut mixture in the
middle and fold up the edges
of the disc to join in a point
on the top. The dumpling
should resemble a large tear-
drop. Seal the top well.

7 Make all the dumplings
similarly. Steam the dumplings for 10 minutes or until
done. The casing will turn
translucent.

8 Gently lift out of the
steamer and serve hot,
drizzled with ghee.

Prunus dulcis

ALMOND

(BADAM)

The almond has always been a symbol of affluence and romance in India. Indian heroines in classical literature and mythology are described as having dark, almond-shaped eyes epitomising beauty and allure. Even in a pack of playing cards, the heart suit is referred to as *badam* or almond in many Indian languages. The Mughal emperors of India were great connoisseurs of art and lovers of food. It was, in fact, the Mughals who introduced the almond to Indian cookery and encouraged the use of the almond motif in textiles, weaving and sculpture. Their royal robes were decorated with gold-encrusted patterns inspired by the almond fruit, leaves and seed.

Whole almonds

HOW IT GROWS

Although the almond is native to the Mediterranean, a small amount is grown in India, mainly in Kashmir. Almond trees are large and shady – they grow up to a height of 15m (50ft) – and bear large, oval leaves tinged with red and fleshy fruits which turn from green to bright red as they mature. The fruits of the tree are extremely fragrant and sweet with an astringent aftertaste and are popular with children. In cultivated orchards, the fruits are picked when mature and the seed is extracted. This is bleached if left whole, but most often, the kernel from

Almond-shaped eyes are the epitome of classic Indian beauty

within is removed. This is the almond we use. There are two basic varieties of almonds: bitter and sweet. Indian almonds tend to be slightly bitter, but the sweet ones are imported into India from Afghanistan in great quantities.

Almond shapes are a popular feature in Indian jewellery

APPEARANCE AND TASTE

Almonds range from 2–4cm (1–1½in) in length and are a pointed, oval shape. They have a thin, variegated skin which can be peeled off after soaking the nuts in water. Almonds are sometimes left in the shell which is pale beige, hard and covered with tiny craters. Delicate and sweet to taste, almonds have no particular smell, but they add a nutty, rich flavour to a dish.

BUYING AND STORING

Mostly used whole or flaked, almonds are also available ground, chopped or powdered (from Indian shops). Almond oil is very popular as a cooking medium or a beauty aid. Look for large, plump nuts. Avoid old almonds which have a film of white dust that smells rancid. Store in a glass or plastic jar for up to 8 months.

Ground almonds

OTHER USES

Almonds are used extensively in beauty products. The oil is used to massage babies to keep their skin soft and supple. Almond paste is used as a face-pack and almond milk, extracted from the nut, is used as a face wash. Almond derivatives are used in commercial beauty products. Burnt almond shells are made into toothpowder.

CULINARY USES

Almonds are ground to a paste for curry bases. They can be fried or blanched as a garnish or used as slivers in sweets. Biryanis, milk desserts and meat curries are dusted with finely chopped almonds. Almond ice cream, made with rich creamy milk, called *kulfi*, is a delicacy. *Badam halwa* made of powdered almonds and sugar, is a traditional sweet and almond sherbet is a cool drink made of almonds, milk, sugar and rose-water.

Skinned almonds

This recipe comes from south India and is one of the richest sweets you can eat. It always reminds me of a famous south Indian restaurant in Bombay where it is served (believe it or not) with breakfast!

BADAM HALWA
(ALMOND FUDGE)

Serves 4
Preparation time 10 minutes +
  5 hours soaking
Cooking time 1 hour

300g (10oz) almonds, soaked
  for 5 hours, blanched
600ml (1pt) full fat milk
6 tablespoons ghee
6 tablespoons sugar
1 teaspoon cardamom powder
2 sheets edible silver foil (varq)

1 Put the almonds in a food processor with half the milk. Grind to a paste, adding more milk a little at a time until all the milk is used up.

2 Heat the ghee in a heavy pan and add the almond paste. Fry over a low heat until it begins to stick.

3 Add the sugar and stir well. Cook until the ghee separates and the fudge is well blended.

Flaked almonds

4 Take off the heat and add the cardamom powder. Stir well and pour onto a flat dish.

5 When it is almost cool, cut it into fancy shapes and decorate with edible silver foil.

This lamb curry from Kashmir is an international favourite and is featured on most Indian restaurant menus around the world. Any number of variations exist. I was given this recipe by a Kashmiri friend.

ROGAN JOSH
(KASHMIRI LAMB CURRY)

Serves 4
Preparation time 40 minutes
Cooking time 1½ hours

5 tablespoons sunflower oil
2 bay leaves
300g (10oz) lean, boneless
  lamb, cubed

Grind to a paste in a coffee grinder:
600ml (1pt) thick yoghurt
2 teaspoons ginger, grated
1 teaspoon aniseed
½ teaspoon cardamom powder
1 teaspoon chilli powder
2 teaspoons garam masala
  powder

Salt
6 tablespoons ground almonds

1 Heat the oil in a heavy pan, add the bay leaves and the lamb and fry until well browned.

2 Add a little of the yoghurt and spice paste and salt and fry until the oil begins to separate. Keep gradually adding the mixture and allowing the oil to separate.

3 Reduce the heat, cover with a tight-fitting lid and cook the lamb in its own steam until tender.

4 Stir in the ground almonds and simmer for a couple of minutes. Serve hot with *naan* bread.

Badam Halwa

Fruits of
the Earth

Lentils and Pulses

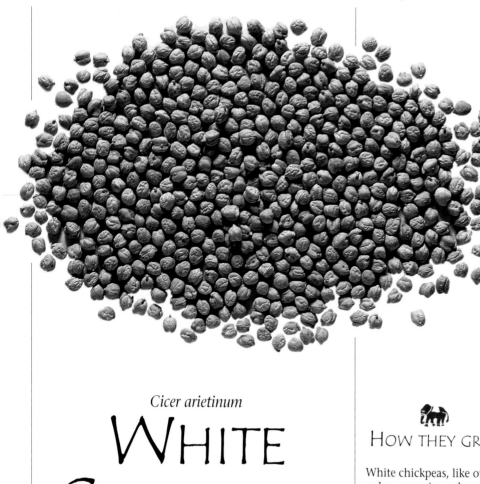

BUYING AND STORING

Chickpeas are available dried or cooked and canned in brine. Buy cans of chickpeas to save cooking time but check the best before date. Dried chickpeas will keep for 4 months.

CULINARY USES

These small peas need to be soaked for at least 8 hours after which they nearly double in size. They are thoroughly boiled before use in curries, salads, rice pulaos and chutneys. White chickpeas go beautifully with garlic, onions and tomatoes and give any dish a thick, creamy consistency. Use them in yoghurt-based salads or raitas, in fresh green salads, and as a garnish over vegetables or rice. They are combined with mixed peppers, tomatoes and a few spices for a tasty, dry dish with rice and lentils. If you have a can of chickpeas, onions, garlic and tomatoes you can make one of the fastest Indian meals possible. Chickpeas are used widely in Mediterranean cookery where they are crushed with garlic, oil and yoghurt to make a dip, or added to soups, salads and stews.

Cicer arietinum

WHITE CHICKPEAS

(KABULI CHANNA)

For the Sikh community of India, rejoicing and feasting is a way of life. These are people whose celebrations are grand extravaganzas of dance, music, food and drink. One of their most special festivals is *Guru Parab*, the birthday of their leader Guru Gobind Singh. Free community kitchens are set up, where you eat *choley-bhature*, a Sikh favourite. Choley are white chickpeas, cooked to a creamy consistency with several spices. Bhature are huge, round puffs of bread that are fried until golden.

HOW THEY GROW

White chickpeas, like other pulses, grow in pods on small, bushy plants. They thrive in cold climates and are cultivated extensively in the cool, dry Indo-Gangetic plains of India. The pods are harvested in the winter, dried and threshed. The peas are further dried in the sun until completely moisture-free.

APPEARANCE AND TASTE

These peas are small, hard, creamy-white and can be halved. The pea has a thick skin which often comes away during soaking and cooking. On their own, chickpeas have little aroma or taste, but when cooked with flavourings and spices, they take on a nutty, creamy flavour.

Sikh religeous function

This recipe is along the lines of the famous Mediterranean dips but with a spicy Indian touch. It can be served with any meal, or spread onto a slice of bread for a quick snack.

CHANNA CHUTNEY
(WHITE CHICKPEA CHUTNEY)

Serves 4
Preparation time 15 minutes + overnight soaking
Cooking time 30 minutes

150g (5oz) white chickpeas, soaked overnight and drained
2 teaspoons sunflower oil
1 teaspoon aniseed
1 large onion, chopped
1 teaspoon garlic, chopped
1 teaspoon mango powder
1 teaspoon chilli powder
Salt
1 teaspoon sugar

1 Boil the chickpeas in water until soft and drain, reserving some of the water.

2 Heat the oil in a pan and fry the aniseed until it pops. Add the onion and fry until golden.

3 Add all the remaining ingredients and fry, stirring all the time

4 Mix in the chickpeas, take off the heat and grind to a thick, smooth paste in a blender, using some of the reserved water to dilute.

This recipe is for a rice dish that is fragrant and easy to make. You can use canned chickpeas for both recipes, which reduces the cooking time dramatically.

CHANNA PULAO
(WHITE CHICKPEAS AND RICE)

Serves 4
Preparation time 10 minutes + overnight soaking
Cooking time 30 minutes

150g (5oz) white chickpeas, soaked overnight and drained
2 tablespoons ghee
4 cardamom
6 cloves
2 bay leaves
8 black peppercorns
300g (10oz) basmati rice, washed and drained
Salt
2 tablespoons sunflower oil
1 large onion, sliced finely

1 Boil the chickpeas until soft, drain and reserve the water.

2 Heat the ghee in a pan and fry the whole spices until they pop.

3 Add the rice and fry until shiny.

4 Pour in 300ml (½pt) of the reserved water, adding more water if there is not enough.

5 Add salt and bring to the boil. Reduce the heat and simmer until the rice is cooked. Then gently mix in the chickpeas.

6 Heat the oil in another pan and fry the onions until dark gold in colour. Pour over the pulao and serve hot.

Channa Pulao

Cicer arietinum

BLACK CHICKPEAS

(KALA CHANNA)

In October, the festival of *Dussera* is celebrated with great drama and fanfare. It is a time when women wear their best saris and jewellery and families attend late-night cultural programmes of music, dance and theatre. Each state makes special *Dussera* feasts. In Bengal, images of the goddess Durga are worshipped amidst scenes of great pageantry and sweets of condensed milk are distributed. In Maharashtra, *Dussera* is celebrated with community feasting at each of the goddess' temples. Here, little puffed poories made of rice flour are served with a spicy curry made of black chickpeas and roasted coconut.

Sprouted black chickpeas

CULINARY USES

Black chickpeas need overnight soaking before boiling. To sprout chickpeas, soak then drain and hang them up in a damp cloth for 8 hours. They can be cooked in a pressure cooker. Combined with ginger, garlic, coconut and spices, the chickpeas are cooked to a thick, soupy consistency and served with bread or mounds of plain, boiled rice. The curry is made fiery with ground red chillies, which are added according to taste. These peas colour the liquid they are boiled in and the resulting curry is rich and brown.

HOW THEY GROW

Found mainly in central and coastal India, black chickpeas are referred to as wild peas in many Indian languages. They grow in pods like fresh green peas on small shrubs. In winter, as the pods mature, they are plucked and sun-dried until brown.

APPEARANCE AND TASTE

A relative of the more commonly seen white chickpea, the black variety is dark brown, small and hard. The peas are perfectly round and smooth. They have a strong, earthy aroma, reminiscent of rich, black, monsoon-drenched soil. They have a thick skin and a pleasant, nutty flavour.

BUYING AND STORING

They are sold whole and dried, though in the region where they are grown, they are also eaten fresh. They are a slightly unusual ingredient, not used by all Indians, but they are worth looking out for in shops. Store in an airtight jar for up to 6 months.

The goddess Durga

These recipes are from my aunt who insists that served with rice flour rotis, they are the best meal a person can have. An excellent cook, her chickpea curry is the best I've ever tasted.

VATANA AAMTI
(BLACK CHICKPEA CURRY)

Serves 4
Preparation time 20 minutes + overnight soaking + 8 hours sprouting
Cooking time 45 minutes

300g (10oz) black chickpeas, soaked overnight and sprouted for 8 hours
1 teaspoon chilli powder
1 teaspoon turmeric powder
Salt
150g (5oz) tomatoes, chopped
6 kokum
5 tablespoons sunflower oil
8 cloves
10 black peppercorns
2 teaspoons coriander seeds
1 large onion, sliced
300g (10oz) coconut, grated if fresh, or desiccated
1 teaspoon black mustard seeds
1 teaspoon cumin seeds

1 Boil the chickpeas in water until soft. Stir in the powder spices, salt, tomatoes and kokum.

2 Heat 3 tablespoons of the oil in a pan and add the peppercorns and coriander seeds. When they pop, add the onion and fry until golden.

3 Stir in the coconut and fry until brown.

4 Grind this mixture to a fine paste in a blender, adding a little water as necessary. Add to the chickpeas, bring to the boil and then take off the heat.

5 Heat the remaining oil in a pan and fry the mustard seeds and cumin seeds. When they pop, pour over the curry and mix well. Do not boil the curry, as the coconut will start to give off an oily flavour.

VATANA USAL
(SPICY BLACK CHICKPEAS)

Serves 4
Preparation time 20 minutes + overnight soaking + 8 hours sprouting
Cooking time 45 minutes

300g (10oz) black chickpeas, soaked overnight and sprouted for 8 hours
3 tablespoons sunflower oil
1 teaspoon cumin seeds
1 large onion, chopped
150g (5oz) tomatoes, chopped
1 teaspoon turmeric powder
1 teaspoon coriander powder
1 teaspoon chilli powder
½ teaspoon sugar
Salt
4 tablespoons coconut, grated if fresh, or desiccated
4 tablespoons coriander leaves, chopped

1 Boil the chickpeas in water until soft, drain and set aside.

2 Heat the oil in a pan and fry the cumin seeds.

3 Add the onion and fry until brown.

4 Stir in the tomatoes and cook until they are soft. Add all the powder spices, sugar and salt and mix well.

5 Add the cooked chickpeas.

6 Take off the heat and add the coconut and coriander. Mix well and serve hot.

Vatana Aamti

Lablab purpureus

VAL

(VALOR)

The state of Gujarat has made an important contribution to Indian cookery – the *thali*. Thali actually means a plate of metal and in culinary terms it has come to mean an extensive meal served on such a plate. The thali consists of accompaniments, dry vegetables with the more liquid preparations in small, metal bowls. The right side of the thali is reserved for the sweet which is served along with the main meal. In the centre, space is left for rotis, poories and rice. On the whole Gujaratis are vegetarians, and as such, they have perfected the cooking of vegetables, lentils and pulses. One pulse included in a thali is val, a variety of bean.

HOW IT GROWS

Val beans grow on flat pods on small bushes. When the pods mature, they are plucked and sun-dried. They are then threshed either by hand or mechanically, and the beans are further dried. Tender val pods are also eaten as a fresh vegetable.

APPEARANCE AND TASTE

Dried val beans are creamy-white to light tan in colour, flat and long. They have a thick, white ridge on one side. On cooking, val acquires a strong, nutty aroma and the taste becomes creamy with a slight, but not unpleasant, bitterness.

BUYING AND STORING

Buy plump firm beans which show no sign of wrinkling or discolouring. Store in a dry, airtight jar for 4 months.

CULINARY USES

Val needs overnight soaking as it is quite hard. It is usually sprouted to enhance its flavour. Just soak it in water then drain and hang up in a clean moist cloth overnight to promote sprouting. The beans need to be peeled to remove the thick, chewy skin. Then they are ready to be cooked. Val goes well with coconut, jaggery and ginger. You can add the sprouted beans to soups and salads.

Food served on a *thali*

The following recipes are from Maharashtra. The first is a kind of coconut curry that goes well with rotis.

VALACHE BIRDE
(VAL AND COCONUT STIR-FRY)

Serves 4
Preparation time 20 minutes + overnight soaking + 8 hours sprouting
Cooking time 25 minutes

3 tablespoons sunflower oil
1 teaspoon black mustard seeds
1 teaspoon cumin seeds
Large pinch asafoetida
10 curry leaves
4 green chillies, slit lengthways, exposing the seeds, but so the chilli is not broken in 2
300g (10oz) val, soaked overnight, sprouted for 8 hours, and skinned
4 tablespoons jaggery, grated
Salt
150g (5oz) coconut, grated if fresh, or desiccated
6 kokum
2 tablespoons coriander leaves, chopped

1 Heat the oil in a pan and add the mustard seeds. When they pop add half the cumin seeds.

2 Add the asafoetida, curry leaves and chillies and fry for a minute.

3 Add the val, a little water, jaggery, kokum and salt and cook on a low heat until the val is soft but not mushy.

4 Grind the coconut and the remaining cumin seeds to a fine paste in a blender. Stir this paste into the curry and simmer for a minute. Serve sprinkled with coriander leaves.

Valache Birde

This dish includes a long reed-like vegetable called drumstick. When cooked the reed is sucked to eat the soft, inner flesh and the fibrous residue is discarded.

VANGI ANI VAL
(AUBERGINE AND VAL WITH COCONUT)

Serves 4
Preparation time 30 minutes + overnight soaking + 8 hours sprouting
Cooking time 30 minutes

2 drumsticks, (optional) cut into 3cm (1in) pieces
3 tablespoons sunflower oil
1 teaspoon black mustard seeds
Large pinch of asafoetida
1 large onion, chopped finely
150g (5oz) val, soaked overnight, sprouted for 8 hours and skinned
150g (5oz) aubergines, cubed
1 teaspoon turmeric powder
1 teaspoon chilli powder
1 teaspoon goda masala powder
Salt
4 tablespoons coconut, grated if fresh, or desiccated

1 Boil the drumstick until it can be easily opened. Drain and reserve.

2 Heat the oil and fry the mustard seeds with the asafoetida. When the seeds pop add the onion and fry till golden.

3 Add the val, aubergines, powder spices and salt. Mix well. Then add a little water and cook until the beans are soft but not mushy.

4 Cook on a high heat to evaporate all the water. Take off the heat and add the coconut and drumsticks.

5 Stir gently and serve hot.

Lens culinaris

BLACK LENTILS

(URAD DAL)

Whole black lentils

Split black lentils

Skinned, split black lentils

Also known as black gram, black lentils are used whole in north Indian cookery and split in the south. Batters made of ground black lentils are prepared every day in many south Indian homes. They are then steamed, fried or roasted to make different breakfast dishes. Nearly all south Indian homes wake up to the smell of black lentils whereas north Indian ones are filled with their aroma at dinnertime. *Maa di dal*, a dark, rich dish served with plain rice and dollops of ghee or clarified butter, is a must on all festive occasions. Visit any Punjabi home on a special day and this hearty dal is sure to be on the table.

HOW THEY GROW

Found all over India, black lentils grow in small pods 2–3cm (1in) long. When ripe, the seed pods are picked, dried and threshed or beaten to separate out the lentils. These are further dried and either left whole or split.

APPEARANCE AND TASTE

Whole black lentils are small and oblong. The black seeds are sometimes flecked with dark green or grey. When they are split, they are creamy-white and matte. The lentils are sometimes split with the skin left on. Black lentils have a strong musky smell and a rich, heavy taste. Split black lentils have a different aroma, subtle and flour-like. The taste is quite bland. All varieties, especially the split lentils, release a glutinous liquid when cooking, which gives the final dish a thick, creamy consistency.

BUYING AND STORING

You will not need great amounts of this lentil. The whole lentils are too heavy to be eaten every day, so buy small amounts and store in airtight jars for up to 4 months.

CULINARY USES

Black lentils are successfully combined with red kidney beans to make the famous Punjabi *maa di dal* or *kali dal*.

The split lentils are eaten with rice or added to hot oil along with mustard seeds and onion before adding vegetables, to give a nutty taste and a slightly chewy texture to the dish. The vegetables should be added when the lentils turn golden but before they become too dark. They tend to soften with cooking and lend flavour to potatoes, beans and cabbage.

Black lentil dishes feature at every Punjabi celebration

There are many different recipes for these 2 south Indian specialities. These are from grandmother's kitchen. When I visited her as a child, she would make me a pancake the size of a large plate. Rice cakes are made in a special steamer which is a 3–4 tiered container with 4 hollow craters in each tier. In the absence of such a steamer, use an egg poacher.

IDLI
(STEAMED RICE CAKES)

Serves 4
Preparation time 20 minutes + 4 hours soaking + 8 hours fermenting
Cooking time 15 minutes

300g (10oz) any variety of rice
440g (1lb) split, skinless black lentils
12 fenugreek seeds
1 teaspoon salt
Water as required

1 Soak the rice, and the lentils mixed with the fenugreek seeds, separately in plenty of water for at least 4 hours.

2 Drain and grind them separately until fine in a blender, adding water as necessary to make a thick, pouring batter. Mix the two batters together and add the salt. (If you grind them together the batter will not be smooth enough).

3 Leave to ferment in a warm place for about 8 hours.

4 Pour the batter into a rice cake steamer or egg poacher and steam the cakes for 15 minutes.

5 To remove, slide a sharp knife under each cake and lift. Set aside and keep warm. Repeat this process until all the batter is used up. Serve warm with garlic chutney and sambhar (see page 89).

A feast of dosas

DOSA
(RICE AND LENTIL PANCAKES)

Serves 4
Preparation time 10 minutes + 4 hours soaking + 8 hours fermenting
Cooking time 20 minutes

440g (1lb) any variety of rice
150g (5oz) split, skinless black lentils
1 teaspoon salt
1 onion, cut in half
6 tablespoons sunflower oil

1 Soak the rice and the lentils separately for 4 hours in plenty of water.

2 Grind to a paste in a blender, adding water as required to make a thick batter. (See step 2 in the previous recipe).

3 Mix the batters, add the salt and leave to ferment in a warm place for 8 hours.

4 Heat an iron griddle or heavy frying pan. Dip the cut half of the onion in the oil and smear over the pan.

5 Stir the batter and pour a ladleful into the middle of the pan. Spread the mixture quickly, pour a few drops of oil around the edges and let it cook until tiny holes appear on its surface.

6 Turn over, cook and remove. In all likelihood, this pancake will be far from perfect. Discard it as the first one serves to 'season' the pan for the following ones.

7 Redo the onion routine. Pour a ladleful of batter onto the pan and spread in quick, circular movements. Cook for a minute and drizzle some oil around the edges.

8 Turn over with a spatula and cook on the other side. Remove and keep warm. Make all the pancakes accordingly. Serve them with garlic chutney and sambhar (see page 89).

Idlis and Dosas

Lens culinaris

GRAM LENTILS

(CHANNA DAL)

Festive food made with gram lentils

One of the most beautiful states of India, Kerala comes alive with the sound of music around the end of August each year to celebrate the festival of Onam. It is celebrated in style – richly-caparisoned elephants are led in endless processions, boat races are held in the backwaters of the villages, homes are decorated with flowers and gleaming brass lamps, and sumptuous feasts are served on fresh, green banana leaves. A highlight of the Onam feast is *channa dal payasam*, a traditional sweet made by cooking gram lentils, jaggery, coconut, cardamom, cashew nuts and raisins in ghee or clarified butter. Gram lentils are associated with festivities. Each Indian festival has its own preparation made from this lentil.

Boat race as part of the celebrations of the festival of Onam, Kerala

HOW THEY GROW

Gram, or Bengal gram as it is also known, is the most widely grown lentil in India. The bushy shrub bears seed-filled pods, each containing 2 or 3 lentils. They are picked in early winter when they turn ripe and brown. Then they are husked and left whole, split or ground into a flour.

APPEARANCE AND TASTE

Matte and yellow, gram lentils resemble yellow lentils but are slightly bigger and coarser. They are stronger in taste than most other lentils with a nutty sweet aroma and flavour.

BUYING AND STORING

Good gram lentils should be plump and bright. Store in an airtight container for about 4 months.

CULINARY USES

All lentils cause flatulence but gram most of all and therefore it is cooked with a good pinch of asafoetida. Gram lentils are cooked in a variety of ways – with onions, spices, tamarind or garlic, or mixed with meat for kababs and koftas. They are used with vegetables, especially squashes, cooked with meats in spicy curries like *dal gosht* and in sweets. Cooked with jaggery and ground to a paste they are used for stuffings in Maharashtrian pancakes called *puranpoli*, fried in squares or cooked with rice. Lentil flour is also a versatile ingredient.

Here, bottle gourd is combined with gram lentils in a classic north Indian recipe. (Bottle gourds are available at all Indian grocers.) This vegetable curry tastes very good with Indian breads and pleasantly disguises the blandness of the gourd.

DOODHI CHANNA
(BOTTLE GOURD WITH LENTILS)

Serves 4
Preparation time 25 minutes + 30 minutes soaking
Cooking time 20 minutes

4 tablespoons sunflower oil
1 teaspoon cumin seeds
1 teaspoon ginger paste
1 teaspoon garlic paste
4 tablespoons gram lentils, soaked for 30 minutes and drained
600g (1¼lb) bottle gourd (lauki/ doodhi), skinned and diced
10 tablespoons tomato purée
1 teaspoon turmeric powder
1 teaspoon chilli powder
1 teaspoon coriander powder
Salt

150ml (¼pt) water
1 teaspoon garam masala powder

1 Heat the oil in a pan and add the cumin seeds. When they pop, add the ginger and garlic pastes.

2 Stir in the lentils and the gourd after a minute, and fry well.

3 Add the rest of the ingredients except the garam masala, cover and cook until the lentils are soft. Sprinkle the garam masala over and mix gently.

4 Serve hot with poories.

This recipe is a basic lentil dish that can be eaten with rice or rotis.

KHATTI DAL
(TANGY LENTIL CURRY)

Serves 4
Preparation time 10 minutes
Cooking time 1 hour

4 tablespoons gram lentils
450ml (¾pt) water
4 teaspoons sunflower oil
1 teaspoon black mustard seeds
1 teaspoon fenugreek seeds
1 teaspoon aniseed
1 teaspoon ajowan seeds
2 bay leaves
1 large onion, chopped finely

1 teaspoon turmeric powder
4 teaspoons lemon juice
Salt

1 Simmer the lentils in the water until soft.

2 Heat the oil in a pan and add the mustard seeds When they pop, add all the other seeds and the bay leaves. Fry for a minute.

3 Add the onions and fry until golden.

4 Pour in the cooked lentils and add the turmeric, lemon juice and salt. Simmer for 5 minutes to blend well.

Khatti Dal

Split red lentils

Lens culinaris

RED LENTILS

(MASOOR)

Perhaps more than anywhere else in the world, a meal in India carries the impress of season, geography, social and religious customs and medical beliefs. The result is an incredible panorama of textures and flavours which reflects a particular regional cuisine. When people from any area travel, they carry with them the legacy of their cuisine. Lentils being everyday fare, it is easy to distinguish people from the different states of India simply by the way they cook them. A south Indian will have his flavoured with fenugreek seeds, curry leaves and tamarind while a Maharashtrian will have his embellished with green chillies, tomatoes and fresh coriander.

Whole red lentils

HOW THEY GROW

Red lentils are the seeds of a bushy plant which grows in cold climates and in non-irrigated conditions throughout northern India, Madhya Pradesh and parts of Maharashtra. When mature, the long pods in which the lentils are contained are plucked, dried and threshed. The seeds within have a casing around them and are kept whole or peeled and split.

APPEARANCE AND TASTE

When whole they are dark brown to greenish-black in colour, round and flattish. The fairly thick skin conceals a pinkish-orange centre. Split red lentils are the familiar orange ones found in shops. Red lentils are delicate in flavour and have a nutty, fresh taste. The whole lentils are muskier, chewy and coarser.

BUYING AND STORING

Whole red lentils and split lentils have quite different qualities so when buying make sure you buy what is asked for in the recipe. Split red lentils are useful as they are fast cooking and make a quick, nutritious meal. Both the varieties store well for up to 6 months in a dry, airtight container.

Red lentils are cultivated in the cool climate of northern India

OTHER USES

During Diwali, every Indian home is decorated with lamps, flowers and floor paintings. Enterprising artists use a wide variety of materials to make colourful and intricate patterns on the floor. All sorts of lentils are used as their different colours can result in an interesting palette of hues. Whenever a lentil *rangoli* or pattern is created, red lentils feature prominently because of their vibrancy and ability to offset the other yellow, brown or black ones.

CULINARY USES

The whole lentils take longer to cook and soaking them overnight helps reduce cooking time. Because of their musky flavour, they are cooked, mashed and added to minced meat for kababs, blended into meat curries or seasoned with powerful flavourings like ginger and garlic. They are also sprouted and cooked. They are versatile and go with onions, coconut, tamarind or tomatoes.

The following recipes are for 2 very popular dishes. The kababs are good for a summer barbecue or as an accompaniment to an aperitif. The second dish can be served with rice or on its own as a filling soup.

SHAMI KABABS
(LAMB AND LENTIL KABABS)

Serves 4
Preparation time 30 minutes
Cooking time 1 hour

3 tablespoons sunflower oil
2-3 onions, chopped very finely
1 teaspoon ginger paste
1 teaspoon garlic paste
1 teaspoon green chillies, minced
300g (10oz) lamb mince
150g (5oz) split red lentils, washed and drained
1 teaspoon turmeric powder
1 teaspoon garam masala powder
½ teaspoon allspice powder
Salt
Sunflower oil for frying
4 eggs, beaten

1 Heat the oil and add the onions. Fry until translucent, then add the ginger, garlic and chillies and fry for a minute.

2 Add the mince and lentils and fry well, then stir in the powder spices and salt and cook until the mince is done and the lentils are soft. Dry the mixture over a high heat. This is important as any moisture will cause the kababs to crack while frying.

3 Remove from the heat and allow to cool slightly. Mix in 1 beaten egg then take a small ball of the meat mixture and shape it into a flat, 1cm (½in) thick disc. Wet your palms if the mixture sticks.

4 Heat a little oil in a heavy pan. Dip the kabab in the beaten egg and shallow fry until golden.

5 Cook all the kababs in the same way.

SABUT PIYAZ KI DAL
(WHOLE ONIONS WITH LENTILS)

Serves 4
Preparation time 10 minutes
Cooking time 30 minutes

220g (8oz) whole red lentils, washed and drained
3 tablespoons sunflower oil
1 teaspoon black mustard seeds
Large pinch of asafoetida
12 curry leaves
4 dried red chillies, stalks removed and deseeded
16 shallots, peeled
2 tablespoons jaggery, grated
1 teaspoon tamarind pulp, diluted in 2 tablespoons water
1 teaspoon turmeric powder
Salt

1 Simmer the lentils in double their quantity of water until soft.

2 Heat the oil in a pan and add the mustard seeds. When they pop, add the asafoetida, curry leaves and red chillies. Fry for one minute.

3 Add the whole shallots and stir-fry.

4 Add a little water, the jaggery, tamarind, turmeric and salt and cook until the shallots turn transparent.

5 Pour in the lentils carefully, adjust the seasoning and serve hot.

Lens culinaris

YELLOW LENTILS

(TOOR/ARHAR DAL)

India has the world's largest number of vegetarians. In a meatless diet, lentils and pulses play an important role, providing all the protein needed for healthy living. Lentils or dals are an integral part of Indian cookery so they are widely grown and are consequently very cheap. Every Indian eats dal daily and the Hindi term *dal roti* has come to mean staple, everyday food. *Dal-roti*, or lentils and bread, are made in thousands of different ways in Indian homes. This may sound boring but lentils can be transformed into any number of dishes – ground into flour for bread, roasted and crushed for sweets, and added whole to vegetables and meats for flavour and texture.

HOW THEY GROW

The yellow lentil plant is a deep-rooted shrubby perennial which is grown from seed. The small flowers give way to long, slim pods which contain seeds. The pods are dried in the sun or mechanically, and husked to separate the seeds which are the lentils. In some parts of India, yellow lentils are slightly oiled to increase shelf-life, more so when the lentils are exported, and therefore Indian shops outside India usually stock the oily variety of yellow lentil.

APPEARANCE AND TASTE

These lentils are yellow and sold split into two round halves. The oily variety is sticky and glossy, the unoily one is matte. They are very easy to digest and have a pleasant, subtle, nutty flavour.

BUYING AND STORING

In India, the unoily lentil is preferred, so if you do buy oily yellow lentils, soak them in hot water for a while and throw away the resulting cloudy, white liquid. Then wash the lentils several times to get rid of most of the oil. Yellow lentils store well for up to 6 months in clean, dry containers. Though lentils are processed before packing, it is a good idea to spread them on a plate and extract any small stones, bits of earth or stalks before use.

Dal-roti: lentils and bread

CULINARY USE

Easy to cook, their cooking time is further reduced if the lentils are soaked for half an hour. Always add salt to the dal at the very last minute or the lentils will stay hard. Yellow lentils are mostly eaten whole, but they can also be puréed after soaking, to make a pancake batter.

The following recipes are for dishes that are common all over India. The first goes with rice and combines the sweetness of onions with the nuttiness of the lentils.

MASALA DAL
(SPICY YELLOW LENTILS)

Serves 4
Preparation time 15 minutes + 30 minutes soaking
Cooking time 40 minutes

220g (8oz) yellow lentils, soaked for 30 minutes
600ml (1pt) water
4 tablespoons sunflower oil
1 teaspoon black mustard seeds
1 teaspoon cumin seeds
Large pinch asafoetida
1 large onion, chopped
1 teaspoon ginger, shredded
1 teaspoon garlic, shredded
150g (5oz) tomatoes, chopped
1 teaspoon turmeric powder
1 teaspoon chilli powder
1 teaspoon garam masala powder
2 tablespoons coriander leaves, chopped
Salt

1 Bring the lentils to the boil and simmer in the water until very soft.

2 Heat the oil in a pan and add the mustard seeds. When they crackle, add the cumin and asafoetida.

3 Stir a few times and add the onion. Fry until golden, then add the ginger and garlic.

4 Add all the other ingredients and cook until a thick paste is formed.

5 Pour in the lentils, add salt and bring to the boil. Reduce the heat and simmer for 5 minutes. Serve very hot.

This recipe is for a main dish which uses the lentils for texture and nutritive value. It is especially popular in Maharashtra where radish is grown in abundance.

MOOLI DAL SUBZI
(RADISH AND LENTILS)

Serves 4
Preparation time 20 minutes
Cooking time 30 minutes

3 tablespoons sunflower oil
1 teaspoon black mustard seeds
Large pinch asafoetida
12 curry leaves
4 tablespoons yellow lentils, washed and drained
600g (1¼lb) Indian white radish (mooli - available in Indian shops), chopped finely
1 teaspoon turmeric powder
1 teaspoon chilli powder
1 teaspoon coriander powder
1 teaspoon cumin powder
Salt
150ml (¼pt) water
4 kokum

1 Heat the oil in a pan and add the mustard seeds. When they crackle, add the asafoetida, curry leaves and lentils. Fry for a minute.

2 Add the radish and stir-fry for 5 minutes.

3 Sprinkle in all the powder spices and salt and mix well. Then add the water, reduce the heat and cook until the lentils are soft.

4 Add the kokum and stir-fry on a high heat to evaporate all the liquid. Serve hot.

Mooli Dal Subzi

Macrotyloma uniflorum

HORSE GRAM

(KULITH)

The farmers of central India are hard-working folk who need robust, wholesome food to sustain them through long periods of hectic activity. One of the main providers of this energy is horse gram. Every day the women of the farming community pack a lunch of rotis, horse gram curry and a raw onion and carry it to the fields where their men are working. The lunch break is spent under a shady tree after which work continues until dusk.

Women carrying meals to the workers in the fields

HOW IT GROWS

Horse gram is grown extensively in India. It is a hardy crop that does well in a wide range of soils where there is little rainfall. When the seed-bearing pods mature, they are picked, dried and beaten with wooden poles. The seeds thus separated are cleaned and sorted.

APPEARANCE AND TASTE

Small, brown and oval, these seeds resemble whole red lentils. Horse gram has a powerful, earthy aroma and a strong, fresh taste. The fragrance is reminiscent of freshly cut hay.

BUYING AND STORING

Horse gram may be a little difficult to find. Do not confuse it with whole red lentils. It is available whole or ground to a grey-brown flour.

Horse gram provides essential protein in farmers' diets

MEDICINAL AND OTHER USES

A teaspoonful of horse gram boiled in about 0.5 litre (¾pt) of water makes an infusion which is prescribed for colds and high blood pressure. Horse gram is also used as cattle feed and as a green manure.

CULINARY USES

Horse gram is sprouted and used in stir-fries or curries. It is also powdered and made into a thick soup which is served with rice and ghee. The seeds go well with fried garlic and are combined with mustard seeds and asafoetida. On the west coast, horse gram is cooked with grated, roasted coconut and peppercorns.

The following 2 dishes are products of the same procedure. The soup is a light dish with a musky undernote which is normally eaten with rice. The stir-fry goes as well with toast as it does with rotis. Although it is considered a main dish, it can quite easily be served as a salad with fried chicken or kababs. Try it mixed with yoghurt for an unusual accompaniment.

KULITH SAAR
(HORSE GRAM SOUP)

Serves 4
Preparation time 5 minutes + 8 hours soaking + 8 hours sprouting
Cooking time 30 minutes

300g (10oz) horse gram, soaked for 8 hours + left to sprout for 8 hours
900ml (1½pt) water
Salt
6 kokum
2 teaspoons sunflower oil
4 cloves garlic, coarsely crushed

1 Simmer the horse gram in the water until soft. Remove from the heat and drain, reserving the gram for the next recipe.

2 Add the salt and kokum to the water.

3 Heat the oil and fry the garlic until it just begins to change colour.

4 Pour over the seasoned gram water. Serve very hot.

Ground horse gram

Kulith Saar and Kulith Usal

KULITH USAL
(HORSE GRAM STIR-FRY)

Serves 4
Preparation time 15 minutes
Cooking time 30 minutes

300g (10oz) cooked horse gram from the recipe above
1 teaspoon turmeric powder
1 teaspoon chilli powder
2 tablespoons sunflower oil
1 teaspoon black mustard seeds
Salt
6 kokum
150g (5oz) coconut, grated if fresh, or desiccated

1 Mix the horse gram, turmeric and chilli powder.

2 Heat the oil in a pan and add the mustard seeds. When they pop, add the horse gram mixture and salt and stir-fry for a minute.

3 Take off the heat and add the kokum and coconut. Mix well and serve hot. Remove the kokum after an hour or so if you are not serving the stir-fry immediately, or it will make the dish too sour.

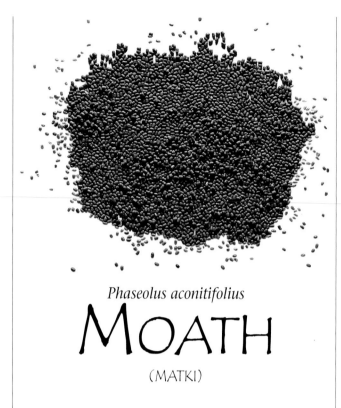

Phaseolus aconitifolius

MOATH

(MATKI)

Pulses are a rich source of protein and carbohydrate. They contain calcium, iron, phosphorus and many other minerals and vitamins. To make these nutrients more digestible, it is necessary to sprout pulses. Moath is one such pulse which improves greatly in taste as well as nutritive value by sprouting.

Moath is served on the street from fast-food stalls

HOW IT GROWS

As it is the most drought-resistant of all pulses, moath is grown widely in dry or sandy areas. It helps prevent erosion of soil by the wind. Moath seeds grow in small pods on thick, matted bushes. In the winter, the pods are picked, dried and threshed, either by hand or mechanically.

APPEARANCE AND TASTE

Small, elongated beans with a brown skin and a brownish-yellow interior, they have a nutty flavour and a strong, earthy smell.

BUYING AND STORING

Because of its size and colour, moath is especially prone to adulteration and almost always has dust and small stones mixed into it. Always pick out the impurities before use. Store in an airtight jar for 3 months.

CULINARY USES

Moath is cooked dry with spices, coconut and fresh coriander. It can also be made into a thick purée to be eaten with rice. Sprouted moath is stir-fried with a few spices and eaten with hunks of freshly-baked bread called *pau*. This makes a filling snack when sprinkled with fine, fried noodles to add crunch. Moath goes particularly well with fried onions which add a touch of sweetness to the nuttiness of the beans.

This recipe comes from the state of Karnataka where it is served with rice and fresh vegetables.

MATKI AMBAT
(MOATH AND COCONUT CURRY)

Serves 4
Preparation time 20 minutes + overnight soaking + 8 hours sprouting
Cooking time 30 minutes

300g (10oz) moath, soaked overnight and sprouted for 8 hours
1 teaspoon turmeric powder
Salt
3 tablespoons sunflower oil
1 teaspoon coriander seeds
4 dried red chillies, deseeded and crumbled
150 (5oz) coconut, grated if fresh, or desiccated
1 teaspoon tamarind pulp, diluted in a little water
1 medium onion, chopped finely

1 Boil the moath in water until soft. Stir in the turmeric and salt.

2 Heat 1 tablespoon of the oil in a pan and fry the coriander seeds and chillies until brown.

3 Grind with the coconut and tamarind to a smooth paste, adding a little water if necessary.

4 Add this mixture to the moath.

5 Heat the remaining oil and fry the onions until golden.

6 Pour over the curry and bring to the boil once. Serve hot.

This second recipe is a nutritious, vegetarian dish that can be served as a salad.

MATKI USAL
(MOATH STIR-FRY)

Serves 4
Preparation time 20 minutes +
  overnight soaking + 8
  hours sprouting
Cooking time 20 minutes

3 tablespoons sunflower oil
1 large onion, chopped
300g (10oz) moath, soaked overnight and left to sprout for 8 hours
4 green chillies, slit lengthways so the seeds are exposed, but the chilli is not broken in 2
1 teaspoon turmeric powder
1 teaspoon coriander powder
1 teaspoon cumin powder
Salt
½ teaspoon sugar

2 tablespoons coriander leaves, chopped
4 tablespoons coconut, grated if fresh, or desiccated

1 Heat the oil in a pan and fry the onions until golden.

2 Add the sprouted moath, chillies, powder spices, salt and sugar and stir well.

3 Add a little water and cook on a low heat until soft but not mushy.

4 Stir over a high heat to dry up any remaining water. Take off the heat and serve sprinkled with coriander leaves and coconut.

Phaseolus aureus

MUNG BEANS

(MOONG DAL)

Split mung beans

Split mung beans, skinned

Mung beans, or green gram, are the most versatile of all the lentils. They are used in *pani-poorie*, a roadside snack of crisp, hollow fritters filled with boiled potatoes, sprouted mung beans and tangy chutneys. At the opposite end of the range, they are cooked over a low heat with generous amounts of clarified butter or ghee, sugar, nuts and spices to make one of the richest desserts ever created. 'Bean sprouts', commonly available everywhere, are actually sprouted mung beans and are easy to grow at home.

HOW THEY GROW

The small mung bean plant grows all over India as a rain-fed crop. The beans, which grow inside pods, are threshed out after the pods are dried – either on the plant or in the sun. Mung beans are left in their skin or split. There is also a variety which is split but left in the skin.

APPEARANCE AND TASTE

Whole mung beans, or green gram, are small, oval, and olive-green in colour. When split, they are small, flattish and yellow. Whole mung beans have a stronger flavour than the split ones. They are rather chewy and musky. The yellow, split mung beans are extremely easy to cook, need no soaking and are easy to digest.

BUYING AND STORING

The whole beans and split ones are quite different and are seldom interchangeable so you will need to get both, depending on what you plan to make. Store in airtight containers for up to 4 months.

MEDICINAL AND OTHER USES

Split mung beans are recommended boiled and mashed for babies as an easily digestible source of protein. They are also useful in geriatric and convalescent diets.

CULINARY USES

Whole mung beans need soaking to reduce cooking time. Split mung beans are soaked overnight and ground with water to make a batter for pancakes and fritters. To sprout mung beans, wash in several changes of water. Then put them into a dish with just enough water to cover them and leave the dish in a warm place. Change the water every morning and night for 1–2 days. By this time the beans will have sprouted. The smaller the sprouts, the better the flavour. In India, lentils and pulses are sprouted by soaking them overnight and then wrapping them in a wet cloth for a day.

Whole mung beans

Mung beans grow all over India as a rain-fed crop

Spiced rice and beans is one of the most complete and quick meals you can make. Served with a hot pickle it is sure to stimulate a dull appetite. This is a dish I make when I come home from a long journey.

MOONG DAL KHICHDI
(SPICED RICE AND BEANS)

Serves 4
Preparation time 15 minutes
Cooking time 30 minutes

1 tablespoon sunflower oil
1 teaspoon cumin seeds
6 black peppercorns
4 cloves
Large pinch asafoetida
16 curry leaves
4 green chillies, slit lengthways
  so the seeds are exposed, but
  the chilli is not broken in 2
300g (10oz) any Indian rice,
  washed and drained
150g (5oz) split mung beans
  (moong dal)
900ml (1½pt) hot water
Salt
2 teaspoons ghee

1 Heat the oil in a pan and add the cumin. When it changes colour, add the peppercorns, cloves, asafoetida, curry leaves and chillies.

2 Fry for a minute, add the rice and mung beans.

3 Fry until shiny, then add the water and salt.

4 Bring to the boil, reduce the heat, cover the pan and simmer until the rice is fluffy and dry.

5 Serve hot, drizzled with melted ghee.

This dish can be served as a lovely snack or accompaniment to a main meal. There are 2 ways of making it – one that is followed in the north and the other in the south. This is the southern version, which is harder to come by outside India.

DAHI WADA
(DUMPLINGS IN YOGHURT)

Serves 4
Preparation time 20 minutes + 2
  hours soaking
Cooking time 30 minutes

600ml (1pt) thick yoghurt
Salt
2 teaspoons sugar
2 teaspoons sunflower oil
1 teaspoon black mustard seeds
1 teaspoon cumin seeds
12 curry leaves
4 dried red chillies, stalks
  removed and deseeded

For the dumplings:
220g (8oz) split mung beans
  (moong dal), washed and
  drained
60ml (2fl oz) water
1 teaspoon ginger, shredded
Large pinch of bicarbonate of
  soda
Salt
Sunflower oil for deep frying

1 Mix the yoghurt with the salt and sugar.

2 Heat the oil in a small pan and add the mustard seeds. When they pop, add the cumin seeds, curry leaves and red chillies.

3 Fry for a minute and pour into the seasoned yoghurt.

4 Grind all the dumpling ingredients except the oil to a thick batter in a blender. You may need to add more water to adjust the consistency.

Dahi Wada made with whole mung beans for a green effect

5 Heat the oil for frying in a kadai or wok. Drop in a ladleful of batter, reduce the heat and fry until it is golden. If the oil is heated to the right temperature, the dumpling should quickly rise to the surface. After frying, remove the dumpling and immerse it in a bowl of hot water. Squeeze out all the water carefully and immerse it in the yoghurt mixture. Proceed similarly for the rest of the dumplings. Chill and serve.

Note: If you plan to serve them later, immerse the softened dumplings in the chilled yoghurt at the last moment.

Phaseolus limensis
BUTTER BEANS
(PAVTA)

Every Indian pantry stores at least 5 different types of pulses. These are cooked on their own or combined with vegetables and meat to accompany rice and rotis. Butter beans are one of the pulses that are as popular in north India as in the south. They often feature in a south Indian wedding banquet along with a variety of vegetables, rice and sweets.

Butter beans are served at wedding banquets

HOW THEY GROW

Butter beans grow in long pods. When the pods mature in winter, they are picked and dried. Then comes the threshing to separate the beans. Butter beans grow all over central India and along the west coast.

APPEARANCE AND TASTE

Butter beans are large (one of the largest beans used in Indian cookery), creamy white and flattish. They have a medium thick skin. The name shows the bean's most obvious characteristic: a buttery, smooth taste. They have a pleasant, nutty aroma.

BUYING AND STORING

You can buy dried or canned beans. Cans are time-saving though the beans may be a bit soft and disintegrate on further cooking. Dried beans are better for intense Indian cooking techniques. When buying dried beans, avoid those that are discoloured or broken. Store in an airtight container for up to 4 months.

CULINARY USES

In the south of India, butter beans are cooked with ground coconut, red chillies and tamarind and then flavoured with fried garlic. They are also combined with vegetables like aubergines, potatoes and gourds. They may be used in salads, stews, fritters or as a filling for a toasted sandwiches.

This first recipe is for a dry vegetarian dish from Maharashtra. Beans and potatoes are a world-famous combination and here they are further enhanced with spices and coconut.

PAVTA BATATA
(POTATO AND BUTTER BEANS)

Serves 4
Preparation time 10 minutes + overnight soaking
Cooking time 30 minutes

150g (5oz) butter beans, soaked overnight
3 tablespoons sunflower oil
1 teaspoon black mustard seeds
Large pinch of asafoetida
1 medium onion, chopped finely
i teaspoon turmeric powder
1 teaspoon chilli powder
1 teaspoon coriander powder
300g (10oz) potatoes, peeled and cubed
Salt
4 tablespoons coconut, grated if fresh, or desiccated
4 tablespoons coriander leaves, chopped

1 Cook the beans in plenty of water until they are cooked but not too soft.

2 Heat the oil in a separate pan and fry the mustard seeds. When they pop, add the asafoetida and onion. Fry until the onion becomes translucent.

3 Add the powder spices, potatoes and salt and mix well. Add a little water and cook until the potatoes are soft.

4 Gently mix in the cooked beans, coconut and coriander leaves. Serve hot.

Note: Any leftovers can be made into the patties in the next recipe, proceeding from step 3.

Wedding feast

This second recipe can be made from the leftovers of the first with a few additions.

PAVTA PATTIES
(BUTTER BEAN PATTIES)

Serves 4
Preparation time 20 minutes + overnight soaking
Cooking time 20 minutes

150g (5oz) butter beans, soaked overnight
300g (10oz) potatoes, peeled, boiled and mashed
1 teaspoon turmeric powder
1 teaspoon chilli powder
1 teaspoon garam masala powder
5 tablespoons sunflower oil
4 teaspoons flour

1 Boil the beans in plenty of water until very soft. Drain.

2 Knead all the ingredients (including the beans), except the flour and oil into a stiff dough.

3 Make equal-sized balls of this dough and flatten slightly.

4 Heat the oil in a frying pan.

5 Roll each patty in the flour, shake off any excess and shallow-fry until crisp and brown.

6 Drain on absorbent paper and serve hot with sweet tamarind chutney.

Phaseolus vulgaris
RED KIDNEY BEANS
(RAJMA)

At the temple dedicated to the goddess Vaishno Devi in Kashmir, a mosaic of roadside restaurants welcomes the weary visitors with a traditional meal of kidney beans and rice. Steaming red bean curry is ladled over snow-white rice and handed to the guests as they warm themselves around a charcoal fire.

Outside the temple of Vaishno Devi

HOW THEY GROW

Kidney beans grow on annual climbing plants, trained on poles or nets, bearing pods which contain seeds. The pods are plucked when mature and dried in the sun or are left to dry on the plant. They are then threshed to remove the beans. Red kidney beans are grown in many places around the world and can be found in the cuisines of Spain and Latin America.

APPEARANCE AND TASTE

Large and deep maroon in colour, good red kidney beans are up to 1.5cm (¾in) long. They tend to lend their colour to the dish in which they are cooked. The beans have a strong musky and nutty aroma and a full, chewy taste. The skin is thick and has a slightly sweet aftertaste.

BUYING AND STORING

Buy brightly coloured, fat beans that are shiny and smooth. Store in an airtight container for 4 months.

CULINARY USES

The beans go into chilli con carne and many wholesome soups and stews. The soaking and cooking of red kidney beans has always been a subject of debate as they contain a poisonous resin that is not destroyed by light cooking. To be absolutely safe, soak the beans in water for 8–10 hours, until they double in size. Then they must be cooked thoroughly, preferably by boiling for at least 12 minutes. In India, city housewives pressure-cook kidney beans to ensure that they are completely done. The beans go well with lamb, onions and tomatoes. Try them in salads or with vegetables.

This first recipe is a slight variation on the Kashmiri dish served at the festival of Vaishno Devi. The addition of black lentils changes its consistency slightly and adds to its nutritive value.

KALI DAL
(CREAMY BLACK LENTILS AND BEANS)

Serves 4
Preparation time 30 minutes + overnight soaking
Cooking time 1½ hours

5 tablespoons sunflower oil
2 teaspoons cumin seeds
1 medium onion, chopped finely
1 teaspoon ginger, shredded
1 teaspoon garlic, minced
300g (10oz) tomatoes, chopped
150g (5oz) red kidney beans, soaked overnight and drained
150g (5oz) whole black lentils, soaked overnight and drained
1 teaspoon turmeric powder
1 teaspoon chilli powder
1 teaspoon coriander powder
1 teaspoon garam masala powder
Large pinch of asafoetida

Salt
Large pinch of sugar
900ml (1½pt) hot water
4 tablespoons double cream
2 tablespoons ghee
2 tablespoons coriander leaves, chopped

1 Heat the oil in a heavy pan and add the cumin. Fry for a minute and add the onion.

2 When it turns golden, reduce the heat, add the ginger and garlic and fry well.

3 Add the tomatoes and fry until they are soft.

4 Stir in the red kidney beans and the black lentils.

5 Mix in all the spices, salt and sugar and add the water. Bring to the boil.

6 Reduce the heat, cover and cook until the beans are tender. You may need to add water to thin down the bean purée. The consistency should be that of a pouring batter.

7 Take the pan off the heat and stir in the cream. Pour the ghee over, sprinkle the coriander on top and serve very hot with boiled rice.

This next salad recipe includes both north as well as south Indian ingredients. This filling dish can be served on its own with roti.

RAJMA KA SALAAD
(RED KIDNEY BEAN SALAD)

Serves 4
Preparation time 15 minutes + overnight soaking
Cooking time 45 minutes

150g (5oz) red kidney beans, soaked overnight and drained
1 large onion, chopped finely
Salt
½ teaspoon sugar
2 teaspoons lemon juice
2 tablespoons sunflower oil
1 teaspoon black mustard seeds
1 teaspoon cumin seeds
Large pinch of asafoetida
10 curry leaves
2 tablespoons coriander leaves, chopped

1 Boil the beans in plenty of water. Drain after checking that they are thoroughly cooked.

2 Mix in the onions, salt, sugar and lemon juice.

3 Heat the oil in a small pan and add the mustard seeds. When they pop, add the cumin, asafoetida and curry leaves.

4 Fry for a minute and pour the spices and oil over the seasoned beans.

5 Add the fresh coriander leaves and stir together.

Rajma ka Salaad

Dried green peas

Pisum sativum

DRIED PEAS

(MUTTER)

Peas are eaten in some form or another in most countries of the world. They are amongst the earth's most versatile vegetables. Cherished for their colour, flavour and adaptability, they lend themselves equally to the salty mildness of Western food or to the fiery zing of Indian cookery. They make good starters, snacks, soups, main courses or salads so it is hardly surprising that they are dried for use when no longer available fresh. The pea plant is believed to have originated in western Asia and was later cultivated by the Hebrews, Greeks, Romans and Persians. In those days of no refrigeration, the only way to store them was to dry them.

Dried white peas

HOW THEY GROW

Peas grow in pods on small bushes. There are different varieties and the ones that are dried are green, black and white. The pods are plucked when mature and laid out to dry in the sun. The thick shells dry until they resemble parchment and become brittle enough to split open. The peas are then extracted.

APPEARANCE AND TASTE

All 3 varieties of pea – black, white and green – are small, round and smooth. Reconstituted peas (soaked and boiled) have an earthy smell and taste quite different from fresh ones.

BUYING AND STORING

Avoid buying dried peas that are wrinkled or discoloured. Good ones should be even in colour and hard. If they are soft to the touch, they are probably old.

CULINARY USES

Dried peas must be soaked for 8–12 hours before use. Don't soak too much at a time because they will absorb water and swell. They go especially well with garlic and coconut. Boil the soaked peas separately in salted water, until completely tender. Drain and add to curries, soups or salads. They can also be puréed and served with the main course. Dried pea purée enriched with milk and cream makes a delicious soup.

Pea and coconut curries are an important part of many coastal communities' cuisine

Dried black peas

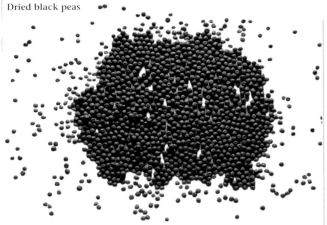

Peas are such an international favourite that every country has a tempting array of dishes based on them. The first of the following recipes is a sinfully rich way of eating peas – steeped in cream, but they taste absolutely scrumptious!

MALAI MUTTER
(PEAS IN CREAM)

Serves 4
Preparation time 20 minutes + overnight soaking
Cooking time 45 minutes

150g (5oz) dried green peas, soaked overnight
3 tablespoons sunflower oil
1 teaspoon cumin seeds
1 large onion, sliced
150g (5oz) potatoes, peeled and grated
1 teaspoon chilli powder
1 teaspoon coriander powder
300ml (½pt) milk
Salt
300ml (½pt) single cream

1 Boil the peas in plenty of water until soft. Drain.

2 Heat the oil in a heavy pan and add the cumin. Fry for a minute and add the onion.

3 When it becomes translucent, add the potatoes and spices. Stir to prevent the potatoes from sticking. Add the milk and cook on a low heat until soft.

4 Add the cooked peas and salt and simmer for a minute.

5 Remove from the heat and add the cream. Reheat gently, without boiling, before serving.

This recipe is a colourful addition to the dinner table and is easy to make.

MUTTER PULAO
(PEA PULAO)

Serves 4
Preparation time 20 minutes + overnight soaking
Cooking time 1 hour

150g (5oz) green, white and black peas, mixed, soaked overnight
Salt
4 teaspoons sunflower oil
1 teaspoon cumin seeds
4cm (1½in) stick cinnamon
300g (10oz) basmati rice
300ml (½pt) hot water
2 tomatoes to garnish

1 Boil the peas in plenty of water with salt until soft, and drain.

2 Heat the oil in a heavy bottomed pan and add the cumin seeds and cinnamon. Fry for a minute.

3 Add the rice and fry until it is translucent and shiny.

4 Add salt and the hot water, stir, cover partially and cook until the rice is fluffy and dry.

5 Gently mix the peas into the rice.

6 Garnish the pulao with decorative wedges of tomato and serve hot with a curry.

Mutter Pulao

Vigna sinensis

BLACK-EYED BEANS

(LOBHIA/CHAWLI)

Feasting and fasting are both equally valued in the Indian scheme of worship and celebration. So while some festivals are marked by sumptuous delicacies, others are days of austere meditation and quiet contemplation. With these days of fasting are associated certain permissible foods which are considered 'pure' and peaceful. Prime among these foods are pulses, fruits and nuts. Sprouted beans, cooked without a trace of spice, sliced fruit and roasted nuts are eaten. A favourite is the black-eyed bean, eaten for its wholesomeness and ability to taste wonderful without any spices. These beans are in demand during feasts as well, when they are added to bubbling curries with any number of spices.

HOW THEY GROW

Produced in pods on small bushy plants, black-eyed beans are grown in the central and northern part of India and vast quantities are sorted, cleaned and packed for export to the USA, Europe and the Middle East.

APPEARANCE AND TASTE

These large, oblong beans are creamy-white, with a black 'eye' on one side. The skin is quite thick. They have a subtle, nutty aroma and a rich, creamy taste that is slightly earthy.

Black-eyed beans feature in women's feasts and fasts

BUYING AND STORING

Old beans sometimes get a rusty-brown tinge and become wrinkled, so avoid these. The best black-eyed beans are plump, even and unbroken. Store in an airtight jar, but consume within 4 months.

CULINARY USES

Soak overnight to soften the pebble-hard beans and boil in plenty of water. They can then be cooked with coconut or curry leaves as in south India, with mustard seeds and asafoetida as in the west and with onions, ginger and garlic as in the north. They are eaten with rotis and rice and make a good, nourishing snack on toast. The flavour of coriander leaves seems to complement black-eyed beans.

The following recipes exploit the musky nuttiness of black-eyed beans to the full. The first dish is a sort of stew that is eaten with rotis or rice. Full of healthy nutrients, it is a meal in itself and leftovers can be mashed up, combined with mashed potatoes and shallow-fried as patties for the next meal.

Pods of black-eyed beans for sale

Lobhia ka Salaad

LOBHIA KI SUBZI
(SPICY BLACK-EYED BEANS)

Serves 4
Preparation time 15 minutes +
  overnight soaking
Cooking time 15 minutes

3 tablespoons sunflower oil
1 teaspoon cumin seeds
Large pinch of asafoetida
1 medium onion, sliced finely
2 teaspoons ginger, shredded
2 teaspoons garlic, shredded
300g (10oz) black-eyed beans,
  soaked overnight
1 teaspoon chilli powder
1 teaspoon turmeric powder
150g (5oz) tomatoes, chopped
1 teaspoon garam masala
  powder
½ teaspoon sugar
Salt
Coriander leaves, chopped, to
  garnish

1 Heat the oil in a wok or kadai. Add the cumin seeds, fry for a minute and then add the asafoetida.

2 Stir once and add the onion. Stir-fry until golden.

3 Add the ginger and garlic and mix well.

4 Drop in the beans, sprinkle in the chilli powder and turmeric and stir. Fry for a minute.

5 Add the tomatoes, garam masala, sugar and salt and mix. Add a little water, cover and bring to the boil. Reduce the heat and simmer until done. The beans should be soft but should retain their shape. Mash a few to add thickness to the sauce.

6 Serve hot, garnished with coriander.

This second recipe is for a salad that works well with any simple meal.

LOBHIA KA SALAAD
(BLACK-EYED BEAN SALAD)

Serves 4
Preparation time 10 minutes +
  overnight soaking
Cooking time 15 minutes

150g (5oz) black-eyed beans,
  soaked overnight
Salt
1 teaspoon sugar
4 tablespoons coconut, grated if
  fresh, or desiccated
2 teaspoons raisins
1 teaspoon lemon juice
2 tablespoons coriander leaves,
  chopped

1 Boil the beans in plenty of water until soft but not mushy. Drain.

2 Cool completely and mix gently with all the other ingredients. Serve at room temperature on a decorative plate.

DAILY BREAD

Cereals and Flours

Oryza sativa

BASMATI RICE

(BASMATI CHAAVAL)

The flavour of basmati rice is celebrated the world over. Its name conjures up visions of lush, green paddy fields being watered by the snow-fed rivers of the Himalayas. Basmati is considered to be the king of rice and, as such, in India it is reserved for special occasions or particular dishes. The ubiquitous *rice kheer,* which is a richer version of the Western rice pudding, is a delightful confection of basmati rice, milk, sugar, spices and nuts cooked on a slow heat until it resembles condensed cream. It is mentioned in ancient Indian epics and scriptures. India was one of the earliest countries to grow rice. From here it travelled first to Egypt, then via Greece, Portugal and Italy, to America. Historians estimate that it was first cultivated at least 3000 years ago.

APPEARANCE AND TASTE

The grains of basmati rice are white, long and very silky to touch. They are even in size and clean-looking. The fragrance is unmistakable. Rich and wholesome, it has a pure scent and a fresh, uncluttered taste.

HOW IT GROWS

Basmati rice grows in the foothills of the Himalayas and some parts of north India. Rice needs a hot climate and plenty of water, so the paddy fields are kept flooded. After the rice is sown, the plantlets are transplanted into the main field. Rice plants grow to a height of about 1.5m (5ft)

The god Rama is said to have been conceived when his mother was given a divine blessing in the form of *rice kheer*

and are thin and wispy. They bear rice seeds in slender ears. When mature, the rice plants are harvested, tied in sheaves and dried. They are then threshed to separate the rice grains. The grains are cleaned, husked and processed by rasping to give white rice. This is further polished to improve its appearance. Rice is an excellent energy-giving food containing 79% starch but needs to be supplemented with lentils, vegetables and fats to make a balanced meal.

BUYING AND STORING

Basmati rice is available whole or as broken grains which are much cheaper. It is not ground into rice flour as it is quite expensive. Rice is like wine – it gets better with age. Good basmati is left to mature in controlled conditions for up to 10 years. Old rice cooks better and remains fluffy whereas new rice becomes sticky when cooked. The only way to know whether the rice is old is to ask, but most brands of packaged rice are suitable. Broken basmati has the flavour but not the texture and appearance of whole rice. Store in the package that the rice comes in or remove to an airtight container and store for up 3 months. Make sure that no moisture or insects get to the rice.

MEDICINAL AND OTHER USES

Kanji is the liquid left after boiling rice and is high-energy nourishment given to patients recovering from influenza, colds and coughs. Rice cooked with a few mung beans is the best food for people with sluggish digestion. Rice is considered sacred in India and forms a part of every ritual. Mixed raw with red *sindoor,* the powder used to paint a red dot on the forehead, it is showered on bridal couples and guests-of-honour.

Paddy fields of basmati rice at the foot of the Himalayas

Basmati rice crop

CULINARY USES

Although there are as many ways of cooking perfect rice as there are rice eaters, one way is to wash the rice gently but thoroughly (to avoid breaking the grains) until the water runs clear. Soak the rice in plenty of water for half an hour. Then drain it and put it along with double its quantity of fresh water and a pinch of salt in a saucepan. Bring to the boil, stirring occasionally. Reduce the heat, cover partially and simmer for 10 minutes. Cover completely and allow to cook for 5 more minutes. Indians always serve rice piping hot. Basmati rice is made into appetising biryanis, pulaos, sweets, stuffings and snacks.

The following recipes depend on basmati rice for aroma. This first dish is an easy-to-make, quick pulao.

GUCCHI PULAO
(MUSHROOM RICE)

Serves 4
Preparation time 15 minutes
Cooking time 25 minutes

4 teaspoons sunflower oil
150g (5oz) mushrooms, sliced
300g (10oz) basmati rice,
  washed and drained
600ml (1pt) hot water
Salt

1 Heat the oil in a heavy-bottomed pan and add the mushrooms. Fry until they turn dark.

2 Add the rice and fry until it is translucent and shiny.

3 Pour in the water, add salt and bring to the boil.

4 Reduce the heat, cover partially and simmer until the rice is fluffy and dry. The mushrooms will rise to the top, so gently fold them into the rice with a fork. Serve hot with a meat or vegetable curry.

Gucchi Pulao

This recipe, from Maharashtra, is full of subtle nuances and tastes.

KESHAR BHAT
(SWEET SAFFRON RICE)

Serves 4
Preparation time 30 minutes
Cooking time 30 minutes

8 tablespoons ghee
6 cloves
4cm (1½in) stick cinnamon
300g (10oz) basmati rice,
  washed and drained
600ml (1pt) hot water
1 teaspoon saffron strands
2 teaspoons warm milk
300g (10oz) caster sugar
½ teaspoon cardamom powder
½ teaspoon nutmeg powder
2 teaspoons raisins
2 tablespoons flaked almonds

1 Heat half the ghee in a heavy-bottomed pan and fry the cloves and cinnamon. Add the rice and fry until it is shiny. Pour in the hot water and bring to the boil. Reduce the heat, partially cover and simmer until fluffy and dry.

2 Mix the saffron into the milk and gently fold into the rice.

3 Add all the other ingredients and mix.

4 Cook on a low heat until all the ingredients are well blended. Serve warm, drizzled with a little ghee.

Oryza sativa
PATNA RICE
(PATNA CHAAVAL)

The harvesting of crops begins when the autumn full moon is ready to rise on the horizon. This event coincides with the festival of *Navanna Purnima* – the moonlit night of new food. On this day, freshly harvested rice is offered to the gods and lamps are lit in the moonlight. Rice has always been a symbol of plenty in Hindu tradition. According to custom, married women in India are honoured and wished a life of plenty by presenting them with a coconut, a handful of rice and a length of fabric on festive occasions. The throwing of rice is associated with all weddings, whether Hindu, Christian or Islamic.

HOW IT GROWS

Patna is the name of a town in north India from which this rice, which grows in the region, takes its name. It is processed in a similar manner to basmati rice.

APPEARANCE AND TASTE

Patna rice is also long-grained but is less hard than basmati rice. It is milky-white in colour, unlike basmati which is translucent. The grains have slightly rounded edges. Pleasant and aromatic, Patna rice has an earthy, mild taste.

BUYING AND STORING

Rice is usually sold in bags, packets or boxes. In India most people buy a large bag of daily rice like Patna and a small one of basmati for special dishes. Store Patna rice in a dry, airtight container for up to 3 months. As it is relatively cheap, it is also ground into a flour for batters and coatings.

At the women's festival of *Otii bharan* gifts of rice and coconut are exchanged

CULINARY USES

It is difficult to imagine an Indian meal without rice and in south and coastal India especially, it is eaten at every meal. It is flavoured with lemon, tamarind, vegetables, lentils, nuts and yoghurt. In India, the rice is always fluffy and a good cook produces cooked rice with each grain light and separate. Patna rice is often soaked overnight with some split lentils and ground into a coarse batter. This is fried to make fritters, poured over a hot griddle and made into pancakes or steamed to make airy, spongy dumplings. The batter is left to ferment and rise which gives even more spring to the finished product.

Patna rice wholesale market

Pulaos add an instant boost to a simple meal and are quite simple to make. This pulao is one of the easiest and adds a delicate fragrance to a meal.

JEERA PULAO
(CUMIN-FLAVOURED RICE)

Serves 4
Preparation time 10 minutes
Cooking time 30 minutes

2 tablespoons ghee
1 teaspoon cumin seeds
300g (10oz) Patna rice, washed
   and drained
½ teaspoon salt
600ml (1pt) hot water

1 Heat the ghee in a heavy-bottomed pan and add the cumin seeds. When they pop, add the rice and fry until it is shiny (about 3 minutes).

2 Add the salt and water, stir and bring to the boil. Cover the pan partially and simmer until the rice is soft and dry. Check that the inside of each grain is cooked by mashing one between your forefinger and thumb. Serve hot with a lentil purée.

This dish is attractive enough to be a centrepiece and adds drama to a special meal. Choose firm, red tomatoes that are evenly shaped and stand upright.

BHARWAN TAMATER
(STUFFED TOMATOES)

Serves 4
Preparation time 15 minutes
Cooking time 5 minutes

2 tablespoons sunflower oil
1 teaspoon cumin seeds
1 large onion, chopped finely
8 tablespoons mushrooms,
   chopped finely
1 teaspoon turmeric powder
1 teaspoon chilli powder
1 teaspoon coriander powder
150g (5oz) cooked Patna rice
2 tablespoons coriander leaves,
   chopped
Salt
4 large tomatoes
Coriander sprigs to garnish

1 Heat the oil in a pan and add the cumin seeds. When they pop, add the onions and fry until translucent.

2 Stir in the mushrooms and the spices and cook for about 5 minutes.

3 Add the rice, coriander leaves and salt and mix well. Take off the heat and reserve.

4 Cut the tops off the tomatoes. Scoop out the flesh inside and set aside to use for some other dish.

5 Fill the tomatoes with the rice and mushroom mixture and serve at room temperature, each tomato garnished with a sprig of coriander.

Bharwan Tamater

OTHER USES

Rice plays a major role in all Hindu rituals and sacraments. It is strewn as a pearly carpet before the images of gods or showered on them as an offering.

Sacks of drying rice

CULINARY USES

Eaten in the same way as basmati, ambemohar and other varieties are also used for making batters, fritters and puddings. Most people eat their local rice and swear by it, claiming that after basmati, theirs is the best! However, most of these local varieties need careful cooking as they can turn out sticky. Do not overcook.

Oryza sativa

AMBEMOHAR

AND ALL OTHER INDIAN RICE

There are innumerable varieties of rice in India and ambemohar is one of the more important ones because it is one of the better tasting. However, it is not readily available outside India. But there are many that are and they include: jeerasul, surti kolam, vambhog, sonachandi, siddha and sella. In a Hindu marriage, when stepping over the threshold of the new home, the bride must overturn a measure of rice with her toe with some force. The resulting spray of rice is a symbol of the good fortune that she has brought with her. Rice is a part of every sacrament and special occasion as it is a sign of purity and fruitfulness.

APPEARANCE AND TASTE

Ambemohar rice has roundish grains that are creamy-white and smooth. It has a pleasant flavour although not comparable to that of the more expensive basmati.

BUYING AND STORING

In India, some houses have a special rice and wheat store-room. Here, big jute sacks of cereals would be stored and an earthy fragrance would linger in the home. Today small bags are available and can easily be accommodated on the kitchen shelf. Ask for old rice – the older, the better – and store in an absolutely dry, airtight container.

Rice used in a *Kutchi*-community wedding ritual, Gujarat

Although I've used ambemohar rice in these recipes you can use any rice that is fragrant and not sticky. The tamarind rice is typical of south India and can be a meal in itself.

PULI SHAADAM
(TAMARIND RICE)

Serves 4
Preparation time 30 minutes
Cooking time 30 minutes

*300g (10oz) ambemohar or any
  Indian rice
600ml (1pt) hot water
5 tablespoons sunflower oil
½ teaspoon fenugreek seeds
Large pinch of asafoetida
4 dried red chillies, deseeded
  and crumbled
1 teaspoon coriander seeds
1 teaspoon split black lentils
1 teaspoon split gram lentils
  (channa dal)
2 teaspoons tamarind pulp,
  diluted in a little water
Salt
1 teaspoon black mustard seeds
2 tablespoons cashew nuts
10 curry leaves*

1 Boil the rice in water and cook until dry and fluffy.

2 Heat half the oil in a pan and fry the fenugreek, asafoetida, chillies, coriander seeds and lentils.

3 When the lentils turn gold, grind coarsely in the blender.

4 Put the tamarind and salt in a pan and add the ground mixture. Cook until the tamarind is thick and the paste is well blended.

5 Mix the rice and the tamarind paste.

6 Heat the remaining oil and fry the mustard seeds. When they pop, add the cashew nuts and curry leaves. Fry for a minute and pour over the rice. Serve hot.

This recipe is for a biryani that is quick and festive. Serve it at parties and wait for the compliments that will follow.

JHINGE KA PULAO
(RICE WITH PRAWNS)

Serves 4
Preparation time 30 minutes
Cooking time 30 minutes

*3 tablespoons sunflower oil
1 teaspoon cumin seeds
1 large onion, chopped finely
1 teaspoon ginger, shredded
1 teaspoon garlic, shredded*

*300g (10oz) raw prawns,
  shelled and deveined
300g (10oz) ambemohar rice
1 teaspoon turmeric powder
1 teaspoon chilli powder
1 teaspoon coriander powder
Salt
4 tablespoons tomato ketchup
600ml (1pt) hot water
4 tablespoons coriander leaves,
  chopped*

1 Heat the oil in a heavy-bottomed pan and fry the cumin seeds. When they pop, add the onions, ginger and garlic and stir fry for a minute.

2 Add the prawns and fry until they turn opaque.

3 Stir in the rice and fry until it is shiny.

4 Sprinkle in all the powder spices, salt and tomato ketchup and mix well.

5 Pour in the hot water, cover the pan partially and cook until the rice is dry and fluffy.

6 Mix gently before serving with the fresh coriander on top.

Oryza sativa

RED PATNI RICE

A traditional, Indian rustic meal includes red rice for its treasury of vital minerals, vitamins and carbohydrates. Considered invaluable as a broad-spectrum cure, people carry a little of this rice while travelling to combat a host of health risks.

Red Patni rice field, Maharashtra

CULINARY USES

Although red rice is coarse, it can be made into several dishes that are tasty but not as sophisticated as those made with the polished varieties of rice. It is combined with ghee and a powdered spice blend made of fenugreek seeds, cumin, turmeric and roasted gram lentils. Cooked with fresh coconut and jaggery, it makes a delicious sweet. It is also cooked on its own and eaten with any curry, preferably spicy ones, flavoured with coconut. Red rice flour is made into a thick batter for pancakes.

The soup is a light, easily-digestible rice dish and can be eaten with any pickle or simple vegetable dish. Made of red rice for added nutrition, it is often given to invalids or children. The second recipe comes from south India. It is simple, fragrant and delicious.

KANJI
(THICK RICE SOUP)

Serves 4
Preparation time 5 minutes
Cooking time 15 minutes

300g (10oz) red Patni rice or
any red rice
900ml (1½pt) water
Salt
2 teaspoons ghee

1 Mix the rice and water and bring to the boil.

2 Reduce the heat and simmer until the rice is very soft. It will be fairly liquid.

3 Add salt and serve hot with the ghee poured over.

HOW IT GROWS

Red rice grows mainly in coastal, central and western India. Much of the produce is consumed locally, but some is packed and distributed to the towns and cities. All rice needs heat and humidity and the fields are characterised by crops standing immersed in water. After red rice is husked, it is parboiled in big, earthen vats and then dried for storage. This shortens the eventual cooking time.

APPEARANCE AND TASTE

The grain is short, thick and streaked with red or maroon. When the grain is milled, it gives a red flour. Red rice has a nutty aroma and a pleasant, chewy texture with a bland flavour that goes with spicy dishes.

BUYING AND STORING

Red rice is fairly difficult to find outside India, but well-stocked grocers may get bags of it from time to time. Store in an airtight jar and use within 4 months.

MEDICINAL USES

Red rice gruel or rice soup is served to convalescents, and country people carry this rice while travelling for instant pep and energy.

Drying rice in the sun

NARIAL KE CHAAVAL
(COCONUT RICE)

Serves 4
Preparation time 15 minutes
Cooking time 30 minutes

*300g (10oz) red Patni rice or
any red rice*
600ml (1pt) water

3 tablespoons sunflower oil
1 teaspoon black mustard seeds
*1 teaspoon green chillies,
chopped*
*2 teaspoons split black lentils
(urad dal)*
Large pinch of asafoetida
150g (5oz) fresh coconut, grated
Salt
2 tablespoons cashew nuts
10 curry leaves

1 Cook the rice in the water until soft, and drain.

2 Heat half of the oil and fry the mustard seeds. When they pop add the chillies, lentils and asafoetida.

3 Stir for a minute and add the coconut. Fry until the colour begins to change to golden.

4 Mix in the rice and salt. Take off the heat.

5 Heat the rest of the oil in a separate pan and fry the cashew nuts until golden.

6 Add the curry leaves and pour over the coconut rice. Serve hot with a vegetable or meat curry.

FLAKED RICE

(POHA/PAWA)

Flaked rice, sometimes known as pounded rice, is most commonly sold as *poha* or *pawa*. It is a simple food and is associated with a story of friendship that is told and retold to every Indian child. Krishna, an incarnation of Lord Vishnu, and Sudama were great friends at school but after completing their education went their separate ways, one to his golden palace, the other to a thatched hut. Several years passed and one day Sudama, now married with children, thought of visiting his friend who had become King of Dwarka. But there was one problem. Sudama was very poor and could not afford a gift for his dearest friend. Nevertheless, his wife tied a handful of moist flaked rice in a bag and gave it to Sudama to give to Krishna. When they met Sudama was ashamed and hid the little packet but Krishna soon found it and ate the simple food with relish. When Sudama returned home he was delighted and surprised to find that his hovel had been turned into a magnificent palace. He knew that his friend Krishna was responsible for the miracle. The story has a special message of friendship and love and on *Janmashtami*, Krishna's birthday, a dish of flaked rice and yoghurt is made to please the god.

MANUFACTURE

There are more than 200 varieties of rice grown in India. The lesser-known, cheaper ones are used for making products like flakes and flour. To make rice flakes, inexpensive rice is husked, cleaned and cooked in hot water. It is then flattened by rollers until wafer-thin. These flakes are mechanically dried. Depending on the weight of the rollers, flakes of varying thickness, from translucent to thick and opaque, are manufactured.

APPEARANCE AND TASTE

Rice flakes are small, about 2mm (⅛in) long, flat and greyish-white in colour. They have uneven, jagged edges and a rough texture. They are extremely light. Rice flakes have no particular aroma and a bland, gentle taste. Depending on the method of cooking, they can be soft or crunchy.

Krishna kneels in welcome to his friend Sudama

राज्य काल - द्वारका

BUYING AND STORING

As both medium and fine rice flakes are readily available, what you are going to make will determine which one you buy. Look for bags that are not too powdery, though some crumbling is inevitable. Store in an airtight jar that is free from moisture. Use up your stock within 3 months.

CULINARY USES

The flakes are very easy to cook and can make a meal in minutes. Fine flaked rice is great for making a snack, where cleaned rice flakes are fried quickly and then mixed with fried chillies, nuts, lentils and seasoned with salt and sugar.

Both the following recipes are commonly served for lunch. For these dishes you need medium rice flakes as the fine ones would disintegrate.

BATATE POHE
(SAVOURY FLAKED RICE WITH POTATOES)

Serves 4
Preparation time 20 minutes
Cooking time 15 minutes

600g (1¼lb) flaked rice, washed and drained
1 teaspoon turmeric powder
Salt
1 teaspoon sugar
2 teaspoons lemon juice
1 tablespoon sunflower oil
1 teaspoon black mustard seeds
1 teaspoon cumin seeds
Large pinch asafoetida
1 teaspoon green chillies, minced
12 curry leaves

4 tablespoons coriander leaves, chopped
4 tablespoons coconut, grated if fresh, or desiccated

1 Mix the rice, turmeric, salt, sugar and lemon juice.

2 Heat the oil in a pan and add the mustard seeds.

3 When they crackle add the cumin, asafoetida, chillies and curry leaves.

4 Fry for a minute and add the rice mixture.

5 Reduce the heat and cook, stirring, for about 10 minutes or until the spices are cooked and well blended.

6 Serve hot, garnished with coriander and coconut.

GUL POHE
(FLAKED RICE WITH JAGGERY)

Serves 4
Preparation time 25 minutes
Cooking time 0

600g (1¼lb) flaked rice, soaked for 15 minutes in water and drained
150g (5oz) jaggery, grated
6 tablespoons coconut, grated if fresh, or desiccated
1 teaspoon cardamom powder

Mix all the ingredients with your hand, kneading lightly to blend. You may need to sprinkle in a little water if the mixture is too dry. There should be no liquid visible. Serve at room temperature.

Gul Pohe

PUFFED RICE

(KURMURA/ MAMRA)

Puffed rice is the essence of many snacks and roadside fare sold in the cities and villages of India. However, in all Hindu weddings it plays a symbolic role. The ultimate witness to the union of the bride and groom is the sacred fire which burns throughout the ceremony. One of the main rituals is the *saptapadi* or the seven steps taken by the couple together around the holy fire. In western India the fire is honoured in a ceremony called *Lahyahome* where the couple pours handfuls of puffed rice into the brightly burning fire as a sacred offering; rice in all its forms is considered holy and is revered.

Sweet-seller, Jaipur

BUYING AND STORING

Once opened, a bag of puffed rice must be finished quickly as exposure to air will take the crispness away. Store in an airtight container.

MANUFACTURE

Making puffed rice is a small-scale industry. Freshly-harvested rice is dried in its husk until completely free of moisture. Then a wok or kadai half-full of sand is heated and when really hot, the rice grains are dropped in. With the heat, they pop out of their husks and puff up. Before they can burst, they are lifted out with a perforated spoon that allows the sand and husk to slip through and neatly separates the puffed rice.

OTHER USES

The husk and sand left behind in the manufacture of puffed rice is used to pack ice for transportation. Factory-made blocks of ice are distributed via bullock-cart to remote villages. To preserve them during their hot journey, the huge blocks are coated in the sand mixture and then swathed in jute cloth.

CULINARY USES

It is mainly used for snacks like *bhelpuri*, a mixture of puffed rice, chutneys and nuts. It is also rolled in melted jaggery and made into light, sweet, crackling balls or slabs. It can be combined with crushed crisps and roasted peanuts to eat with drinks. Try it as a garnish over any dry savoury dish to add contrast in colour and texture.

APPEARANCE AND TASTE

Puffed rice looks like long, white, translucent popcorn. It is light, papery and very fragile. It has no aroma and a crunchy, bland taste.

Bridal couple performing *Lahyahome*

The first of the following recipes is sold on nearly every street corner of Bombay. It is a perfect party dish. It consists of several individual ingredients that give it its sweet, salty, tangy and hot tastes.

BHEL
(SNACK MIXTURE)

Serves 4
Preparation time 45 minutes
Cooking time 0 minutes

600g (1¼lb) puffed rice
1 large onion, chopped finely
300g (10oz) potatoes, boiled, peeled and cubed
300g (10oz) chiwda (page 117) or shop-bought Bombay mix
6 tablespoons coriander leaves, chopped
4 tablespoons of unripe mango, peeled and chopped finely (optional)
150ml (¼pt) sweet tamarind chutney (Meethi Chutney page 125)
150ml (¼pt) onion chutney (Piyaz ki Chutney page 111)
Salt

Mix all the ingredients together, varying the amounts of chutneys according to taste. Make up small quantities of the mixture as required, as it becomes soggy with keeping. This dish depends entirely on your own preferences so feel free to adjust the quantities of any of the components.

Bhel

This recipe is for a crispy sweet that must be eaten with your fingers.

KURMURA LADDOO
(SWEET PUFFED RICE BALLS)

Serves 4
Preparation time 5 minutes
Cooking time 20 minutes

150g (5oz) jaggery
2 tablespoons ghee
300g (10oz) puffed rice

1 Melt the jaggery over a low heat and add the ghee.

2 Take off the heat and add the puffed rice.

3 Cool down enough to handle and shape the mixture into balls about the size of a golf ball.

4 Cool completely and store. These rice balls will keep for up to a fortnight or longer if they are stored in an airtight container.

RICE NOODLES

(CHAAVAL KE SEV)

Thirty years ago, the traditional Indian kitchen was equipped to cater for large numbers of people. There would be long afternoon sessions of snack, pickle or poppadom making and the women of the house would spend hours bottling and drying products for later use. This is changing and ready-made ingredients are fast replacing homemade ones. Rice noodles are a prime example of this shift. Exclusively made at home earlier, they are now nearly always bought.

MANUFACTURE

Rice noodles are made by cooking rice flour in water until a soft, spongy dough is formed. This is passed through perforated machines which shape the noodles. This procedure used to be performed by means of a hand-held device which operated on a corkscrew mechanism and had holes in its base. This perforated base sheet was removable and came with various sizes of hole. After shaping, the noodles were dried until hard, either in long strips or in coils.

APPEARANCE AND TASTE

Fairly thick, white and translucent, rice noodles are hard and rough-textured. They snap quite easily. Although they have little aroma, they have a pleasant taste that can be enlivened both by sugar and by salt.

BUYING AND STORING

Commonly available in Indian grocery shops, rice noodles must be consumed within 2 months of opening the pack.

CULINARY USES

Rice noodles are made into dishes in the same way as vermicelli. However, as they are thicker, they make a more filling, substantial snack. They are first stir-fried in ghee or oil and then made into a sweet with milk and sugar or into a savoury with salt and spices. They are sometimes boiled and added to sweet milk drinks as a garnish. On cooking, rice noodles become soft and slippery.

Roadside snack seller

The first recipe is from south India and can be served for breakfast or tea. It also makes a good snack while travelling and it always reminds me of long train journeys.

NOODLE UPMA
(SOUTH INDIAN NOODLES)

Serves 4
Preparation time 15 minutes
Cooking time 20 minutes

300g (10oz) rice noodles, broken into short lengths
1 tablespoon sunflower oil
1 teaspoon black mustard seeds
10 curry leaves
2 teaspoons split black lentils, (urad dal) *washed and soaked for 5 minutes*

4 green chillies, slit lengthways so seeds are exposed, but the chilli is not broken in 2
Salt
Sugar

1 Put the noodles in a pan of water and bring to the boil. Take off the heat and drain.

2 Heat the oil and fry the mustard seeds. When they pop, add the curry leaves.

3 Add the lentils and fry until golden, then add the chillies.

4 Stir in the noodles, season with salt and sugar and sprinkle some water on top. Cook until the noodles are soft.

This recipe is an Indian version of a dish that is borrowed from the neighbouring country of Myanmar.

NOODLE KI BURMESE SUBZI
(BURMESE NOODLES)

Serves 4
Preparation time 15 minutes
Cooking time 20 minutes

300g (10oz) rice noodles, broken into short lengths
3 tablespoons sunflower oil
150g (5oz) carrots, diced
4 tablespoons fresh or frozen peas, shelled
2 teaspoons dark soya sauce
2 teaspoons distilled vinegar
2 teaspoons tomato ketchup
1 teaspoon chilli powder
1 teaspoon garam masala powder
Salt
2 tablespoons coriander leaves, chopped

1 Boil the noodles in plenty of water until soft. Drain.

2 Heat the oil and add the carrots and peas. Stir-fry for a minute.

3 Add all the other ingredients, except the coriander, and mix well. Cook until the vegetables are tender but still crisp.

4 Add the cooked noodles, mix gently and serve hot, sprinkled with coriander.

Noodle Umpa

RICE FLOUR

(CHAAVAL KA ATTA)

Rice is by far the most popular cereal in India. Though wheat comes a close second, it is rice that is consumed daily in some form or another in most parts of the country. Being such a prominent and versatile ingredient, it is processed into a multitude of forms which are all equally popular and handy. Rice flour is one of these products.

MANUFACTURE

Rice flour is made from the innumerable cheap varieties of rice that are grown all over India. The rice grains are husked, washed, soaked, thoroughly dried and ground into a flour that has the texture of very fine sand. It is widely available commercially but it can also be made at home in an efficient grinder. The flour is raw and has to be cooked before consumption.

APPEARANCE AND TASTE

Rice flour is white and powdery but if rubbed between the thumb and forefinger, it feels slightly grainy. The aroma is subtle and the taste is smooth and gentle.

BUYING AND STORING

Store in a dry, airtight jar and use within 4 months. There is no need to buy vast quantities – you don't need much and the fresher you buy it, the better.

OTHER USES

Rice flour is used in many surprising and novel ways especially in south India. On special occasions, Indian homes are richly decorated – garlands of fresh flowers adorn doorways, tiny lamps flicker on windowsills and intricate motifs of flowers, fruits and birds are painted in stark white on red, mud-washed floors. The 'paint' used is a mixture of rice flour and water which sets when dry and is easily removable with water. At the other end of the spectrum is its use as make-up. Women use rice flour paste to draw fine patterns on the forehead as a fashionable and yet traditional alternative to the more commonly seen red dot. The classical dance of the southern state of Kerala is performed wearing masks made of a paste of rice flour and water dried to a resilient hardness.

CULINARY USES

Rice flour can be used as a thickening agent or to make a dough or batter. When cooked, the texture it imparts to the dish depends on the method of cooking. It can be

Floor decorations painted with rice flour

soft and slightly grainy if used to thicken dishes, elastic in doughs and crisp in batters. When it is used to thicken, it is cooked exactly like corn flour. The flour is mixed into a little cold milk, stock or water depending on the recipe, and added to the dish when it is very hot and still cooking. A good stir ensures that the rice flour cooks evenly.

Rice field just before harvesting, southern India

The first dish given here is a festive dessert perfumed with rose-water. The other recipe, for crunchy fried okra, uses rice flour in the same way as one would use breadcrumbs – for a crisp finish.

FIRNI
(CREAMED RICE)

Serves 4
Preparation time 10 minutes
Cooking time 10 minutes

90g (3oz) rice flour
450ml (1pt) milk
120g (4oz) sugar
2 teaspoons rose-water
2 teaspoons flaked almonds
1 sheet edible silver foil (varq)
– optional

1 Mix the rice flour with a quarter of the cold milk. Heat the remaining milk with the sugar. When it comes to the boil, reduce the heat and stir in the rice flour mixture. Keep stirring until a thick batter-like consistency is achieved.

2 Remove from the heat and cool to room temperature, stirring occasionally to prevent a skin from forming.

3 Stir in the rose-water and transfer to individual serving bowls.

4 Refrigerate until required. Just before serving the creamed rice, which will have set, sprinkle with the almonds and decorate with silver foil if desired.

TALI HUI BHINDI
(CRISP OKRA)

Serves 4
Preparation time 10 minutes
Cooking time 15 minutes

600g (1¼b) okra
2 teaspoons cumin powder
1 teaspoon turmeric powder
1 teaspoon mango powder
1 teaspoon coriander powder
1 teaspoon chilli powder
Salt
120g (4oz) rice flour
5 tablespoons sunflower oil

1 Wash the okra and dry thoroughly. Cut off the tops and then cut into halves lengthways.

2 In a separate dish, mix together the powder spices and salt. Add the okra and coat well. Sprinkle in the rice flour and mix.

3 Heat a little oil in a frying pan. When it is hot, reduce the heat and drop in a few okra at a time. Keep turning frequently until crisp, golden and done. Serve hot as the okra will become leathery when cold.

Kathakali dancer painting his face mask

Firni

WHEAT FLOUR

(ATTA/MAIDA)

Wheat was ground into flour about 6000 years ago. Rough grinding-stones have been unearthed in excavations in India, the British Isles, Switzerland and elsewhere. The Romans invented conical millstones that were turned by a beast or slave and they passed the flour through horsehair sieves to produce different grades. Watermills came next, around the time of the birth of Christ, and by AD 1300, windmills. The invention of the steam engine in 1760 changed the course of milling for ever. By 1836, roller mills had been perfected in Switzerland and these, after many mechanical improvements, are still used in commercial mills today. Everywhere in India, people still buy whole wheat, clean it and take it to the nearest *chakki* or mill to make sure they get the freshest, purest flour possible.

MANUFACTURE

The wheat kernel is composed of three parts, the endosperm, germ and bran. The object of milling is to separate the endosperm from the other two, because this is the source of white flour. After being cleaned the wheat is moistened and allowed to 'temper', when the bran hardens and can be easily separated. The wheat is passed between rollers, winnowed and sifted several times over. Freshly milled white flour is pale yellow but changes colour with age. To quicken this process, mills bleach the flour and then replace lost nutrients. Wholemeal flour contains the entire seed except a portion of the bran.

Ears of wheat

APPEARANCE AND TASTE

Refined wheat flour is used for cakes and bread, and is fine, white and soft. Wholewheat flour is brownish, and coarser because it contains more bran. Both grades of flour have a bland flavour that can be sweetened, spiced or salted.

BUYING AND STORING

Flour can be bought in any supermarket. The flour you buy will determine the texture of your roti: brown gives a thicker, coarser product whereas white will be finer. Health-conscious people believe that wholewheat flour is better because of the fibre it provides. An airtight container will keep insects away and it is best to use up all stock within 4 months.

OTHER USES

A stiff dough made of flour, salt and water can be moulded into decorative shapes, baked, painted and varnished to make wall hangings and other objects of beauty. If you ever break a glass, a ball of dough used as a mop will pick up all the shards, and is easily discarded.

CULINARY USES

Although white flour is also used for rotis, it produces a sticky, leathery dough and wholewheat is more popular. Flour is used in steamed or fried sweets and snacks, in curries as a thickener and in milk desserts. Fish, cutlets and patties are rolled in it before deep frying, to give a crisp coating. A dough made of flour is used to seal cooking pots effectively to steam the contents. Around the world, flour is used in every cuisine to make bread, cakes, pies, pastry, soups, stews, batters and sauces.

Grains of wheat

There are countless breads eaten in India and unlike their Western counterparts, they are cooked fresh for each meal. Rotis are made every day whereas the more complicated breads are saved for special occasions. The following recipes are for two basic breads – *poorie* and *rotis*. Even these are made in different ways in each house and every chef will swear by his or her own method.

POORIES
(FRIED PUFFY BREAD)

Serves 4
Preparation time 15 minutes
Cooking time 30 minutes

450g (1lb) wholewheat flour
1 tablespoon sunflower oil
220ml (scant ½pt) warm water
Sunflower oil for deep frying

1 Mix the flour and a tablespoon of the oil with your fingers and bind into a stiff dough, adding water a little at a time. You may need more or less water than the quantity given.

2 Heat the oil in a deep kadai or wok. Test the temperature by dropping a tiny ball of dough into the oil. It should float at once.

3 Divide the dough into equal sized balls. Smear your palm with some oil and shape each ball smoothly.

4 Roll out each ball to a flat disc about 3cm (1in) in diameter, flouring the board as necessary.

5 Gently lower the disc into the hot oil and press down with the back of a slotted spoon. It will puff up only if the oil is hot enough and it is submerged.

6 As soon as it has puffed,

Roti/Chappati

turn it over and fry for a minute.

7 Lift out with a slotted spoon, and drain on absorbent paper.

8 Cook all the poories in the same way. Serve warm.

ROTI/CHAPPATI
(EVERYDAY BREAD)

Serves 4
Preparation time 10 minutes
Cooking time 20 minutes

450g (1lb) wholewheat flour
2 teaspoons sunflower oil
Warm water as needed
Ghee if desired

1 Blend the flour and oil. Bind into a pliable dough with warm water. Knead for 5 minutes (the more you knead the dough, the softer the rotis).

2 Divide the dough into portions the size of a table tennis ball. Coat lightly with flour, shape into a ball in your palm and flatten slightly.

3 Roll out into flat discs, 10cm (4in) in diameter, flouring the board as necessary.

4 Heat a griddle or shallow pan. Roast the discs on the griddle until the surface becomes bubbly. Turn over and press the edges down with a clean cloth to cook evenly. As soon as brown spots appear the roti is done.

5 Remove and smear with ghee. Keep warm by enclosing in a tea towel or foil.

6 Cook all the rotis in the same way. Serve warm or reheat under a hot grill, taking care not to burn them.

SEMOLINA

(SOOJI)

Even the most progressive Indian respects the power and influence of the stars and planets. The *Navagraha*, or nine planets, are worshipped with an opening invocation to the sun. Each of these stars and planets are linked with specific colours, gems and grains. The sun is associated with the colour red, rubies and wheat. Semolina is therefore linked with religious ceremonies in India. It is cooked with other 'pure' ingredients like milk, sugar, ghee and bananas to make ritual food called *prasad*. At large religious gatherings, a little spoonful of this is wrapped in squares of banana leaves and given to every devotee present.

Semolina is used in worship of the stars and planets

MANUFACTURE

Semolina is made by processing wheat into tiny grains. The wheat is cleaned, the wheatgerm is separated and the remainder is coarsely milled into semolina.

APPEARANCE AND TASTE

Semolina resembles sand. Different varieties of semolina have different sizes of grain. Semolina has no aroma but a lovely, smooth flavour that is slightly textured on the palate. Because of its bland taste, it is suited equally to sweet and savoury dishes.

BUYING AND STORING

Semolina is widely available. In hot weather, it is best to dry-roast or refrigerate semolina to increase its shelf-life. If kept properly, it should last for about 4 months.

CULINARY USES

One of the best south Indian snacks is *upma* made of semolina and spices. It is a kind of savoury cake sprinkled with fresh coconut and fragrant coriander. Or semolina can be made into a sweet with sugar, raisins and ghee (halwa). Fish or vegetable patties are rolled in semolina before frying to give a crisp coating. Semolina cooked in milk is given to babies as a weaning food. It is also made into a batter and fried on a griddle to accompany curries. Several crisp sweets are made of semolina blended with flour, sugar and spices and then fried or baked.

The sun is associated with the colour red, rubies and wheat

Satyanarayan Sheera

This sweet recipe is for *prasad*, or blessed food, which is served at religious functions.

SATYANARAYAN SHEERA
(RICH SEMOLINA PUDDING)

Serves 4
Preparation time 10 minutes
Cooking time 20 minutes

150ml (¼pt) ghee
150g (5oz) semolina
150g (5oz) sugar
150g (5oz) banana, peeled and
  mashed
450ml (¾pt) warm milk
½ teaspoon cardamom powder
2 teaspoons raisins

1 Heat the ghee and add the semolina. Fry until it becomes pink and fragrant. Reduce the heat and add the sugar and stir until it melts.

2 Add the banana and mix well. Pour in the milk.

3 Partially cover the pan and cook until the mixture is dry and the semolina is cooked.

4 Take off the heat and add the cardamom powder and raisins. Serve warm.

This dish is a version of a steamed pudding that is served in rural India with a big dollop of ghee.

BOMBAY PUDDING
(STEAMED SAFFRON PUDDING)

Serves 4
Preparation time 10 minutes
Cooking time 20 minutes

300g (10oz) plain flour
6 tablespoons ghee
6 tablespoons semolina
6 tablespoons sugar
½ teaspoon saffron strands,
  soaked in 2 teaspoons milk
½ teaspoon nutmeg powder
1 teaspoon extra ghee
2 teaspoons raisins

1 Mix all the ingredients except the raisins and the extra ghee.

2 Grease a deep dish with the extra ghee, sprinkle the base with the raisins and pour in the mixture.

3 Cover the dish with greaseproof paper and tie down to seal.

4 Steam the pudding for 15 minutes or until a knife inserted into the centre comes out clean.

5 Cool slightly and cut into squares. Serve warm.

CRACKED/ BROKEN WHEAT

(LAPSI)

Porridge is considered an ideal breakfast dish the world over. In India, a porridge that is eaten regularly is made of broken wheat. It is also made into a series of unusual snacks and traditional sweets that can be enjoyed throughout the day.

The first dish is easy on the digestion during convalescence. It can be eaten with a savoury pickle and a vegetable curry.

MANUFACTURE

Broken wheat is made by milling wheat coarsely. It is cleaned and husked and then processed to the required size. When wheat is made into flour, during the process of sieving, some broken grains remain behind along with some husk. These are also collected and sold as broken wheat. They are highly nutritious as they do not undergo refining. Sometimes they are partially cooked and then dried to reduce the cooking time.

APPEARANCE AND TASTE

Broken wheat is available in small, brown, hard nibs that are uneven and rough. When cooked, broken wheat has a very hearty, warm aroma and a grainy taste that is delightful. It is slightly nutty, chewy and filling.

BUYING AND STORING

As broken wheat undergoes very little processing, it is a healthy food and therefore a good breakfast cereal. Store in an airtight jar and consume within 4 months.

MEDICINAL USES

As it is easy to digest, it is included in geriatric or convalescent diets.

CULINARY USES

A superlative sweet is made of broken wheat by frying it in ghee and then cooking it with milk and sugar. It is also cooked with spices, curry leaves and salt to make a teatime snack. Broken wheat can be partially boiled and added to batters for fritters and pancakes. Try it in puddings and cakes.

LAPSI
(SAVOURY PORRIDGE)

Serves 4
Preparation time 0
Cooking time 20 minutes

2 tablespoons ghee
300g (10oz) broken wheat
1200ml (2pt) water
½ teaspoon salt

1 Heat the ghee and lightly fry the broken wheat.

2 After a minute add the water and salt and cook on a low heat until the grains are soft. Serve hot.

This is a pudding from south India and is made on festive occasions.

LAPSI KHEER
(BROKEN WHEAT PUDDING)

Serves 4
Preparation time 30 minutes
Cooking time 20 minutes

150g (5oz) broken wheat
300ml (½pt) water
4 tablespoons jaggery, grated
300ml (½pt) coconut milk
1 teaspoon cardamom powder

(To make coconut milk, finely grate a fresh coconut, add 150ml (¼pt) of hot water and squeeze to extract the thick milk. You should get roughly 300ml (½pt) of coconut milk from a coconut.)

1 Cook the broken wheat in the water until soft.

2 Stir in the jaggery and cook until blended.

3 Add the coconut milk and cardamom powder. Bring to the boil once and remove from the heat. Serve warm.

Wheat field

Lapsi Kheer

VERMICELLI

(SEVIAN)

How and why this Italian pasta got incorporated into the Indian cuisine is not known and it is probable that the name was borrowed and applied to a similar product already in existence in India. Muslims consider the month of Ramadan as the holiest in their calendar. Austerity reigns in every home and the devout keep a fast from sunrise until sunset. A traditional sweet to eat after moonrise in Ramadan is made of fine vermicelli, milk, saffron and nuts.

MANUFACTURE

Like all pasta, vermicelli is made from wheatflour. The dough is passed through machines with perforated cylinders which shape it into fine needles. These are fan- or oven-dried until hard and carefully packed to avoid breakage. Sometimes they are sold broken or roasted.

APPEARANCE AND TASTE

As the name suggests, vermicelli is worm-like. It is fine, hard, pale beige in colour and sold in sticks measuring nearly 30cm (1ft). Vermicelli has a pleasant, biscuit-like aroma and taste which develops when it is fried in ghee or roasted.

Vermicelli is used in Muslim festive food

BUYING AND STORING

Packed in cellophane or cardboard , vermicelli is widely available. It should keep well for 4 to 5 months.

CULINARY USES

Vermicelli milk pudding is extremely popular all over India. Vermicelli also makes a lovely addition to clear soups and some stews. It makes a great quick snack.

These 2 recipes are always popular. They are easy to make and can be prepared well in advance. They are made all over India and can be quite simple or really rich with the addition of ghee and nuts. These are my versions.

SEVIAN SANJA
(DRY, SWEET VERMICELLI)

Serves 4
Preparation time 15 minutes
Cooking time 20 minutes

4 tablespoons ghee
4 tablespoons raisins
4 tablespoons flaked almonds
300g (10oz) vermicelli, broken
*   into short lengths*
60g (2oz) caster sugar
1 teaspoon cardamom powder

1 Heat the ghee in a pan and fry the raisins and the almonds until golden. Remove with a slotted spoon.

2 In the same ghee, fry the vermicelli until golden, without allowing it to brown.

3 Add the sugar and mix well.

4 Sprinkle in a few drops of water, stir and cook until soft, adding a little water as necessary.

5 Take off the heat and stir in the cardamom powder. The dish should be dry.

6 Serve warm, garnished with the fried raisins and almonds.

SEVIAN KHEER
(VERMICELLI MILK PUDDING)

Serves 4
Preparation time 15 minutes
Cooking time 20 minutes

4 tablespoons ghee
2 teaspoons cashew nuts
2 teaspoons raisins
150g (5oz) vermicelli, roughly
    broken
300ml (½pt) milk
150ml (¼pt) evaporated milk
5 tablespoons sugar
2 teaspoons chirongi nuts
    (optional)

1 Heat the ghee and fry the cashew nuts and raisins until golden.

2 Add the vermicelli and fry until golden. Taking care not to brown.

3 Add all the milk and bring to the boil, scraping down the sides of the pan and stirring all the while.

4 Simmer until the vermicelli is soft, then add the sugar. Stir well and remove.

5 This pudding can be served hot or cold, garnished with nuts.

JOWAR FLOUR

U tensils play an important role in an Indian kitchen. Crafted out of brass, iron, steel, wood, stone or clay, each item is used for a specific purpose or a particular dish. For example rotis, which are made from a range of cereals in some form or another all over India, are cooked on a *tava* or concave iron griddle, in the *tandoor* or clay oven, on an open fire or on flat earthenware pots. Jowar rotis, called *bhakris*, are moulded and patted flat by hand and roasted on a hot griddle. They are then stored until needed, in a flat brass box, tied in a clean cloth.

Cooking jowar *rotis* or *bhakris*

CULINARY USES

It is used to make bread traditionally eaten with a chutney made of desiccated coconut, garlic and dried red chillies. This bread is served piping hot with a dollop of butter for extra taste. The flour is also used for coating foods before frying to give a crispy outer cover.

This dish is a tasty snack and a more nutritious alternative to crisps!

BATATA KAAP
(FRIED POTATO DISCS)

Serves 4
Preparation time 25 minutes
Cooking time 20 minutes

300g (10oz) potatoes, peeled, cut into thick slices
Salt
½ teaspoon chilli powder
Sunflower oil for deep frying
60g (2oz) jowar flour

1 Mix the sliced potatoes, salt and chilli powder and set aside for 10 minutes.

2 Heat the oil in a deep kadai or wok.

3 Roll each seasoned slice in the flour, shake off the excess and deep fry on a low heat until crisp and cooked. Fry a few slices at a time to ensure even cooking.

4 Drain on absorbent paper and serve hot with onion chutney.

HOW IT GROWS

Jowar grows all over peninsular and central India. When the ears of grain mature the tender stalks of jowar are cut and the tiny green seeds roasted in a shallow pit made in the soil. These are eaten with many accompaniments like jaggery, coconut and lemon. After the harvest, threshing, cleaning and drying makes the grains ready for the market. The grains are further milled into flour.

APPEARANCE AND TASTE

Often compared to creamy, round pearls, jowar fields glisten with a pale yellow, radiance. The grains are about the size of sago and have a slight indentation on one side, like a grain of corn. The flour is creamy-white to yellow.

BUYING AND STORING

Although in India most people buy jowar whole and have it ground into flour, bags of jowar flour are becoming increasingly easy to find. Store in a dry, airtight jar for up to 4 months.

Jowar flour

Bhakris must be eaten hot so try and make them as close to mealtime as possible.

BHAKRI
(FRESH JOWAR BREAD)

Serves 4
Preparation time 15 minutes
Cooking time 30 minutes

300g (10oz) jowar flour
Water to mix
2 teaspoons sesame seeds

1 Make a stiff dough with the flour and water as needed.

2 Divide it into portions the size of a table tennis ball.

3 Line a flat surface with a small plastic sheet. (A cut up carrier bag will do.) Take a portion of the dough, roll it into a ball and place it on the plastic sheet.

4 Wet your hands with water and pat the ball into a thick, flat disc, keeping the disc wet at all times.

5 Heat a griddle and place the disc on it. Sprinkle with some of the sesame seeds.

6 When the bottom is crisp, turn over and cook the other side. Remove when crisp and cooked.

7 Cook all the bhakris in the same way.

Ear of jowar grains

BAJRA FLOUR

The Arabian Sea is a source of livelihood for the fisher-folk who live on India's west coast. From its azure depths they catch giant prawns, lobsters and a host of multi-coloured fish. They leave in their boats at night and have their supper on board, which is usually a meal of thick, flat bread made with bajra flour and a hot and sour curry with fish hauled fresh from the sea. Their food is cooked on a tiny coal stove by the light of a lantern.

West coast fishermen

Bajra crop

HOW IT GROWS

When the bajra crop is ripe and ready to be harvested, the tall, slender plants are cut, tied in and allowed to dry. The bundles are then threshed to separate the grain. The grains are laid out to dry in the sun. Most of the produce is consumed by the locals but some of it is processed into flour.

APPEARANCE AND TASTE

Bajra grains are very pretty, small, tear drop shaped and a mixture of silver grey and canary yellow in colour. The flour is grey too. It has a strong, nutty aroma and a very slightly bittersweet aftertaste. The flavour is stronger than that of wheatflour.

BUYING AND STORING

As with jowar, buy a small bag of ready made flour to try. Store in a dry jar.

CULINARY USES

Bajra and jowar flours are often combined to make bhakri or other breads. Jowar and bajra are also pounded with spices, rolled out into thin discs and dried to make poppadoms.

Most cookery books describe the more common Indian breads that are served in restaurants and are representative of north Indian cookery. The following recipes are for relatively uncommon breads. Try them for a change from the usual naan and roti.

ROTLA
(BAJRA BREAD)

Serves 4
Preparation time 30 minutes
Cooking time 30 minutes for all the bread

600ml (1pt) water
300g (10oz) bajra flour
Large pinch salt

1 Bring the water to the boil and stir in the flour.

2 Cook on a low heat until a ball is formed.

3 Take off the heat, cool slightly and knead to a soft dough, wetting it if it gets dry.

4 Divide the dough into equal sized portions, each about as big as a table tennis ball.

5 Wet your palms and roll a portion into a ball. Pat into a flat disc, wetting the dough to keep it pliable.

6 Heat a griddle and put the bread onto it. Reduce the heat and cover, allowing it partly to cook in its own steam.

7 Turn over to cook the other side until brown. The final rotla will be dry. Cook the remaining rotlas in the same way. Serve hot.

Preparing snacks, Pushkar, Rajasthan

THALIPEETH
(SEASONED BAJRA BREAD)

Serves 4
Preparation time 15 minutes
Cooking time 30 minutes for all the bread

Rotla

300g (10oz) bajra flour
1 teaspoon salt
1 teaspoon green chilli, minced
2 tablespoons coriander leaves, chopped
1 teaspoon turmeric powder
300ml (½pt) yoghurt
6 tablespoons sunflower oil

1 Mix all the ingredients except the oil to make a thick batter.

2 Heat a griddle and pour a ladleful of the batter in the centre.

3 Spread the batter to make a flat, round disc. Pour a little oil around the edges and cook the disc.

4 Turn over and cook the other side. There should be brown spots on both sides.

5 Remove to a warm plate and cook the remaining breads in the same way.

GRAM FLOUR

(BESAN)

Gram flour is made from chickpeas and is used in a variety of ways in the kitchen, quite often being used to enhance curries. The word curry comes from *kari*, which in south India means a blend of vegetables and spices. Apparently the 18th-century British viceroy, General Clive, added water and meat to the *kari* to make what is now called Madras curry. However, not all curries are fiery. The Sindhi curry, typical of the immigrant Sindhi community from the province of Sind in pre-partition India, is a delicate medley of vegetables and spices held together by a gram flour sauce.

MANUFACTURE

Many people in India buy split chickpeas or Bengal gram, clean them and take them to the nearest miller to have them ground. This flour is called *besan*. Big commercial mills in India also grind the dried chickpeas between huge rollers, producing quantities of flour for home use and export.

APPEARANCE AND TASTE

Gram flour has an unmistakable, dull yellow colour and matte texture. Its aroma is earthy and dry. The taste is pleasant, rather nutty and heavy.

BUYING AND STORING

Gram flour can be used in various ways so it is a good idea to buy a 450g (1lb) bag. Remove to an airtight container and it will keep for about 6 months. In hot climates like India, it is slightly roasted and stored in the refrigerator.

OTHER USES

Baby care in India relies on many natural products and homemade remedies. One of the gentlest skin cleansers, used for babies' baths as well as for face masks, is a paste made of gram flour and milk.

CULINARY USES

Curries, fritters and sweets can all be made from gram flour. Blended with yoghurt, curry leaves and spices, it becomes the delicate Gujarati kadhi. If mixed with sliced onions or vegetables, flavoured with cumin and ajowan and deep fried, it is seen all over the world as onion or vegetable bhajis. Cooked gently with jaggery and cardamom it features in many mouthwatering sweets.

Gram flour is still used in women's beauty preparations

The following recipes use gram flour in different ways. The first dish is from rural Maharashtra and here, the flour is added for taste and texture. It is cheap and easy to make.

KOBI ZUNKA
(CABBAGE WITH GRAM FLOUR NIBS)

Serves 4
Preparation time 20 minutes
Cooking time 20 minutes

6 tablespoons gram flour
4 tablespoons sunflower oil
1 teaspoon black mustard seeds
1 teaspoon cumin seeds
Large pinch of asafoetida
10 curry leaves
900g (2lb) cabbage, shredded finely
1 teaspoon chilli powder
1 teaspoon turmeric powder
1 teaspoon coriander powder
Salt

1 Heat a heavy pan and dry-roast the gram flour, stirring all the while to prevent it from burning. As soon as the aroma and colour changes, take it off the heat.

2 Heat the oil in another pan. Add the mustard seeds. When they crackle, add the cumin, asafoetida and curry leaves. Fry for a minute.

3 Add the cabbage, the powder spices and salt and mix well.

4 Reduce the heat and add a little water. Cook until the cabbage is cooked but slightly crunchy.

5 Increase the heat to dry off any liquid, then add the roasted gram flour. Stir well. It will absorb any liquid and oil to form clumps. Break up the clumps to cook them.

6 When the flour is cooked take off the heat. Serve hot.

This recipe is for a popular snack – bhajia. Although onion *bhajias* are the most common (as 'onion bhaji'), you can use any firm vegetable.

PHOOLGOBI BHAJIA
(CAULIFLOWER FRITTERS)

Serves 4
Preparation time 20 minutes
Cooking time 15 minutes

For the batter:
150g (5oz) gram flour
1 teaspoon chilli powder
1 teaspoon turmeric powder
1 teaspoon cumin seeds
½ teaspoon ajowan seeds
2 teaspoons fenugreek leaves, dried
2 tablespoons coriander leaves, chopped
Large pinch of bicarbonate of soda
Salt

Sunflower oil for frying
300g (10oz) cauliflower, cut into medium-sized florets

1 Make a thick batter of all the batter ingredients and water as needed.

2 Heat the oil in a deep kadai or wok until it smokes.

3 Dip each floret into the batter and gently add to the hot oil. Reduce the heat to allow the cauliflower to cook through.

4 Fry until golden, then drain on absorbent paper.

5 Fry 2–3 bhajias at a time, regulating the heat to ensure even cooking.

6 Serve hot with coriander chutney and tomato ketchup.

CORNFLOUR/ CORNMEAL

(MAKKI KA ATTA)

Indian bread is always served freshly baked. The origin of the roti or bread can be dated back to Aryan times when early migrants settled along the fertile Indus valley. The Punjabis of that region soon assimilated the roti into their own cuisine, making it a staple food. Today it is common to see a family sitting down to fresh rotis, mostly of cornmeal, served piping hot.

Grain-studded cob

APPEARANCE AND TASTE

Cornflour is fine, white and soft. It is odourless and has a mild taste. Cornmeal on the other hand is coarse, grainy and pale yellow in colour. It gives a chewy texture to the dish. If fried, both the flours become very crisp.

MANUFACTURE

In India corn is commonly called maize and is grown as a vegetable or for grinding into flour. Native to South America, corn is grown in several countries. The golden grain is studded on cobs which are enclosed in a lime green, fibrous casing with wispy tasselled tops. Coarse milling of the dried grain gives cornmeal and finer milling produces cornflour, which is rich in fats and carbohydrates.

Rotis are a staple of many rural Indian community diets

BUYING AND STORING

As cornmeal has a high proportion of oil, it does not keep very well. Buy small amounts and use up within 4 months. Commercially available cornflour has additives to increase its shelf-life and as such, it can be kept for up to a year.

CULINARY USES

Although cornflour is opaque and remains white when dissolved in water, heat turns the solution transparent. That is why it is sometimes used to thicken curries without changing the colour or flavour. Cornmeal is added to batters and vegetables. Both are kneaded into a hard dough to make fresh bread or rotis. In other countries, cornflour is made into porridge, cakes or bread. Cornflour with milk and sugar sets to form a quick, cold pudding. The flour is always first dissolved in cold liquid and then poured into hot liquid to cook it.

In India, the first dish is traditionally made with chickpea flour, but this version is innovative and appetising. It is crunchy and remains so with keeping. Serve it as a snack with a sweet chutney. The second is a typical Maharashtrian dish.

METHI VADA
(FENUGREEK FRITTERS)

Serves 4
Preparation time 30 minutes
Cooking time 30 minutes

300g (10oz) fresh fenugreek (the leaves must be plucked off the stalks, a slightly laborious process)
220g (8oz) cornmeal
1 teaspoon turmeric powder
1 teaspoon chilli powder
1 teaspoon cumin seeds
1 teaspoon ajowan seeds
1 teaspoon ginger, grated
1 teaspoon sesame seeds
Salt
6 tablespoons sunflower oil

1 Mix all the ingredients except the oil and add enough water to make a thick batter.

2 Heat the oil in a shallow frying pan and drop in little balls of batter from a ladle.

3 Fry until brown, then turn the fritters over, cover and allow to cook in their own steam on a low heat. Serve hot.

PITHACHI MIRCHI
(PEPPERS WITH CORNMEAL)

Serves 4
Preparation time 20 minutes
Cooking time 30 minutes

150g (5oz) cornmeal
4 tablespoons sunflower oil
1 teaspoon black mustard seeds
Large pinch of asafoetida
10 curry leaves
1 teaspoon turmeric powder
1 teaspoon chilli powder
1 teaspoon coriander powder
600g (1¼lb) green peppers, diced
Salt
1 teaspoon lemon juice
2 tablespoons desiccated coconut
2 teaspoons sesame seeds, roasted and coarsely crushed

1 Dry-roast the cornmeal on a low heat until golden.

2 Heat the oil in a pan and add the mustard seeds. When they pop, add the asafoetida, curry leaves and powder spices.

3 Stir for a minute then add the peppers and salt. Mix well, add a little water and cook until the vegetable is done but crisp.

4 Add the cornmeal, lemon juice, coconut and sesame seeds and mix well.

5 Cook until the flour has absorbed all the liquid. Serve hot.

Methi Vada

Occasional Treats

Miscellaneous Ingredients

POPPADOMS

(PAPAD)

Poppadoms are round, wafer-thin discs made of various lentil or cereal flours. The word 'poppadom' is a legacy of the British Raj in India and a time when the British would move to the cool hill stations to escape the heat of the cities. In the evenings they would meet on well-kept lawns and white terraces to sip gimlets and nibble on poppadoms. Poppadoms are served roasted or fried as accompaniments to pre-dinner drinks or the main course. Eating papads, or *pappadam* as they are called in south India, with pickle or sweet chutney as a starter seems to be a trend started by Indian restaurants outside India.

A selection of poppadoms

In India poppadoms are often made at home, though in the cities the trend of buying ready-made ones is increasing. They are available plain, or flavoured with herbs, garlic, peppercorns or chillies. The crisp crunchiness provides a change of texture in a meal. Various titbits which are fried can also be classified as papads as they serve the same purpose. Different flours are made into an incredible number of decorative shapes. Sometimes they are pressed into balls which are deep-fried before eating. Sago seeds are coloured green and pink and rolled into rounds, strips or triangles. Lotus root, from the lotus flowers which grow in ponds all over India, is dried for storage and then fried before use. This unusual 'crunchie' is woody, crisp and has five hollow chambers that give it the appearance of cut okra. When you bite into this *bhain*, the woodiness seems to crumble, leaving a beautiful crispness on the palate.

The making of poppadoms at home is an art and requires skill as well as plenty of sunshine. The variously flavoured doughs are soft when fresh, but dry to a brittle hardness. They are laid out to dry on a clean cloth in strong, summer sun and then packed in plastic bags for storage.

Poppadoms need careful storage. As they are extremely brittle, they are best stored in a flat container and should be eaten within 3 months of purchase.

Poppadoms can be cooked in advance as they taste good warm or cold. However, don't make them more than an hour before the meal because they will wilt and go leathery.

TO COOK POPPADOMS

FRYING

Fried poppadoms are definitely tastier but not for the calorie-conscious. Heat oil in a large wok or kadai. When nearly smoking, reduce the heat and drop in the poppadom. It will instantly change colour. The whole process takes seconds so have your slotted spoon and absorbent-paper lined plate ready. Do not allow the poppadom to turn brown or black. Drain the poppadom well and remove to a plate.

ROASTING

The poppadom is held between tongs and roasted over an open flame. Quick and frequent turning is required to prevent burning. As soon as the papad has changed colour, curled up and become crisp, it is done.

GRILLING

Place under a medium grill until bubbles appear on the surface and the colour turns from translucent to opaque. Turn over and repeat the process. Place at least 4cm (1½in) away from the grill to prevent burning.

It is also possible to cook poppadoms in the microwave oven. It should take about a minute but this may vary slightly depending on your oven.

Fry in hot oil for 5 seconds, or
Place under medium grill until golden brown, or
Microwave for 90 seconds.
Braten 5 Sekunden unter mittlerem Öl, oder
bräunen unter mittlerem Grill oder
90 Sekunden im Mikrowelle.
Frire 5 seconds dans l'huile bouillante, ou
Dorer à feu moyen ou
Placer 90 secondes au four à micro-ondes.
Produce of India
T. Choithram and Sons (Stores) Ltd.
Mx. HA0 2BG U.K. Fax 081 900 1426

kept in strong sunlight to mature them. They are made with pickling spices, which almost always include mustard (whole, powdered or crushed), and vinegar or oil. They last for years and get better with age.

APPEARANCE AND TASTE

Most pickles resemble a thick oily curry and are brown, yellow or white in colour. Some vinegar-based ones are translucent and have a thin consistency. Pickles are designed to stimulate the palate, which is why they are always strongly-flavoured. They are sharp, hot, tangy or sweet and smell pungent. Bought pickles are available mild, medium or hot which denotes the level of chilli heat.

BUYING AND STORING

If you've never tasted Indian pickles before, go for the safe mango or lemon. Experiment with garlic, prawn and peppercorn pickles later. Store in a dry jar at room temperature. Never use a wet spoon in pickles or they will spoil and develop fungus. Don't use the same spoon for two different pickles. Keep away from strong light.

CULINARY USES

They can be mixed into yoghurt to make an unusual dip for crisps or raw vegetable fingers. If you are adventurous, spread some mild pickle on a slice of bread - it makes a lively snack.

PICKLES
(ACHAAR)

Eaten in tiny amounts, pickles are an intrinsic part of any Indian meal. Seasonal vegetables and fruits are preserved in spices, oil and salt to be eaten when no longer in season. This custom has given rise to a whole panorama of relishes and pickles that add a touch of tang, fire or sweetness to a meal. As with all other Indian food, pickles are regional, each recipe reflecting the cuisine of a state.

MANUFACTURE

There are literally thousands of pickles, and it would be impossible to list them all. Indians use mangoes, lemons, limes, apples, amla, figs, chillies, carrots, cauliflower, aubergines, green peppercorns, radish and many other fruits and vegetables in pickles. Even within these groups, there are countless variations. Meat and fish pickles are popular in some communities – Goan prawn pickle, coastal lamb pickles and pickled chicken from Punjab, for example. Indian pickles are usually

Grocer's stall

Cycas circinalis/Metroxylon sagu

SAGO

(SABUDANA)

The rainy months from June to September are considered holy in India. The 4 month period is a time when devout Hindus eat no meat or fish. Special fasting foods are made from sago, bananas, peanuts, yoghurt and root vegetables.

HOW IT GROWS

Sago is made from the viscous sap of a tall, shady tree. The tree thrives in hot, dry conditions. As with rubber trees, a groove is cut in the trunk of the sago palm at intervals and the sap which oozes out is collected. It is strained through special sieves which form it into little, soft droplets. These are dried until hard. Depending on the size of holes in the sieve, different sizes of sago are produced.

APPEARANCE AND TASTE

Sago balls are like small pearls, white and hard. On soaking in water, they turn soft and as they absorb more and more fluid they become mushy. When cooked they change from opaque to translucent. The taste is bland but creamy. When cooked, sago pearls have the texture of caviar – spongy and slightly slippery.

BUYING AND STORING

Indian shops stock sago as well as a close relative, tapioca. Store in a dry jar for up to 4 months.

MEDICINAL AND OTHER USES

Indian medicine believes that sago and rice cool the system, counteracting the heat produced by other foods. A thin sago gruel is given to patients who complain of excess bile due to body heat. The liquid left after boiling sago in water is used to starch clothes.

CULINARY USES

Sago is always washed and left to soften. Once it is soft and can be squashed between 2 fingers, it is made into savouries or sweets. Kneaded together with seasoned, mashed potatoes into a dough, it gives texture and flavour to *vadas* or small patties that are shallow-fried. It is also made into poppadoms that can be deep-fried. Sago poppadoms look like sheets of bubbles and are sometimes tinted pink or green for decoration.

Monsoon time

Sabudana Kheer

This recipe is a traditional fasting food but makes a tasty, exotic snack.

SABUDANA KHICHDI
(SAGO SAVOURY)

Serves 4
Preparation time 30 minutes
Cooking time 20 minutes

150g (5oz) sago
4 tablespoons sunflower oil
1 teaspoon black mustard seeds
1 teaspoon cumin seeds
2 green chillis, slit lengthways
  so the seeds are exposed, but
  the chilli is not broken in 2
12 curry leaves
Salt
1 teaspoon sugar
4 tablespoons roasted peanuts,
  roughly crushed
4 tablespoons coconut, grated if
  fresh, or desiccated
4 tablespoons coriander leaves,
  chopped
2 teaspoons lemon juice

1 Wash the sago, drain and spread out thinly on a kitchen towel. Leave for 10 minutes.

2 Heat the oil in a pan and add the mustard seeds.

3 When they crackle, add the cumin, green chilli and curry leaves. Fry for a minute.

4 Reduce the heat and drop in the sago. Stir quickly to prevent lumps from forming.

5 Add the salt, sugar and peanuts and stir well.

6 Cook on a very low heat, stirring, until the sago is cooked. You may need to sprinkle in some water from time to time.

7 Serve hot garnished with coconut and coriander. Spinkle over the lemon juice.

Many countries have a recipe for sago pudding. This is the Indian one. This simple dessert is turned into something special by the addition of spices and nuts. It also makes an unusual breakfast food.

SABUDANA KHEER
(INDIAN SAGO PUDDING)

Serves 4
Preparation time 20 minutes
Cooking time 30 minutes

150g (5oz) sago
600ml (1pt) milk
100g (3oz) sugar
1 teaspoon cardamom powder
2 tablespoons cashew nuts
150ml (¼pt) evaporated milk

1 Wash the sago, drain and allow to stand for 15 minutes.

2 In the meantime, mix the milk and sugar and bring to the boil. Reduce the heat and simmer for 5 minutes.

3 Take off the heat and add the cardamom powder, cashew nuts and evaporated milk. Cover and reserve.

4 Add 300ml (½pt) water to the sago and bring to the boil. Reduce the heat and simmer until the sago is cooked.

5 Take off the heat, cool slightly and pour in the milk mixture.

6 Serve cold, adjusting the consistency with some water if necessary.

Saccharum officinarum

JAGGERY

(GUR)

Sugar cane grows in abundance in the tropical heat of central India. The deliciousness of sugar cane juice has caused many *ras ki dukan* or juice shops to open purely for the sale of this drink. But sugar cane also provides another substance which is very important – jaggery. During the manufacture of sugar from sugar cane, as the cane turns to crystal, several by-products are formed: molasses, alcohol and jaggery. Jaggery is dehydrated sugar cane juice and is mostly produced by small cultivators in huge, rural crushers run by bullocks. The jaggery is not purified and therefore has all the quality of the juice itself. Jaggery is as important as sugar in Indian cookery. It has a special flavour that cannot really be substituted for by sugar, although brown or demerara sugar is the closest equivalent.

Making jaggery

APPEARANCE AND TASTE

Jaggery ranges from mustard-yellow to deep amber in colour, depending on the quality of the sugar cane juice. It is sticky but can be crumbled easily. It is made up of big lumps which melt to form a thick, gooey paste. Jaggery has a heavy, caramel-like aroma which is slightly alcoholic, like sweet sherry or port. The taste is very sweet and musky.

BUYING AND STORING

Different varieties of jaggery are available, some stickier than others, but they are mostly interchangeable. Buy a small amount to try first and look for reputable brands like Kolhapur jaggery. (Kolhapur is a town in Maharashtra where quality jaggery is produced). You will find that the jaggery is moulded in various sizes and wrapped in plastic or in jute cloth. To store, make sure that the container is dry or the jaggery will go mouldy. Use within 6 months.

OTHER USES

Jaggery is used for making liquor in the villages of India. It is also distilled into ethanol, used in environment-friendly petrol.

Moulded jaggery waiting for distribution

Crushing sugar cane

CULINARY USES

You only need small amounts of jaggery for most dishes. It goes well with lentils and tamarind. Jaggery is melted over heat and blended with other ingredients. For sweets like the south Indian *payasam*, jaggery is simmered with cooked rice and a variety of spices and nuts. Brittle is made by adding nuts to melted jaggery and then cooling the mixture in thin slabs. Sesame *laddoos*, or puffed rice balls covered in jaggery, are eaten enthusiastically. In rural India, tea is sweetened with jaggery instead of sugar. The resulting beverage is thick and sweet, and gives an instant boost of energy to farmers and workmen. Many drinks are sweetened with jaggery which makes the consistency and taste rather syrupy.

In rural south India guests are welcomed with a drink of hot jaggery tea and bidden farewell with a piece of jaggery for the homeward journey. This recipe is for a dish made on festive days.

KARANJI
(FRIED JAGGERY PASTIES)

Serves 4
Preparation time 40 minutes
Cooking time 30 minutes

300g (10oz) plain flour
2 teaspoons sunflower oil
Large pinch of salt

For the filling:
150g (5oz) jaggery
300g (10oz) coconut, grated if fresh, or desiccated
2 teaspoons white poppy seeds, dry-roasted
2 teaspoons raisins
1 teaspoon cardamom powder

Sunflower oil for frying

1 Make a stiff dough with the flour, oil, salt and water as needed.

2 Melt the jaggery in a heavy pan on a low heat. As soon as it has completely melted, add the rest of the filling ingredients and stir well.

3 Cook for 5 minutes. Take off the heat and allow to cool a little.

4 Divide the dough into equal sized balls about 2cm (¾in) in diameter.

5 Roll each one out to a thin disc, dusting it with a little flour if necessary.

6 Place a little of the coconut mixture in the centre of the disc. Fold the disc in half to make a half-moon shape. Seal

Sugarcane grows in Uttar Pradesh

the edges properly.

7 Make all the pasties. Heat the oil in a deep kadai or wok.

8 Deep-fry each pasty individually until golden. Remove with a slotted spoon and drain on absorbent paper. Serve at room temperature.

This is an unusual drink that can be served in tiny amounts to finish off a meal.

RAS AMRIT
(JAGGERY MILK)

Serves 4
Preparation time 30 minutes
Cooking time 0

300g (10oz) coconut, grated
450ml (¾pt) water
4 tablespoons jaggery, grated
½ teaspoon cardamom powder

1 Grind the coconut with the water in a blender. Squeeze out the thick milk. Discard the residue.

2 Stir in the grated jaggery and mix well. Strain.

3 Add the cardamom powder and mix. Serve well chilled.

AGAR-AGAR

(CHINA GRASS)

Bombayites love the colourful jellies, custards, yoghurts and cream desserts served in the restaurants set up by Parsees at the beginning of the century. Specialities are jellies with three layers, all of different colours, studded with shredded fruit and served in a glass, thick sweet yoghurt, and china grass. China grass is the name given to a dessert made by dissolving agar-agar in sweet milk. It is flavoured with spices, coloured, set and served cold.

MANUFACTURE

Agar-agar is obtained from various seaweeds also known as Japanese or Ceylon moss. It is also called Bengal isinglass, but in India, most people know it as china grass.

APPEARANCE AND TASTE

Agar-agar is sold as thin, crinkly, translucent white strips that are difficult to break, have no aroma and a neutral taste. Powdered agar-agar is also available.

BUYING AND STORING

Agar-agar is used for jellies and because of its blandness, can be flavoured with any essence. That is why it is a versatile dessert ingredient in the Indian pantry. It can be stored for up to a year if kept away from moisture.

CULINARY USES

Used primarily for making sweets, the strips, which swell slightly in cold water, are immersed in boiling water to dissolve them completely. The resulting, transparent liquid is sweetened and flavoured and then left to set in the refrigerator. It is worth experimenting with agar-agar to make tiny transparent shapes as garnishes.

Children love these cool, creamy desserts and they are also a favourite at summer parties. They look as good as they taste and make an attractive finale to a light meal. You can also try your own combinations and flavourings.

ELAICHI CHINA GRASS

(CARDAMOM SNOW)

Serves 4
Preparation time 10 minutes
Cooking time 15 minutes + setting time

10 agar-agar strips or 4 tablespoons of powder
900ml (1½pt) milk
Sugar
1 teaspoon cardamom powder
2 tablespoons almonds, chopped finely

1 Break up the agar-agar if using strips and sprinkle into the milk. Stir well.

2 Bring the milk to the boil in a heavy pan, stirring to prevent the agar-agar from sticking to the bottom. Reduce the heat and cook until it has completely dissolved.

3 Strain to remove any lumps, then add the sugar. Stir until dissolved.

4 Cool completely and add the cardamom powder.

5 Pour into a flat dish and refrigerate until set.

6 Cut into fancy shapes with different biscuit cutters. Decorate with almonds sprinkled in an attractive pattern on top. Serve cold.

GULABI CHINA GRASS

(ROSE DIAMONDS)

Serves 4
Preparation time 10 minutes
Cooking time 15 minutes + setting time

10 agar-agar strips or 4 tablespoons powder
900ml (1½pt) milk
Sugar to taste
1 teaspoon rose essence
A few drops pink food colouring
Pink rose petals, sprinkled lightly with water to give a dewy effect, to decorate

1 Proceed as for the above recipe through steps 1-3.

2 Cool and add the rose essence and pink colouring.

3 Pour into a flat dish and refrigerate until set.

4 To serve, cut into diamond shapes and place a pink rose petal on top of each diamond. Serve cold.

Gulabi China Grass

Osimum basilicum

SUBJA SEEDS

The Muslims in India have an all-time favourite dessert, *falooda*, a cold milky drink that combines the sublime smoothness of ice cream, the wholesomeness of milk, the sweet perfume of rose syrup and the wonderful texture of noodles and subja seeds.

Falooda

HOW THEY GROW

Subja seeds grow on a variety of basil plant. This is found wild all over India, and has dark green leaves and a branched, erect stem. The plant grows to a height of 1m (3ft). The flowers grow in slender spikes and give way to tiny seeds. These dry on the plant or are dried in the sun.

APPEARANCE AND TASTE

The seeds are tiny, black and tear-drop shaped. When dropped into water, they first develop a whitish-grey bloom and then the skin swells, appearing furry. The outer coating is translucent and pale grey so the black seed within can be easily seen. Once they get to this stage, they are ready to be eaten. They have no aroma or taste but a strange, pleasant combination of contrasting textures. The outer fur is slippery and soft whereas the centre is crunchy.

BUYING AND STORING

Subja seeds may not be very easy to find but look for them in good Indian grocery shops. A little amount puffs up to a lot and will go a long way, so a bag of seeds seems to last for ever. Store in a dry, airtight jar for up to a year.

MEDICINAL USES

Subja seeds are considered to be diuretic, tonic and an excellent remedy for constipation and piles. The plant is recommended for coughs, worms and stomach complaints and the juice of the leaves is applied externally for skin disorders.

A *falooda* shop

CULINARY USES

Subja seeds are used in milk-based drinks like *falooda* and on top of desserts like *kulfi* (Indian ice cream). You can experiment with them as a garnish for other puddings, fruit salad or even clear drinks. They need no cooking.

This makes the perfect end to a meal.

FALOODA
(ROSE MILK DRINK)

Serves 4
Preparation time 15 minutes
Cooking time 0

6 tablespoons rice noodles,
   broken into short lengths
4 teaspoons subja seeds
900ml (1½pt) milk
Sugar
4 teaspoons rose cordial
   (available in Indian shops)
4 scoops vanilla ice cream

1 Boil the noodles in water until soft and drain.

2 Soak the subja seeds in 150ml (¼pt) milk.

3 Mix the remaining milk and sugar and then pour into 4 tall glasses.

4 Divide the subja seeds, milk and noodles between the glasses. Then gently pour in the rose syrup which, being heavier, will settle to the bottom.Chill well. Before serving, float a scoop of ice cream on top of each glass.

This is a nightcap that is reputed to be soothing and soporific.

RAAT KI RANI
(NIGHT COOLER)

Serves 4
Preparation time 15 minutes
Cooking time 0

4 teaspoons subja seeds
600ml (1pt) milk
4 teaspoons honey
½ teaspoon cardamom powder
4 ice cubes

1 Mix all the ingredients and chill for 15 minutes. Serve cold.

Soaked subja seeds

GHEE AND OILS

(GHEE AUR TAIL)

Just as every region in India has its own special cuisine, so each area uses a particular cooking medium to lend a particular flavour. This largely depends on what grows there. Coastal India is full of coconut palms, so obviously coconut oil is the standard oil used in coastal cooking. In West Bengal mustard oil is used in many fish dishes. Groundnut, mustard, coconut, sesame, rapeseed, kardi seed, cotton seed, sunflower and corn are the principal oil seeds. Sunflower seed oil is very popular because of its subtle taste, ability to be reheated without any effect on its flavour and for its low cholesterol count. Unless another oil is specifically called for, it is best to use sunflower or corn oil for Indian cookery.

Ghee can almost be classed as a distinct ingredient apart from fats and oils. This fat is derived from milk. Traditionally, it is made at home but is becoming increasingly available in the shops.

Groundnut

Sesame

Walnut

COCONUT OIL

This is extracted from the dried kernel, or copra, of the coconut. It is particularly used in south and west Indian cookery where its rather strong coconut smell complements coconut-based vegetable and fish curries. A little is also poured on top of some dishes for added flavour. Coconut oil tends to solidify to a white mass when cold. Gently warming the bottle will bring it back to its pale yellow, liquid state. Most Indians use coconut oil on their hair to encourage lustrous growth. It is also good for massage.

GROUNDNUT OIL

Full of proteins, groundnut oil is used in Maharashtra and Gujarat. It is nearly colourless and odourless and therefore goes well with any dish.

MUSTARD OIL

This oil is greatly favoured in Bengal and eastern India. Certain Punjabi dishes get their flavour from this strong-smelling, viscous oil. Mustard grows widely in Punjab. The oil has a pungent taste and smell and is deep gold in colour. Punjabis normally heat the oil almost to smoking point and then cool it for use to tone down its smell. People swear by its ability to promote thick, lustrous hair growth and it is often massaged into the scalp.

Mustard

Ghee

SESAME OIL

Indian sesame oil is light and colourless and should not be confused with Chinese sesame oil which is dark and aromatic. The Chinese one is made of roasted sesame seeds and cannot be used instead of the Indian oil.

Rapeseed, cotton seed and kardi seed oils are cheaper and not highly recommended.

Oilseed rape

Homemade butter

GHEE

Ghee is the purest form of butter-fat. It is mentioned in ancient texts which have been dated by historians to around 8000 BC. In the days when there was no refrigeration, milk was converted to ghee to lengthen its storage life. Ghee is clarified butter and is made from the milk of cows and buffaloes. In India, buffalo milk is preferred because of its higher fat content and because the ghee it yields has a cleaner taste and colour than cows' milk ghee. Because of its unique flavour, there is no real substitute for ghee.

Ghee is made by converting full cream milk into yoghurt and then churning this to separate out the solid butter from the liquid which is called buttermilk. This is traditionally done with a wooden or ceramic churner called a *ravi*. The butter is then placed in a heavy-bottomed pan or kadai and melted. It is simmered until the dusky sediment settles to the bottom and separates from the clear, golden ghee. The froth which keeps appearing at the top is skimmed off and discarded. The fragrance of fresh ghee is powerful and suffuses the house. Cool the ghee slightly and strain into a metal or glass jar taking care to only use a metal strainer. Cover and store once the ghee is completely cool. Ghee solidifies when cool but is still creamy like soft margarine. In cold climates, it becomes quite hard and can be melted by gently warming the whole container. Clarifying the butter stops it going rancid and it is also able to withstand high temperatures and constant reheating. Ghee can be stored for several years.

Alternatively, ghee can be made from bought, unsalted butter. Just melt the butter in a heavy pan and simmer on a low heat for about 30 minutes until all the water evaporates and the sediment settles. Then proceed as before.

Every Indian pantry has a store of ghee. It is used for desserts, for frying and to smear on top of rotis. A spoonful is poured on top of lentils to give them a lift. Ghee is available commercially, packed in metal cans. Although it is very good, it loses some of its original flavour because of intensive processing. Of the oils available in the West, most can be used for Indian cooking. However, olive oil is not recommended.

Sunflowers

A versatile chef will keep 2 or 3 different oils in the store-cupboard. Along with the countless spices that give Indian food its flavour, these oils and especially ghee are valuable flavouring agents and an indispensable part of the Indian pantry.

Oils and ghee

Silver artefacts

EDIBLE SILVER FOIL

(VARQ)

For thousands of years, gold and silver have been part of daily life in India. Children are given tiny silver cups, spoons and plates as gifts, married couples buy whole dining sets of crafted silver and even the poorest of the poor save to buy thin silver anklets. In fact silver is even used in food. Added as a garnish over sweets, edible silver foil can be seen shimmering in the glass cases of any sweetmeat shop. It is so popular that India converts 13 tonnes of pure silver into edible silver foil each year.

MANUFACTURE

Although it is hard to imagine biting into silver, edible silver leaf is quite different. Small balls of gold or silver are placed between sheets of tissue paper laid flat in a leather pouch. This is beaten repeatedly, but carefully with a heavy, metal hammer flattening the balls into paper-thin sheets.

APPEARANCE AND TASTE

Silver foil is as thin as the best chiffon and lustrous. It is extremely fragile and often breaks up during use. It has no aroma or taste.

BUYING AND STORING

It is sold between sheets of tissue paper usually in boxes. Each sheet contains so little silver that it is not prohibitively expensive. Gold foil is also available. Both have a shelf-life of many years.

OTHER USES

It is used as an amalgam in arresting tooth decay.

CULINARY USES

Edible silver foil is used only as a garnish. It embellishes sweets, rich biryanis, meat curries and kababs. Carefully lift off a sheet of silver foil along with its lower sheet of tissue paper. Then turn it over on top of the prepared dish so that the foil sticks to the food. Bits will remain on the paper which can be pressed on the food similarly. It is nearly impossible to stick on a uniform coating of silver foil.

The first recipe is for a rice dish whose very name conjures up exotic visions. This pulao has a glamour that is aptly complemented by the addition of silver foil.

ZAFFRAN PULAO
(SAFFRON PULAO)

Serves 4
Preparation time 15 minutes
Cooking time 30 minutes

2 tablespoons ghee
6 black peppercorns
6 cloves
300g (10oz) basmati rice, washed and drained
600ml (1pt) hot water
1 teaspoon saffron strands soaked in a little hot water
1 teaspoon fresh orange zest, grated
Salt
1-2 sheets edible silver foil (varq)

1 Heat the ghee in a heavy pan and add the peppercorns and cloves.

2 When they pop add the rice and fry until aromatic.

3 Stir in the water, saffron, orange zest and salt. Bring to the boil and reduce the heat. Simmer until the rice is fluffy and dry.

4 Take off the heat and gently mix with a fork, taking care not to break the delicate grains of rice.

5 To serve, arrange on a decorative platter and float the silver foil on top.

Burfis are little cakes, made of a vast array of ingredients. Milk burfi is very popular and keeps for about a month in the refrigerator. It can be served as a dessert or as a teatime snack.

MILK BURFI
(CREAMY MILK SQUARES)

Serves 4
Preparation time 15 minutes +
  3 hours draining
Cooking time 15 minutes

900ml (1½pt) full fat milk
4 teaspoons fresh lemon juice
4 tablespoons dried milk powder
6 tablespoons caster sugar
6 tablespoons ghee
1 teaspoon cardamom powder
2 sheets edible silver foil (varq)

1 Heat the milk slightly and curdle it by adding the lemon juice. Then hang it up in a muslin or fine cotton cloth to drain for 3 hours.

2 The milk solids are now a fresh cheese called paneer.

Knead this well with the milk powder and sugar.

3 Heat the ghee in a heavy pan and add the paneer mixture. Stir-fry on a very low heat until the ghee separates.

4 Take off the heat and mix in the cardamom powder. Allow to cool slightly.

5 Knead again to blend. Pat into a flat cake and cool completely.

Indian sweets

6 Cut into squares and decorate with silver foil.

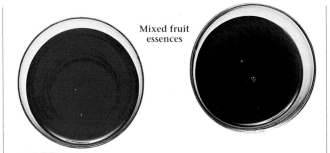

Mixed fruit essences

Kewra essence

Rose essence is extracted from dark pink and red rose petals

ESSENCES

(ITTARS)

Essences have been a part of Indian cookery since antiquity. The ittars of the Mughal emperors of India were famous and rare flowers would be grown in the royal greenhouses to be converted into perfume. Some of these were used in the kitchen, others in toiletry. Ittars came to symbolise romance and prestige and their addition to food was considered luxurious. Even today, they are used at festive functions, in ritual worship and at traditional weddings.

Rose-water

MANUFACTURE

Floral essences are the most popular. The rose reigns supreme, closely followed by screwpine or *kewra*, jasmine and *khus* which is a highly fragrant grass. The best blooms or herbs are selected and the essence is distilled. This is mixed with water to make rose-water, kewra-water, etc. Rose essence is extracted from cultivated, dark pink and red roses. Jasmine grows widely all over India and is converted into a strong perfume. Sandalwood perfume is also used in the kitchen.

APPEARANCE AND TASTE

Different essences have different colours – rose is colourless, kewra (screwpine) is yellow or transparent and khus is deep green. They are always powerful-smelling and must be used very sparingly. They have no particular taste.

BUYING AND STORING

Some essences like rose are easier to find than others. You only need tiny amounts and it is a good idea to try 1 essence at a time. Store in a dark place with the cap tightly screwed on. They last for 2–3 years.

OTHER USES

Essences are also used to liven up pot-pourris, scent homes and to make preserves. Rose petals are packed in sugar to make a jam. This is enhanced with a drop of rose essence for fuller flavour. Khus essence is sprayed on curtains woven out of khus grass to perfume the surroundings. Hindu deities are anointed with perfume concentrates as part of worship. Women all over India use ittars as part of their beauty regimen.

Kewra (screwpine) flower

CULINARY USES

The easiest way to use an essence is to dilute a few drops in a little water or milk and sprinkle over the food. Rose essence is used to flavour many milk sweets like cottage cheese balls in sugar syrup. Kewra essence adds a hint of colour and fragrance to some pulaos and sweets. All essences are also made into refreshing drinks. A few drops mixed with sugar, lemon juice and cold water makes an unusual, fragrant summer cooler or appetiser.

The following recipes are for 2 completely different drinks. One is thick and creamy while the other is light and refreshing. Lassi is a popular drink in India and in places where the heat is extreme it is served in big jugs – 1 jug per person! It tastes good sweet or salted but the addition of an essence usually means that it is sweet.

LASSI
(YOGHURT COOLER)

Serves 4
Preparation time 10 minutes
Cooking time 0

600ml (1pt) natural yoghurt
300ml (½pt) water
Sugar
2 teaspoons rose essence
8 ice cubes

1 Blend all the ingredients except the ice cubes in a liquidiser. Chill well.

2 Pour into individual glasses and add 2 ice cubes to each.

This sherbet is one of the many that are served in India. Countless seasonal sherbets made of exotic fruits like lychees, guavas and papaya are stored in the pantry but when the best fruits are no longer available essences are used instead.

KEWRA SHERBET
(SCREWPINE COOLER)

Makes 1 bottle (20-25 glasses)
Preparation time 0
Cooking time 20 minutes

900ml (1½pt) water
300g (10oz) sugar
6 tablespoons lemon juice
6 teaspoons kewra (screwpine)
essence

Kewra Sherbet

1 Heat the water and sugar in a pan, stirring until all the sugar has dissolved.

2 Take off the heat, cool slightly and add the lemon juice and essence.

3 Cool completely and bottle. Store in the refrigerator.

4 Dilute some of the sherbet with water and serve with plenty of ice.

CITRIC ACID

(LIMBUPHOOL)

Sweet limes, Bombay market

All Indians are fond of snacks which are served at teatime or with drinks. One of the most popular snacks is *chiwda* or a mixture of cereals, nuts and spices, somewhat like a savoury muesli. Perhaps the best-known outside India is Bombay mix. All these chiwdas are a mixture of tastes, hot, sweet, salty and tangy. Being dry preparations, the sourness needs to come from an ingredient that will provide taste without moisture. That ingredient is citric acid. It is used in different chiwdas made of potatoes, chickpea flour, flaked or puffed rice and sago.

MANUFACTURE

Citric acid is an organic acid found in many fruits like lemons, oranges, raspberries, gooseberries, etc. For use in the kitchen, it is extracted from lemon juice or it is prepared commercially by fermenting glucose.

APPEARANCE AND TASTE

Citric acid is available in the form of a fine, white, shiny powder or as large, fragile crystals that break easily. It has no aroma and a pleasant, sour, acidic taste.

BUYING AND STORING

It keeps well when dry. If it gets wet, it is liable to go mouldy.

CULINARY USES

The grains of citric acid are sprinkled into chiwdas or snacks. When made into a solution, they can be added to rice, lentils or vegetables. Citric acid is a good substitute for lemon juice and gives a tang to homemade lemonade.

The first dish is eaten with rice. It comes from one of the best restaurants in Gujarat.

KUTCCHI DAL DHOKLI
(LENTILS WITH WHEAT PASTA)

Serves 4
Preparation time 25 minutes
Cooking time 30 minutes

220g (8oz) split yellow lentils (toor dal), washed and drained
1 teaspoon chilli powder
1 teaspoon turmeric powder
1 teaspoon cumin powder
1 teaspoon coriander powder
Salt
1 teaspoon sugar
1 teaspoon citric acid
4 tablespoons sunflower oil
1 teaspoon black mustard seeds
½ teaspoon fenugreek seeds
10 curry leaves

For the dough:
150g (5oz) wholewheat flour
2 tablespoons sunflower oil
1 teaspoon turmeric powder
½ teaspoon chilli powder
Salt

2 tablespoons coriander leaves

1 Simmer the lentils in water until soft.

2 Stir in the powder spices, salt, sugar and citric acid.

3 Heat the oil in a small pan and add the mustard seeds. When they pop add the fenugreek and curry leaves. Fry for a minute and pour over the dal.

4 Make the dough by kneading all the ingredients with some water.

5 Roll out thinly and cut into diamond shapes with a sharp knife.

6 Set the lentils to boil and add the dough shapes one at a time.

7 Simmer for 10 minutes.

8 Serve hot garnished with coriander leaves.

Chiwda - 'Bombay mix'

The following recipe is one of the innumerable rice dishes from south India. It is light and fragrant and goes well with a vegetable curry and poppadoms.

LIMBOO BHATH
(LEMON RICE)

Serves 4
Preparation time 15 minutes
Cooking time 30 minutes

4 tablespoons sunflower oil
2 teaspoons split gram lentils (channa dal)
10 curry leaves
1 teaspoon cumin seeds
1 teaspoon black mustard seeds
Large pinch of asafoetida
1 teaspoon green chillies, chopped
1 teaspoon turmeric powder
300g (10oz) basmati rice, washed and drained
Salt
1 teaspoon citric acid
600ml (1pt) hot water
4 tablespoons fresh coconut, grated (optional)

1 Heat the oil in a pan and add the lentils, curry leaves, cumin, mustard and asa-foetida. Fry until the seeds pop.

2 Add the chillies, turmeric and rice and fry until the rice is glossy.

3 Add salt, citric acid and hot water and bring to the boil.

4 Lower the heat, partially cover the pan and simmer until the rice is fluffy and dry.

Citric acid

5 Serve hot, garnished with coconut shavings.

VINEGAR

(SIRKA)

'Brown' or malt vinegar

Vinegar was relished by ancient Greeks and Romans who would place vinegar vessels on the dining table for guests to dip their bread in. Thirteenth-century street vendors in Paris were known to sell barrels of vinegar to hoteliers and housewives. In India, the inclusion of vinegar in cookery is more recent. India is home to people of many different communities, Hindus, Muslims, Christians, Buddhists, Parsees, Jains, Sikhs and Jews.

'White' or distilled vinegar

Each of these communities has their own way of cooking which is greatly enjoyed by the rest. Of these, the Parsees and the Goans have been most influenced by international cuisines and use many 'Western' ingredients like pasta, marzipan and vinegar. Where Hindu cookery uses tamarind or lemon as souring agents, Parsee or Christian fare in India gets its tang mainly from vinegar.

Indian women use vinegar to give gloss to their hair

Grinding stone for masala

MANUFACTURE

Vinegar is made by the fermentation of any alcohol. As sugar-cane grows plentifully in India, alcohol, a by-product in the manufacture of sugar from the cane, is fermented to produce vinegar. India does not produce vast amounts of vinegar as its use is fairly limited.

APPEARANCE AND TASTE

Vinegar is clear and transparent or dark brown and has a characteristic sour, acidic aroma and taste. The dark variety is heavier.

BUYING AND STORING

Good vinegar is not cloudy. Although in the West vinegars flavoured with herbs and fruits are popular, in India plain vinegar is preferred. Store bottles of vinegar away from the light and they will be stable for several years.

OTHER USES

Vinegar makes an excellent finishing rinse for the hair, leaving it soft, shiny and manageable. Use clear vinegar for fair hair and brown vinegar for dark hair.

CULINARY USES

A traditional way of using vinegar in curries is to grind the curry spices with it. Gourmets claim that the best flavour is achieved when this is done on a rough grinding stone. The resulting paste is used as a marinade or fried in hot oil before adding meat or fish. Alternatively, vinegar can be added to the dish during cooking. Vinegar is also used for pickling. North Indians make a delicious preserve of carrots, turnips and cauliflower, flavoured with crushed mustard in vinegar.

The recipe that follows is from Goa and is made with pork, prawns, chicken, lamb or beef. Known all over the world as a medium hot curry, it has come to denote a certain level of chilli heat in a dish.

KOMDI VINDALOO
(SPICY GOAN CHICKEN CURRY)

Serves 4
Preparation time 20 minutes
Cooking time 30 minutes

6 tablespoons sunflower oil
4 small potatoes, peeled and halved
2 large onions, chopped finely
8 pieces of chicken, skinless
6 cloves
8 black peppercorns
6 cardamom
4 green chillies, slit lengthways, so the seeds are exposed, but the chilli is not broken in 2
1 teaspoon sugar
Salt

Grind to a paste:
1 teaspoon cumin seeds
1 teaspoon coriander seeds
½ teaspoon turmeric powder
1 teaspoon garlic, chopped
1 teaspoon ginger, chopped
4 dried red chillies, deseeded, softened in water and drained
Large pinch cinnamon powder

4 tablespoons malt vinegar

1 Heat the oil in a pan and fry the potatoes until golden. Remove with a slotted spoon and reserve.

2 Fry the onions in the same oil. When they are translucent, add the chicken, cloves, peppercorns, cardamom and green chillies.

3 Fry until the chicken is well browned. Add sugar and salt and stir-fry for about 5 minutes.

Mutton Dhansak

Goan carnival – Goan recipes use a lot of vinegar

4 Add the potatoes and the ground spice paste and cook until the chicken is done.

5 Stir in the vinegar and simmer for 5 more minutes. Serve hot with boiled rice.

The second recipe is for a famous Parsee dish that is served with brown rice, made by cooking rice with a little caramel.

MUTTON DHANSAK
(PARSEE LAMB WITH LENTILS)

Serves 4
Preparation time 30 minutes
Cooking time 1 hour

2 large onions, chopped finely
150g (5oz) tomatoes, chopped
150g (5oz) bottle gourd, chopped finely (squash can be substituted)
4 tablespoons red pumpkin, chopped
4 tablespoons fresh fenugreek leaves, chopped
6 tablespoons coriander leaves, chopped
6 tablespoons mint leaves, chopped
150g (5oz) split yellow lentils (toor dal)
300g (10oz) lamb, trimmed and cubed
1 teaspoon turmeric powder
1 teaspoon chilli powder
Salt
1 teaspoon sugar
450ml (scant 1pt) water
4 tablespoons distilled vinegar
1 tablespoon sunflower oil
1 teaspoon cumin seeds

1 Put all the ingredients from onions to water in a heavy pan and cook until the lamb and lentils are soft.

2 Mash the vegetables and lentils with a wooden spoon, taking care not to break the meat.

3 Add the vinegar and stir. Heat the oil and fry the cumin seeds. Pour over the curry.

4 Simmer for 5 minutes and serve hot.

BIBLIOGRAPHY

H. K. Bakhru – *Herbs that Heal*, India 1992
Dr S. K. Jain – *Medicinal Plants*, India 1968
Jill Norman – *The Complete Book of Spices*, London 1990
Vimla Patil – *Dal Roti*, India 1985
Vimla Patil/Monisha Bharadwaj – *Prestige Festival Cookbook*, India 1992
J. S. Pruthi – *Spices and Condiments*, India 1976
Meera Taneja – *Good Housekeeping Indian Cookery*, London 1983

INDEX

PHOTOGRAPHIC ACKNOWLEDGEMENTS

Key

J.C.	Jean Cazals
J.D.	Julie Dixon
M.G.	Michelle Garrett
M.Gro.	Marcus Grover
J.H.	Jacqui Hurst

A-Z	A-Z Botanical Collections
DPA	Dinodia Picture Agency
IoI	Images of India
KC	Kyle Cathie Limited
Link	Link Picture Agency
NHPA	Natural History Photography

All recipe photography by Julie Dixon

1: J.H.
2-3: J.D.
5: top right J.H. bottom left J.D.
6-7: J.C.
9: J.C.
10: DPA (Sunil S. Kapadia)
12: J.C.
14: M.Gro.
15: J.H.
16-17: J.C.
18: top left J.H.; top right, M.Gro.; bottom left J.H.
20: top left, J.C.; centre left and right J.H.; bottom right DPA (V.H. Mishra)
22: top left and bottom left J.H.; top right DPA (R. A. Acharya) bottom right DPA (B.P. Maiti)
23: top left, J.H.
24: top left, top right, centre, centre right and bottom left, J.H.; bottom right DPA (Pramod Mistry)
26: top left DPA (Nitin Jhaveri); bottom DPA (A.D. Cheoolkar)
27: Link (Orde Eliason)
28: top right Link (Orde Eliason); bottom right J.H.; bottom left M.G.
29: top left M.G.
30: top left DPA (A.D. Cheoolkar); bottom left DPA (Vinay Parelkar)
32: top and bottom right J.H.; bottom left KC (Ashvin Mehta)
34: top, centre and bottom left J.H.; top right DPA (N.M. Kelvalkar); bottom right M.G.
35: top left DPA (A.D. Cheoolkar)
36: top left J.H.; top right DPA (R.A. Acharya); bottom right J.H.
37: bottom left DPA (Rajesh Vora); top right DPA (Shashikant Mehta)
39: bottom left and top J.H.; bottom right DPA (V. I. Thayil)
40: top left DPA (I.D.); top right J.H.; bottom KC (Ashvin Mehta)
41: centre left J.D.
42: top right J.H.; top right KC (Ashvin Mehta); bottom left M.Gro.
44: top and centre J.H.; bottom right M.Gro.
46: centre left DPA (R. A. Acharya); top right J.H.; bottom DPA (A.D. Cheoolkar)
48: top KC (Ashvin Mehta); centre J.H.; bottom DPA (A.D. Cheoolkar)
50: top J.H.; bottom DPA (Rajesh Vora)
52: bottom left DPA (Jagdish Agarwal); top right J.H.; bottom right IoI. (Andy Leyshon)
54: top left J.H.; top right M.Gro.; bottom left A-Z
56: top left and centre left J.H.; bottom right A-Z (John Banurji)
58: top DPA (Rajesh H. Sharma); centre DPA (Nadish Naoroji); bottom J.H.

59: top right DPA (R.A. Acharya)
60: top left and top right J.H.; bottom right KC (Ashvin Mehta)
61: top left KC (Ashvin Mehta); bottom left DPA (Prashant Bokaria); top right J.H.
62: top left, top right DPA (Anil A. Dave); bottom left J.H.; bottom right A-Z (Dan Sams)
64: top right M.G.; bottom left KC (Ashvin Mehta); top left J.H.
66: top right M.G.; bottom left DPA (Ashvin Mehta)
67: bottom right M.G.
68: top left, top right and centre left M.G.; bottom right A-Z
70: top right DPA (H. Mahidhar); bottom right M.G.; bottom left DPA (Dinodia)
71: all top and bottom right DPA (P.R. Gansham)
73: top left and centre M.G.
74: top left M.G.; top right M.G.; bottom right and bottom left DPA (Jagdish Agarwal)
76: left DPA (Anil A. Dave); right DPA (Pramod Mistry)
77: top DPA (A.D. Cheoolkar)
78: top DPA (A.D. Cheoolkar); bottom DPA (M.M. Navalkar)
80: top left, centre left and top right J.H.; bottom right KC (Ashvin Mehta)
82: top right M.G.; bottom right M.Gro.
84-85: J.C.
86: left J.H.; top right DPA (Ravi Shekhar)
87: right DPA (M.M. Navalkar)
88: left and top right J.H.; bottom right DPA (Imtiaz Dharkar)
89: bottom left DPA (Ravi Shekhar)
90: left and top J.H.; bottom right DPA (Imtiaz Dharkar)
91: top centre DPA (N.M. Kelvalkar); bottom left DPA (Nitin Jhaveri)
92: left and right J.H.; top M.Gro.
94: all J.H.
95: bottom right J.H.
96: right J.H.; bottom left DPA (S.T. Parashar)
98-99: J.C.
100: left, top centre left and top centre right J.H.; top right DPA (Rajesh Vora); bottom right DPA (Imtiaz Dharkar)
102: left J.H.; top right DPA (Anil. A. Dave); bottom right M.G.
103: top J.H.
104: top J.H.; left IoI (Roderick Johnson); bottom right DPA (Viren Desai)
106: top and centre right DPA (V.H. Mishra); bottom right DPA (H. Mahidar); bottom left J.D.
108-109: J.H.
110: top DPA (F. Mistry.); all bottom J.H.
111: bottom left DPA (Anil A. Dave)
112: top J.H.; bottom DPA (N.G. Sharma)
113: top and bottom left J.H.
114: bottom and top left J.D.; top and bottom right DPA (Anil A. Dave);
115: top DPA (M.A. Ketkar); centre J.H.
116: top right, top left and bottom left J.H.; bottom right DPA (P.R. Gansham)
118: top right DPA (R.A. Acharya); bottom left J.H.
119: bottom DPA (R.A. Acharya); right

J.H.
120: top J.H.; bottom M.Gro.
121: bottom M.G.
122: top and bottom J.H.
123: top left J.H.
124: top left, centre and bottom right J.D.; bottom left DPA (Anil A. Dave)
125: bottom left DPA (S.D. Manchekar)
126: top left J.H.; top right DPA (Anil A. Dave); bottom right DPA (M.M. Navalkar); bottom left DPA (N.G. Sharma)
128: top left and centre left DPA (Anil A. Dave); top right J.H.; bottom right DPA (Anil A. Dave)
130: top and bottom left J.H.; top right DPA (H. Mahidhar)
132-133: J.C.
134: top DPA (Vinay Parelkar); bottom DPA (M. Amirtham)
135: top DPA (P. Karunakaran)
136: top left and centre left J.H.; top right DPA (Imtiaz Dharkar); bottom DPA (Ravi Shekar)
138: top M.G.; bottom DPA (Miland A. Ketkar)
139: bottom right M.G.
140: centre left M.G.; top right A-Z (Robert J. Erwin); bottom right DPA (Ashvin Mehta)
142: centre left, top left, top right and centre right and bottom right J.D.; bottom left DPA (N. Madhwani); centre M.Gro.
143: left DPA (Anil A. Dave)
144: top left and bottom right M.G.; top right A-Z (Michael Ward); bottom left DPA (P.R. Gansham)
145: bottom left DPA (P.R. Gansham)
146: top right, bottom right and centre left J.H.; top centre DPA (H. Mahidhar); bottom left DPA (Nadrish Naoroji)
147: top J.H.
148-149: J.C.
150: top left and bottom right DPA (Anil A. Dave)
152: centre DPA (R.K. Vaghela), top right DPA (Anil A. Dave) bottom right DPA (D. Banerjee)
154: top and bottom left DPA (Anil A. Dave); bottom right DPA (D.A. Chawda)
156: bottom right DPA (Ravi Shekar); top right, top centre right and centre right DPA (Anil A. Dave)
157: top DPA (Ravi Shekar)
158: top right DPA (M.M. Navalkar), left J.H.; bottom DPA (Miland A. Ketkar)
160: top DPA (Anil A. Dave); bottom right DPA (M. Amirtham); bottom left J.H.
162: top DPA (Ravi Shekar)
163: top left DPA (S.G. Gavali)
164: top DPA (Jagdish Agarwal); centre J.H.; bottom M.Gro.
165: bottom left M.G.
166: top left DPA (Anil A. Dave); bottom left DPA (M.M. Navalkar)
168: top left, top right, bottom right DPA (Anil A. Dave); bottom left DPA (R.J. Production)
170: top right M.Gro.; bottom left DPA (Anil A. Dave)
171: top right DPA (Hari Mahidhar)
172: top right DPA (Anil A. Dave); left DPA (R.K. Makharia)
174: top and bottom left DPA (Anil A. Dave); bottom right M.Gro.
175: top left DPA (Anil A. Dave)

176: top right DPA (Anil A. Dave); bottom DPA (B.P. Maiti);
177: bottom left A-Z (Jiri Loun)
178-179: M.Gro.
180: top right J.H.; centre DPA (N.M. Kelvalkar); bottom right DPA (S. Bhise)
181: top left DPA (N.M. Jain)
182: top left DPA (P.R. Gansham); top right DPA (S. Mehta); bottom right DPA (Rajesh H. Sharma)
184: top left DPA (Aravind Teki); centre right DPA (V.H. Mishra); bottom right DPA (H. Mahidar)
186: top left J.H.; centre DPA (V.H. Mishra); bottom DPA (D.A. Chawda)
188: top J.H.; bottom DPA (V.H. Mishra)
190: bottom left DPA (M.M. Navalkar); centre J.H.; top right Link (Orde Eliason)
192: top J.D.; bottom right J.C.
194: left J.D. top right DPA (Suraj N. Sharma); bottom right NHPA (K. Ghani)
195: top right DPA (Pramod Mistry)
196: top left J.H.; top right DPA (M.M. Navalkar); bottom right DPA (Aravind Teki)
198: top left DPA (Anil A. Dave); bottom left J.H.; bottom right J.C.
200: top J.H.; bottom right DPA (H.Mahidhar)
202: top J.D.; centre DPA (M.M. Navalkar)
204: centre DPA (Nadish Naoroji); bottom right J.H.
205: bottom right DPA (N.M. Kelvalkar)
206: centre left DPA (Rajesh H. Sharma); top centre J.H.; top right DPA (V.I. Thayil); bottom right IoI (James Mitchell)
208: top right J.H.; bottom right DPA (Dinodia)
210: top right J.H.; bottom DPA (R.A.Acharya); centre left DPA (Rajesh H. Sharma)
212-213: J.H.
214: top and bottom J.D.
215: J.D.
216: top left DPA (N. Jain); centre J.D.; bottom right DPA (Rajesh H. Sharma); centre J.D.
218: top right DPA (Anil A. Dave); bottom left and bottom right DPA (Suresh G. Gavali)
219: top DPA (M.M. Navalkar)
220: top J.D.
221: top left J.D.; bottom left J. C.; bottom right M.G.
222: top right J.D.; bottom left J.H.; bottom right DPA (V.I. Thayil)
223: top left DPA (V.H. Mishra); top right DPA (Suraj N. Sharma)
224: top left DPA (Chelna Desai); bottom J.H.
225: top right DPA (P.R. Gansham)
226: top and bottom left J.H.; top right DPA (Milind A. Ketkar); bottom right KC (V. Muthardman)
228: left and bottom right J.H.; top right DPA (Suresh G. Gavali)
229: top right J.H.
230: top left and centre left J.H.; top right DPA (Nadish Naoroji); bottom left DPA (I. Dharkar)
231: top left DPA (Vinay Parelkar)
232: DPA (Anil A. Dave)
238-239: J.C.